AN UNHOLY ROW

Popular Music History
Series Editor: Alyn Shipton, journalist, broadcaster and lecturer in jazz history at the Royal Academy of Music.

This series publishes books that challenge established orthodoxies in popular music studies, examine the formation and dissolution of canons, interrogate histories of genres, focus on previously neglected forms, or engage in archaeologies of popular music.

Published

Handful of Keys: Conversations with Thirty Jazz Pianists
Alyn Shipton

The Last Miles: The Music of Miles Davis, 1980–1991
George Cole

Jazz Visions: Lennie Tristano and His Legacy
Peter Ind

Chasin' the Bird: The Life and Legacy of Charlie Parker
Brian Priestley

Out of the Long Dark: The Life of Ian Carr
Alyn Shipton

Lee Morgan: His Life, Music and Culture
Tom Perchard

Being Prez: The Life and Music of Lester Young
Dave Gelly

Lionel Richie: Hello
Sharon Davis

Mr P.C.: The Life and Music of Paul Chambers
Rob Palmer

Trad Dads, Dirty Boppers and Free Fusioneers: A History of British Jazz, 1960–1975
Duncan Heining

Soul Unsung: Reflections on the Band in Black Popular Music
Kevin Le Gendre

Jazz Me Blues: The Autobiography of Chris Barber
Chris Barber with Alyn Shipton

An Unholy Row

Jazz in Britain and its Audience, 1945–1960

Dave Gelly

SHEFFIELD UK   BRISTOL CT

Published by Equinox Publishing Ltd.

UK: Unit S3, Kelham House, 3 Lancaster Street, Sheffield, South Yorkshire S3 8AF
USA: ISD, 70 Enterprise Drive, Bristol, CT 06010

www.equinoxpub.com

First published 2014

British Library Cataloguing-in-Publication Data

A catalogue record for this book is available from the British Library.

ISBN: 978 1 84553 712 8 (hardback)

Library of Congress Cataloging-in-Publication Data

Gelly, Dave.
   An unholy row : jazz in Britain and its audience, 1945-1960 / Dave Gelly.
      pages cm. -- (Popular music history)
   Includes bibliographical references and index.
   ISBN 978-1-84553-712-8 (hb)
  1. Jazz--Great Britain--1941-1950--History and criticism. 2. Jazz--Great
Britain--1951-1960--History and criticism. 3. Jazz--Social aspects--Great
Britain--History--20th century. I. Title.
  ML3509.G7G45 2014
  781.650941'09045--dc23

                  2013038365

Typeset by Atheus
Printed and bound by Lightning Source Inc (US), La Vergne, TN; Lightning Source UK
Ltd, Milton Keynes; and Lightning Source AU Pty Ltd, Scoresby, Vic.

Contents

In the absence of a commemorative plaque on the premises, I dedicate this book to the memory of Pete Payne's Music Shop, Catford, south-east London (opposite the bus garage and the marmalade factory), where I passed my teenage Saturday afternoons, and to Chris, Harry, Del, Bix, and all my fellow neophytes, living or dead.

Acknowledgements

My thanks to the following for helping me write this book – even those who didn't realize it at the time.

- The British Library
- David Nathan & all at the National Jazz Archive
- Paul Wilson, Curator of Radio, National Sound Archive
- Brian Blain
- Digby Fairweather
- Dave Green
- Freddie Legon
- John Minnion
- Joe Mudele (formerly Muddell)
- Michael Pointon
- Don Rendell
- Art Themen
- Peter Vacher
- Val Wilmer
- Peter Yorke

My late friends Peter Vicary (formerly pianist with the Second City Jazzmen of Birmingham) and Eddie Harvey (trombonist, pianist, arranger and pedagogue). Their reminiscences enlivened many a convivial evening – plus the occasional afternoon.

1 An Unholy Row

I think there were five of us, all aged about fourteen, gathered in the "games room" of a substantial family villa on the leafy southern fringes of London. We were equipped with musical instruments – battered cornet, decrepit clarinet, miscellaneous bits of a drum kit – and we were doing our best to emulate our heroes, Humphrey Lyttelton and his Band. We had been at it for some time when the door burst open to reveal our unwitting host, the cornettist's father. "Will you kindly stop making that unholy row?" he demanded, in a voice more weary than irate, and withdrew.

The 1950s, as we are often reminded, was an age of deference. Accordingly, we shut up at once, abashed but not entirely surprised. By any standards, "an unholy row" was a pretty fair description of our efforts, but even if we had been competent musicians, even if we had been Humph and his Band themselves, I wouldn't mind betting that, as far as the cornettist's father was concerned, it would still have been an unholy row. The whole thing was offensive to ears attuned to the BBC Midland Light Orchestra or the swing-and-water piano of Charlie Kunz. There was nothing startlingly new in this. Ever since the 1920s British voices had been calling jazz music far worse names. The insults hurled at Louis Armstrong by the popular press during his visit in 1932 had been positively blood-curdling. There had been a dedicated coterie of jazz lovers in those days, too, but we were only dimly aware of all that. As far as we were concerned, jazz was something marvellous that we had found for ourselves. Furthermore, it possessed the happy incidental virtue of getting up the noses of adults. It was a phase, they said, and we would grow out of it. But we knew we wouldn't.

If teenagers find something marvellous for themselves nowadays there's a beady-eyed entrepreneur standing by who knows a commercial opportunity when he sees one. In no time he will have stolen it and sold it back to them, with a free T-shirt thrown in. Jazz itself has grown respectable now. The years covered by this book were ones in which it was more or less left to its own devices to make its unholy row — alternately ignored and patronised by the arts establishment, sniffed at by educationalists, tolerated by anxious parents and viewed with suspicion by the forces of law and order.

We didn't know how lucky we were.

2 Trumpet in a Handcart

And so we take our last look at this occasion on this most historic night . . . The crowd – I can watch them up the Mall there – pouring into this great space in front of the forecourt. And there's a trumpet playing somewhere down below me.

It was 8 May 1945, VE Day, one of the golden dates in British history, and the BBC's Howard Marshall was describing the scene in front of Buckingham Palace, where Their Majesties and Mr Churchill had been acknowledging the ecstatic cheers of the people. And the trumpet? Its sound emanated from a handcart, from which precarious perch a young captain of the Grenadier Guards, somewhat red in the face and fortified by celebratory champagne, was blowing lusty choruses of 'Roll Out The Barrel'. His name was Humphrey Richard Adeane Lyttelton, aged twenty-three, grandson of the 8th Viscount Cobham. He was not to know it at the time, as he was trundled euphorically around the Victoria Memorial, but this was the perfect debut for a life as an old-Etonian, ex-Guards officer, jazz trumpeter, bandleader, cartoonist, writer, broadcaster, humorist and, eventually, National Treasure. By far the most important of these many distinctions was his life in jazz. Lyttelton was to become not only one of Europe's most gifted jazz musicians, but a leading figure in a new kind of artistic and social movement, one in which the sentiments, dissatisfactions and aspirations of a generation, however vaguely felt, were embodied and celebrated in a form of popular music. Britain in the post-war years was a place of such confusing social upheaval that the new enthusiasm for jazz among young people was noted, if at all, as just one more outlandish sign of the times, but it marked the earliest beginnings of what came to be called "youth culture".

At that time, for a Guards officer to be seen playing the trumpet in public, never mind a handcart, would almost certainly have been a breach of King's

Regulations, had it not been so bizarre as to be unthinkable. So how had Lyttelton come to be doing it in the first place? To answer that we must look briefly into the early life of this remarkable man and also the pre-war world of British jazz which had captured his youthful enthusiasm.

Humphrey Lyttelton was born on 23 May 1921 at Eton College, where his father, George Lyttelton, was a housemaster. His family roots were firmly established among the aristocracy and the landed gentry. One of his grandfathers was Lord Lieutenant of Cambridgeshire and the other, as he put it, "owned half of Worcestershire". As a small boy he was much attracted by military music and took percussion lessons from a former drum-major. By the age of ten he could read drum notation and was competent on the side-drum. At Sunningdale preparatory school and later at Eton he managed to stay afloat without showing any great academic distinction, "being ill-equipped with the power of concentration". His most noticeable talent was for sketching and drawing caricatures, although his early efforts at this were not always successful, his "Adolf Hitler" being mistaken for Charlie Chaplin and his "Mahatma Gandhi" for Jimmy "Schnozzle" Durante. At Eton he took up the harmonica, on which, with his ready repertoire of military marches, he achieved sufficient expertise to be appointed unofficial one-man band of the school's Officers' Training Corps.

His discovery of jazz came by way of popular dance music.

> I already knew quite a lot about dance music. It had been introduced into the nursery when I was still quite young by the procession of dance band-struck nurserymaids who had crooned the latest hits over me in my bath. And when I became old enough to lay my hands on the family radio set, I began to listen regularly to the broadcasts of Jack Payne and Henry Hall . . . I reached jazz – proper jazz – in several easy progressions. From Jack Payne and Henry Hall to Harry Roy and his lively Rag Bag selections, next to Nat Gonella and his Georgians, and then to Louis Armstrong.[1]

This process, at the end of which teenage boys and young men with a liking for lively rhythmic music (this was overwhelmingly a male interest) experienced a sudden jazz epiphany, was quite common. It was disturbingly like instant religious conversion and, at that time, usually involved Louis Armstrong. It came to the fifteen-year-old Humphrey Lyttelton in 1936, when a school friend acquired a copy of Armstrong's recording of 'Basin Street Blues'. "After playing it fifteen times we tottered out into the daylight with the incredulous, stunned expressions of the newly converted. Poor Nat Gonella's number was up. From that moment on we were fully initiated Jazz Lovers."[2] A year or two later, at Stowe School, a teenaged George Melly (1925–2007) "was passing an open window and heard the most beautiful sound in the world. It was Louis Armstrong playing 'Drop That Sack'".[3]

The phenomenon was not confined to the great public schools, to the upper classes, to England, or even to the Anglo-Saxon world. It was beginning to occur all over Europe during the 1930s. Django Reinhardt (1910–1953), a Roma man, born in Belgium, experienced his Armstrong moment in 1930, at the age of twenty. He was already a professional guitarist, playing a kind of Gallic novelty version of American hot dance music, when hearing an Armstrong recording for the first time reduced him to tears and he was heard to murmur "*mon frère!*"[4] Similarly, Stéphane Grappelli (1908–1997), a Frenchman of Italian descent, declared towards the end of his long life that hearing Armstrong as a young man had "changed my destiny".[5] When its results began to impinge upon families, neighbours and non-converts generally, the Armstrong moment was often followed by complaints and protests leading to an Unholy Row moment, but true converts were not deterred.

It was not only would-be performers to whom the Armstrong moment occurred. The poet Philip Larkin declared, when introducing his own reading of his poem in praise of Sidney Bechet, "I think to me and other members of my generation the great jazz players had the same emotional effect as perhaps a hundred years ago the great poets had."[6] His contemporaries Kingsley Amis (1922–1995) and John Wain (1925–1994) expressed similar ideas. The emotional effect on members of older generations was different, sometimes alarmingly so. In his *Letter from America* broadcast following Louis Armstrong's death, in 1971, Alistair Cooke (1908–2004) recalled what happened when, in 1931, he first brought an Armstrong record into his family's Blackpool home. He had ordered a copy of 'St James Infirmary' and, when it eventually arrived, bore it proudly home from the gramophone shop:

> I hustled it onto the turntable. My mother was intrigued by its title, which she thought odd, not to say gruesome . . . It began with a shattering chord and the trumpet taking off like a supersonic jet. Long before it was over I took it off the machine, because I saw that my mother was sitting there in tears. She was not moved by the beauty of the piece or the artistry of the mad trumpeter. She was frightened by it, and aghast that her son could listen to this jungle band without a blush. To her, in those remote days, it was as if, today, a mother had seen her son nonchalantly take out a needle and give himself a shot of heroin . . . In my youth it was the normal thing for people over fifty to be either frightened by jazz or contemptuous of it. Old soldiers, doctors, schoolmasters and other establishment figures made a point of equating the word "jazz" with the adjectives "negroid" and "decadent".[7]

These experiences all came via the medium of recording. Gramophone records were heavy but fragile discs which revolved 78 times a minute. They came mostly in two sizes: twelve inches across, containing about five minutes of music on each side, and ten inches, containing about three minutes. Jazz records were almost exclusively ten-inchers, and in the early days they were marketed simply as "dance", or even "novelty" items. The first British release by Jelly Roll Morton's Red Hot Peppers ('Black Bottom Stomp' / 'The Chant'), for instance, appeared in HMV's 1927 dance-music list. The same year saw the release of 'Drop That Sack' by Lil's Hot Shots (actually Louis Armstrong's Hot Five, going under his wife's name), Frankie Trumbauer's 'Singin' The Blues' (with Bix Beiderbecke), plus records by Fletcher Henderson, Joe Venuti and others. The number of such releases gradually increased through the thirties, as the jazz audience grew. In 1929, Parlophone brought out its "New Rhythm Style" (later "Super Rhythm Style") series specifically for jazz, and other labels followed suit. British jazz lovers certainly spent money on records. Between 1933 and 1936, the American record producer John Hammond was able to record such American artists as Joe Venuti, Benny Goodman, Bud Freeman and Jimmy Noone in New York, purely for the British market. This was at a time when the Depression had all but wiped out the record industry in the US. The discs were extremely cheap to record, and Hammond, a rich man, paid his own expenses, including transatlantic travel, but even so, with all these releases added together the supply was still fairly small. This meant that enthusiasts had time to get to know each of their purchases intimately. It is a characteristic of European jazz lovers whose attachment dates back to the days of 78 rpm discs that most of them can whistle, hum or otherwise retrace the progress of their favourite recordings in some detail. This intimacy enabled the would-be players among them to learn the jazz idiom in the way children learn language – vocabulary, pitch, rhythm, timbre, inflection – all of a piece, by ear. The most gifted among them, like Lyttelton, eventually developed the fluency of native speakers.

Having acquired a trumpet, and the one free lesson that came with it, he set about teaching himself to play, as far out of general earshot as possible. Then came the inevitable schoolboy band of fellow-converts, together with more formal musical efforts at Eton. At the age of eighty-six, Lyttelton still proudly recalled his spirited rendition of the fanfare in Handel's *Judas Maccabeus*, which overpowered both the choir and the College organ, and drew a stricken croak of "Good God!" from the music master. Thereafter he was never to be parted from the trumpet – not while performing an early version of "work experience" in a South Wales steel works, nor even throughout a wartime career in the Grenadier Guards. It stayed with him during the assault and eventual landing at Anzio, through a series of spells in military hospitals in North Africa, and eventually at Caterham Barracks, from which he sallied forth for his unheralded appointment with the radio public on VE Day.

Opportunities for pre-war novice jazz-lovers in Britain to experience live jazz were few. The music flourished mainly in a louche *demi monde* of dives, joints and semi-secret "bottle parties". In *I Play as I Please*, his first volume of autobiography, Lyttelton recalled his fleeting experience of that world.

> Once, when I was still a 17 year-old at Eton, I did make a pilgrimage to London to take in the Bag O' Nails and the Nest Club . . . I went with another jazz-minded schoolmate during one of the midterm weekend holidays known as Long Leave . . . At the Bag O' Nails, rows of "hostesses" sat round and gazed at us like birds of prey as we sipped our drinks, but our eyes were on the band, and we could not spare them a glance . . . We were hearing jazz – in the flesh – for the first time. The rest could wait!

They moved on to the Nest, "a long, low-ceilinged room, thick with smoke and almost pitch dark", where the band sat crammed onto a tiny stand, improvising on standard jazz tunes. "When we came in they were just coming up to the fifteen-minute mark in a half-hour version of 'Crazy Rhythm'. This was it! We found a secluded, dark spot near the bandstand and stood there, rather nervous but very happy, until the place closed."[8]

Because they were so closely allied, the dividing line between jazz and what was called "dance music" (the equivalent of what might later be called "pop music") was not at all obvious. To use Lyttelton's boyhood examples, it was the line which separated Armstrong clearly from Jack Payne and Henry Hall, less clearly from Harry Roy, and hardly at all from Nat Gonella, who was himself an Armstrong devotee. Invention came into it, and inspiration, but principally a quality, difficult to define, which had something to do with honesty of purpose and a desire to communicate beyond the limits of pure entertainment. Armstrong himself certainly possessed it, and was aware of the fact, although he didn't agonise over the matter. He firmly believed that he had been put on this earth "to make people happy", and left it at that.

The Armstrong moment, which touched and inspired Lyttelton and many others in the 1930s, amounted to a recognition of this quality. The unanswerable question is, why did members of that generation become sensitized to it? It left older people unaffected, and only a minority of the population ever came within its gravitational field. But that minority grew to sizeable proportions in the years that followed, and with it an almost desperate desire to draw a clear distinction between "real jazz" and mere "dance music". It was the French, with their penchant for critical theory, who led the way in this, notably Hugues Panassié, co-founder of the Hot Club de France. His books *Le Jazz Hot* (1934) and *Le Vrai Jazz* (1936) enjoyed a wide readership, especially in English translation. They were still to be found on the shelves of English suburban public libraries more than two decades later.

British jazz lovers were kept up to date by the weekly *Melody Maker*, essentially a trade newspaper for the dance-band profession but with a strong pro-jazz bias in its record reviews and features. At first founded as a monthly in 1926, it provided an informal basic education in jazz (who played what, names of established artists, jazz terminology) and acted as a focus or rallying-point for what would nowadays be called the "jazz community". It was the *Melody Maker* that introduced serious, detailed criticism of jazz *as music* in its regular columns, beginning in 1931. The author was the bass player and band leader Spike Hughes, writing under the pen-name "Mike". In contrast to the French theorists, Mike directed his attention to the nuts and bolts of the subject, in particular to the element which distinguished jazz from all other forms of Western music, the rhythmic phenomenon known as swing. Ignoring all the nonsense about "jungle drums", "savage rhythms", and so on, which was still rife, he listened carefully and got down to details. Impressed, for instance, by the marvellous elasticity of rhythm on records by Ellington and Luis Russell, he explained how the interlocking bass and drum parts worked to achieve their effect, even going so far as to transcribe a few bars by way of illustration.

To read the *Melody Maker* regularly was to declare oneself a serious devotee. This applied from the early 1930s until some indeterminate point in the 1970s. With the *Melody Maker* acting as their focus and notice-board, there had grown up in the 1930s a number of jazz enthusiasts' societies, scattered around the country. The British have a fondness for setting up formally constituted clubs through which to pursue their hobbies and interests. The "Rhythm Clubs", as they were known, conformed to this pattern. They flourished modestly throughout the pre-war years, even uniting briefly into a national federation. Initially, they concentrated almost exclusively on recorded music. Their membership was overwhelmingly male and largely middle-class, and they met in an atmosphere redolent of pipe smoke and the saloon bar. Among them was a left-inclined sub-group, which saw jazz as an aspect of the struggle for socialism. This could be a difficult balancing act, because in the Soviet Union, with which they felt an affinity, the Party line tended to waver between viewing jazz as, on the one hand, an expression of the downtrodden masses and, on the other, a product of American capitalism designed to drug those same masses into acceptance of their plight. This left-wing tendency was to become more prominent in the post-war years. Curiously, although jazz was sometimes lumped together in fashionable discourse under the heading of "Modernism", along with Picasso, *The Waste Land* and "experimental" art of various kinds, that whole aspect seems to have aroused little interest among the majority of pre-war British jazz lovers.

There were in 1930s Britain professional musicians renowned for their ability to play jazz, but few if any would have called themselves professional jazz musicians. The distinction is narrow but crucial. The playing of popular dance music was a skilled, professional activity, and the playing of jazz calls for many of the same basic skills, using the same instruments. It comes as no surprise, therefore, to find the best jazz musicians of the period – Tommy McQuater, George Chisholm, Billy Munn, Sid Phillips, Buddy Featherstonehaugh, Harry

Gold – listed among the ranks of some of the top dance orchestras. For musicians in "name" bands, music occupied a position somewhere between a highly skilled trade and a profession, with an added element of show-business. If their anecdotes and fond recollections are anything to go by, they certainly considered themselves to be an elite corps. This pattern would be repeated, rather more modestly, down through the ranks of lesser professional and semi-professional bands around the country, many of which would contain a player or two ready and eager to "shoot a chorus", as the jargon of the time had it. As they became established, rhythm clubs would stage jam sessions featuring such local players, and in London some of the best-known names would be invited to perform. Some rhythm clubs, although much reduced, continued to meet throughout the war. In November 1941, the No.1 Rhythm Club, based in central London, put on a public jam session at Abbey Road recording studios, which resulted in three twelve-inch discs, the proceeds going to Forces' charities. Among those taking part were trumpeters Leslie "Jiver" Hutchinson and Dave Wilkins, clarinetist Carl Barriteau and guitarist Joe Deniz. These were all survivors of Ken "Snakehips" Johnson's West Indian Dance Orchestra, which had been playing at the Café de Paris, near Leicester Square, on the night of 4 March that year, when it was bombed with great loss of life. The chaotic wartime conditions and the consequent loosening of social restraints, indeed the very uncertainty of life itself, combined to create a demand for the kind of fun which goes with drink and lively music. Musicians, especially those who could play "hot", did well. The fever abated with the arrival of peace, but it had planted an unselfconscious fondness for swingy music in many of that generation.

At the end of the war Britain resembled one of the disused vending machines then to be found on railway station platforms – a dilapidated relic of the late 1930s. In 1947, the Office of National Statistics produced its first "typical shopping basket" of items bought by the average British shopper. As an evocative glimpse into living conditions in Austerity Britain it would be hard to beat – coal and coke, condensed milk, table mangle, galvanised bucket, plimsolls – but towards the end of this grim list come, interestingly, "gramophone record" and "radio licence".

The radio, or "wireless", as it was still commonly called, continued to play an immensely important role in everyday life. The BBC Light Programme came into being on 27 July 1945, replacing the General Forces Programme (GFP), with the express intention of providing radio entertainment, popular music and comedy in particular, to maintain civilian morale at a difficult time. The vast bulk of its musical diet consisted of dance bands, popular singers such as Vera Lynn, cinema organs, light orchestras, brass and military bands and "songs from the shows". Public taste, as revealed in the two leading record-request programmes, *Family Favourites* (launched 1945) and *Housewives' Choice* (launched 1946), was remarkably diverse. It extended from Richard Tauber singing 'We'll Gather Lilacs' to Bing Crosby and the Andrews Sisters with 'Pistol Packin' Mama'. However, the most evident difference between the popular music of 1939 and that of 1945 lay in the degree of American influence. The war in Europe had broken out at a time when the swing era was at its peak in the US. This had already made some impact in Britain, notably on the performance style and repertoire of popular dance bands. Towards the end of the thirties, the restrained tones of the more genteel bands had begun to be replaced by a sharper, more assertive approach. This was particularly noticeable in the sound of saxophone sections, where the characteristic warbling tone, created by precisely matched vibratos, was no longer universally adhered to, even by such masters of the genre as Carroll Gibbons and his Savoy Orpheans.

When, from early 1942, a tidal wave of American military might engulfed the British Isles in the long build-up to D-Day, it came complete with a cultural undertow of irresistible proportions. The presence, towards the end of the war, of American service bands, most famously Major Glenn Miller's Band of the Allied Expeditionary Force (AEF), but also Sam Donahue's US Navy Band and others, had a powerful effect on their British counterparts. British service bands were largely composed of young professional musicians in uniform, and close personal contact with the Americans brought them new ideas and new standards to aim at. Wartime recordings by the Squadronaires (official title, the RAF Dance Orchestra) and the Skyrockets (officially No. 1 Balloon Centre Dance Orchestra) reveal how valuable this quite brief period of practical encouragement proved to be. The next musical generation, too, were deeply impressed by the Americans, especially when they had the chance to hear them in person and at close quarters. The saxophonist Don Rendell, then aged eighteen, later recalled:

> Sam Donahue's Navy Band was in town. Hearing the whole band at the Queensbury All-Services Club was a thrill that is still vivid to my mind . . . The Donahue men, such as trombonist Dick Le Fave and clarinetist Ralph La Pola, would go around the clubs after the gig when they were in London . . . It seemed to me then that the Americans had more fundamental ability to produce sound – probably through more college training in the early stages of learning instruments. The sax players, too, had more power than anyone I knew over here.[9]

By the end of the war musical tastes, particularly among servicemen, had shifted markedly in the direction of the swingy American style. This can be observed quite clearly in the output of the GFP. Taking, for example, the two months leading up to VE Day, there were thirty-six separate programmes that fell broadly within the jazz/swing category. They included shows by dance bands, such as those of Frank Weir, Buddy Featherstonehaugh and Carl Barriteau, known for their leaning towards swing; the weekly half-hour

Swing Session, with such groups as the Vic Lewis–Jack Parnell Jazzmen and Harry Hayes and his Band; little quarter-hour spots devoted to records by Louis Armstrong, Art Tatum and Mary Lou Williams; numerous half-hours by a unit drawn from the American Band of the AEF, under the leadership of Sgt. Mel Powell; two shows, alternating fortnightly, aimed at jazz enthusiasts – Swing Club (a record miscellany presented by Spike Hughes) and Radio Rhythm Club (programmes on specific topics, such as "Ragtime", "Blues", and so on). In addition, jazz names (Harry Hayes, Nat Gonella, Victor Feldman) appeared as guests in shows by Britain's own band of the AEF (led by George Melachrino) and similar programmes. Nor was jazz ignored by the civilian Home Programme. Over the same couple of months it featured the weekly quarter-hour Swing Sextet, led by Mel Powell and featuring Peanuts Hucko on clarinet (described by the *Melody Maker* as "swing chamber music . . . sheer virtuosity in modern-style small-band music"), presented the Squadronaires five days running as Band of the Week, and devoted half-hour programmes to "Ladies of Jazz" and trumpeter-vocalist Wingy Manone. There was an ambitious series called "Jazz Is Where You Find It", specially recorded for AEF stations in occupied Europe, featuring members of Sam Donahue's US Navy band, together with "a dozen of Britain's star soloists", including Kenny Baker, Woolf Phillips, Ronnie Chamberlain, Aubrey Frank, Pat Dodd, Vic Lewis, Lauderic Caton, Carlo Krahmer and Stéphane Grappelli, who was a wartime British resident.

The sheer amount of jazz and near-jazz to be heard on British radio, most of it contemporary in style and not aimed specifically at dedicated jazz fans, shows that this music had become genuinely popular. The names of some musicians were instantly recognizable by the general public, usually as a result of radio exposure. The Welsh clarinetist Harry Parry, sometimes called "Britain's Benny Goodman", was one of these. He had been resident bandleader on Radio Rhythm Club in the early war years and was a frequent star guest on variety shows. His records on the Parlophone label sold well and, from 1945 to 1947, his sextet was resident at the smart Potomac Restaurant in Jermyn Street. Some measure of his public profile may be gained from the fact that, at a time when manufactured toys were in short supply, a vaguely clarinet-shaped, recorder-like instrument in moulded Bakelite, labelled "Harry Parry Clarinet", was on sale at Woolworth's.

Nowhere was the American influence more apparent than in the work of a new band, Ted Heath and his Music. In 1942, Heath, a trombonist with Geraldo's orchestra, wrote a hit song, 'That Lovely Weekend', which caught to perfection the sense of fleetingly snatched joy which characterized wartime romances. With the proceeds he was able to fulfil his ambition of forming a band of his own. As the war drew to a close, and the musicians of his choice became available, he assembled a remarkably authentic-sounding sixteen-piece swing band. As a measure of just how far some British musicians had come in grasping the essence of big-band swing, it is instructive to compare

Heath's 1945 recording of Sy Oliver's *Opus One* with Tommy Dorsey's American original. The differences are really quite small. Heath's brass section has none of the genteel timidity which hampered even the best British bands in the thirties, and the rhythm section has a real lift to it. Dorsey, although somewhat handicapped by a pointless string section, still has the edge, with that impression of eagerness which comes from phrasing right on the very front of the beat, and he does have the unfair advantage of a young Buddy DeFranco as clarinet soloist. Nevertheless, on an initial hearing Heath's could easily be mistaken for an American band.

Equally impressive, but now largely forgotten, was a small band led by the alto saxophonist Harry Hayes. Formed in 1944, it recorded regularly for HMV, each release being greeted with serious attention in the *Melody Maker*. Hayes played in a style which fell somewhere between Benny Carter and Johnny Hodges, with a warm, slightly fluffy tone and impeccable technique. Born in 1909, he had enjoyed a successful career in the top dance bands of the thirties before joining the regimental band of the Welsh Guards in 1940. His eight-piece band appears to have been modelled on the small groups occasionally formed around members of Duke Ellington's orchestra. Among its many virtues was a charming lightness of touch in the arrangements, with none of the footling detail, redundant key-changes and general over-writing which had often marred similar efforts before the war. It also had some of the very best young players to emerge in the early 1940s, most notably the bravura trumpeter Kenny Baker and pianist Norman Stenfalt, whose sparkling introductions and purposeful solos still sound bright and fresh after the passage of many years.

Both of these bands seem entirely at home with the jazz idiom. They had grown up with it, absorbed it, and were able to relax into it. Kenny Baker, who was in his early twenties at the time, always maintained that the solos he recorded with Hayes were among the best he ever played, because they were "spontaneous and full of ideas". That is the impression one often gains from British jazz recorded during those few years around the end of the war – a kind of youthful bursting forth, despite the surrounding gloom. Baker was a prodigy. While serving in the RAF he managed to play and record regularly with most of the leading players on the wartime jazz scene, including the bands of Harry Parry and Buddy Featherstonehaugh, both regulars on *Radio Rhythm Club*, and with a quintet led by the pianist George Shearing – perhaps the most remarkable figure of all in British jazz during the war years. Blind from birth, possessing the gift of perfect pitch, a phenomenal memory and immense natural facility, Shearing made his first solo broadcast in 1939, at the age of nineteen, and almost immediately assumed the mantle of national jazz phenomenon. He was voted "Top Pianist" six times in succession in the annual poll conducted by the *Melody Maker* among its readers, moved to the United States in 1947 and, in less than two years, made the first in a string of hit records with his quintet. He remained active and successful into extreme old age, hung on to his British citizenship and was knighted in 2007. He died in 2011, at the age of ninety-one.

There were no record charts in those days, but some of the most popular records of the first few post-war years contained a strong element of one kind of jazz or another. These included Pee Wee Hunt's stylized Dixieland version of 'Twelfth Street Rag' (1948) – a very big hit indeed, early harbingers of rhythm and blues in Nellie Lutcher's 'Hurry On Down' (1947) and Louis Jordan's 'Open The Door Richard' (1947), Frankie Laine's 'Shine' (1948), complete with Armstrong-style scat intro, and several more. Even 'Cocktails For Two' (1945), Spike Jones's sublime concoction of mayhem and silly noises, was served up in a ramshackle Dixie sauce. Bundled together, all types of jazz, swing, near-jazz, and anything else which could conceivably be squeezed into the same package, attracted a sizeable segment of the post-war population below the age of thirty. None of the above records, I venture to suggest, would have met with much success before the war (except, perhaps, 'Cocktails For Two', which is a masterpiece for all time). Sensibility had shifted, and the change helped bring to light a veiled but palpable friction between the generations.

To put it crudely, although older people wanted living conditions better than those of the 1930s (which was why they voted Labour in the landslide election of 1945), they wanted tastes, manners and social life in general to be more or less as they used to be, minus the slums and the snobbery – "back to normal", as the popular phrase had it.[10] They tended to harp on nostalgically about "before the war", a habit which very young people, who had little significant memory of that time, found increasingly irksome. In cramped and constrained post-war conditions, small expressions of individuality would regularly lead to conflict, and the battleground was to become familiar territory in the decades that followed – music, dress, "going out" (i.e. away from the family circle) and choice of companions. The discord was regularly acted out in British films of the period. For instance, in *It Always Rains On Sunday* (Ealing Studios, 1947), set in the East End of London, the main drama proceeds against a domestic background of low-level warfare between a woman and her two teenage step-daughters over petty questions of going out, unsuitable dress and keeping the wrong company (in one case with the shady proprietor of a music shop, who also runs a dance band). This leads to an atmosphere of frustration and claustrophobia so powerful that it lingers in the mind long after details of the plot have been forgotten. It was often around such situations that a kind of shamefaced, creeping anti-Americanism made its appearance. Sour jokes about the success of GIs with British women during the war ("Overpaid, oversexed and over here", "One Yank and they're off", and so on) persisted because they concealed a deeper resentment that we were now the poor relations, that British ways were in danger of being supplanted by American ways, and that our young people preferred them – preferred going out and having dubious fun with strangers. The alien nature of this fun was epitomised in the conflict over styles of dancing. Along with the cinema, public dancing was a favourite social activity. At weekends village halls, town halls, hotel ballrooms and Palais de Danse were crowded with dancers of several generations. For the most part, the popular dance forms – waltz, quickstep, foxtrot, and so on – had survived from pre-war days, but the GI invasion had introduced an energetic, free-form style, derived from a Harlem speciality, the Lindy Hop, commonly known as the "jitterbug" or "jive". This proved to be the cause of endless dark complaints about young people "jumping around like a bunch of savages". There is a moment in the Ealing film *Dance Hall* (1950) when a couple of girls begin jiving rather sedately in a corner of the hall, only to be interrupted by the manager with the words, "Ladies, ladies, please! Come out of that jungle!" In view of attitudes like that, perhaps it is not surprising that the one truly objectionable aspect of the American wartime presence, its institutionalized and officially sanctioned racism, was scarcely ever mentioned.

None of the manifestations mentioned above – popular music, popular cinema, social dancing – would have been recognized at the time as constituting any part of "culture". Despite the levelling effect of war on the home front and the broad political consensus of the immediate post-war years, cultural interests were still largely determined by social class, as the new shape of BBC radio clearly revealed. There was the Third Programme for "serious" or high culture (opera, symphony concerts, talks on "highbrow" subjects and so on) for the upper crust and its associated intelligentsia. Then came the Home Service (plays, current affairs, light music), the preserve of the middle classes. The Light Programme (variety turns, dance bands, comedy shows packed with catch-phrases) provided for the cheerfully uncouth majority. Jazz, and the growing enthusiasm for it, did not fit neatly into any of these categories. This was to prove its great strength and attraction in the years to come.

Back in post-war London, now kicking his heels at Chelsea Barracks, Humphrey Lyttelton made for the Nuthouse, one of the surviving representatives of a thirties-style club, and asked to sit in with the band. At such places there was a long tradition of young, upper-class revellers pestering bandleaders for a chance to sit-in, usually on the drums. The former King Edward VIII, as Prince of Wales, had famously been one of these.

> There passed over the musicians' faces an expression which in later years I have come to know well. It is a special look, registering consent with the minimum degree of encouragement . . . I was never a Society type, but I was on this occasion wearing the uniform of a Grenadier Captain, which to them amounted to very much the same thing . . . They nodded glumly in answer to my request, so I climbed up onto the stand and suggested one of the standard jazz tunes. I won't say that my playing brought them to

their feet cheering and applauding, but it was certainly better than they had expected, and from that time on I was allowed – even invited – to sit in quite regularly.[11]

The leader of the band at the Nuthouse was the drummer Carlo Krahmer, described by Lyttelton as "the sort of unofficial Dean of the London jazz world". Everyone seemed to know him and he kept open house at his basement flat, which also housed his gigantic record collection. It was Krahmer who provided Lyttelton with his entrée to the jazz scene, acting as his guide and mentor. Indeed, it is no exaggeration to say that Carlo Krahmer launched Humphrey Lyttelton's career. As to the style of jazz, as far as Lyttelton knew there was only one:

> When I first began to play the trumpet, the word "jazz" was still quite a simple term, roughly describing the "hot" dance music coming from America. The jazz fan of the thirties didn't bother much with definitions, apart from vaguely distinguishing the music of the large bands, which he called "swing", from that of the small improvising bands and informal jam session groups, which he called "pure jazz".[12]

According to this definition, the Nuthouse band played "pure jazz", as did the ad hoc bands that would assemble to play at rhythm-club evenings. Their repertoire consisted of what Lyttelton called "standard themes". These were popular songs of the 1920s and '30s whose candid melodies and robust harmonies made them particularly amenable to jazz improvisation. Everybody knew 'Crazy Rhythm', 'Tea For Two', 'Whispering', 'Lady Be Good', 'Honeysuckle Rose', and so on, and no one with a moderately musical ear should have had any difficulty following improvisations on them. Since jam sessions are, by definition, unprepared, off-the-cuff affairs, the tunes played had to be ones which all the players already knew. In practice this severely limited their choice to a common pool of a few dozen numbers in most cases. The simple and unvarying form of each performance – theme, string of solos, theme – relied on the inventiveness of the individual soloists to hold the listeners' attention. In its native habitat, places such as the Nuthouse, this arrangement worked perfectly well, since the music wasn't so much listened to as enjoyed as part of an agreeable ambiance. Sources of inspiration included Armstrong (of course), Goodman, Coleman Hawkins, Artie Shaw, Gene Krupa, Jack Teagarden, Teddy Wilson, and so on. Only towards the very end of the 1930s did the supple, blues-inflected style of Kansas City begin to reveal its influence, when 'Doggin' Around' and a few other Count Basie numbers joined the list of jam-session favourites.

A significant innovation, which was to set a pattern for the presentation of jazz in the post-war period, appeared in London in October 1942.

The Feldman Swing Club was the first club in Britain dedicated purely to presenting live jazz. It was financed by Joe Feldman, a clothing manufacturer with four musical sons – Robert, saxophonist, who ran the club with his pianist brother, Monty, together with Arnold, a trumpeter, and Victor, the baby of the family and an infant prodigy, first as a drummer and later as pianist and vibraphonist. The club operated, initially on Sunday evenings and later on Saturdays as well, in a large basement at 100 Oxford Street, premises which on weekdays housed a quick-lunch establishment for office workers, known as Mac's Restaurant. With an annual membership of five shillings (25p) and a modest admission charge thereafter, it was regularly filled to capacity. With no drinks licence and opening hours of 7.30–11pm, it could by no means be described as a night club. Although there was dancing, the music itself was its *raison d'être*. Robert Feldman picked the band – on opening night it included Kenny Baker on trumpet, Jimmy Skidmore and Frank Weir on saxophones and Tommy Pollard on piano – and the Feldman Trio (Robert, Monty and eight-year-old Victor, sometimes dubbed "Kid Krupa") played during the interval. The Feldman Club soon became established as a regular haunt of US service musicians seeking to sit-in. An appearance at the Feldman Club was valued by aspiring British players as a mark of acceptance into the jazz world. Needless to say, Carlo Krahmer's name was prominent among the regular performers. The club continued for twelve successful years in its subterranean West End venue.

The ideological problem of the 1930s had been to establish the distinction between jazz and dance music; the problem of the post-war years was to make sense of the wildly divergent styles of jazz which now began to appear. An early attempt to sum up this development appeared in *Melody Maker* on 11 March 1946. The writer, Seymour Wyse, introduced himself as a Briton who had returned to the country after eight years in the US and he was responding to some remarks (now irretrievable) which had been made in a recent Radio Rhythm Club broadcast. There were now, he wrote, four types of jazz: (i) New Jazz (or bebop, of which Britain was almost entirely ignorant as yet) (ii) Jump Music (roughly corresponding to Lyttelton's "pure jazz"), which he identifies with the great soloists of the thirties – Armstrong, Hawkins, Eldridge, Carter, and so on (iii) Dixieland (white Chicago style), including Muggsy Spanier, Eddie Condon, Jack Teagarden, Bobby Hackett, and so on (iv) "Phantom Jazz" (revivalism), which, in his view, was a matter more of myth than of reality. This is a remarkably shrewd summary. It foretells in general outline the shape of things to come. Wyse makes some astute observations, too, on the "clubbish" nature of British jazz enthusiasm and its "fetish" of record collecting, understandable though this may be in the circumstances. The *Melody Maker*'s weekly column on jazz records bore the title "Collectors' Corner" and assumed a distinctly scholarly air.

The bulk of jazz records bought and of jazz played both live and on the radio at the time came under Wyse's headings of "jump music" and "Dixieland".

There can be little doubt about the popularity of the former, going by the jazz content of radio broadcasts and record releases already mentioned, and by winners of the *Melody Maker* readers' poll. In 1946 these included the bands of Ted Heath, Jack Parnell, Harry Hayes, Harry Gold and Harry Parry. Among individuals named were Kenny Baker, George Chisholm, Carl Barriteau and Norman Stenfalt. An "All-Star Jazz Rally", held at Abbey Road studios the following year, featured much the same cast and the paper carried a photograph of an impressively long queue awaiting admission.

In the case of "Dixieland", two American bands falling into this category had made a particular impression: Bob Crosby's orchestra and Muggsy Spanier's Ragtime Band. In 1935, Bob Crosby, younger brother of the singer and film star Bing Crosby, became leader of a big band, succinctly described by the *Radio Times* in 1940 as "one of the foremost American white bands, [which] specialises in a modern version of the vigorous Dixieland style". Contained within it was a small band called the Bob Cats. Its members included several native New Orleans musicians, and their spirited, open-textured ensemble playing attracted a sizeable following, even at the height of the swing era. In 1939, the cornettist Muggsy Spanier, whose jazz recording pedigree reached back as far as 1924 Chicago, put together an eight-piece band to play the kind of music he loved best of all, the kind he had played as a young man. The unexpected, if modest, success of Muggsy Spanier's Ragtime Band led to its making eight records, sixteen numbers in all, for Victor Records. They were released in Britain by HMV in 1940, at the rate of one per month. All members of the band, including Muggsy himself, had spent time working in big bands, and there is a distinct sense of release and an infectious joie de vivre about these pieces, known to posterity as the "Great Sixteen".

These bands, the Bob Cats particularly, had their direct counterparts in Britain, the best-known being Harry Gold's Pieces of Eight. Gold (1907–2005) was perhaps the first Briton to experience a species of Armstrong moment, although in his case the cause was the Original Dixieland Jazz Band, which he had heard live in 1920, at the age of thirteen. It certainly determined the course of his long life. After an early career with the bands of Roy Fox, Oscar Rabin and others, he formed the Pieces of Eight in 1945 and its debut was in a VE-Day broadcast from the grounds of the British Embassy in Paris. The Pieces of Eight quickly became one of the most popular bands in Britain. Its music, like its founder, was irrepressibly cheerful, and Gold's mastery of the bass saxophone a source of wonder, partly because, at 5 ft 2 in, he was practically invisible behind the instrument's mighty bulk. He launched a spirited defence of Dixieland in the *Melody Maker* (9 November 1946), following a further article by Seymour Wyse who claimed that such old-fashioned music was "dead". Gold aptly compared the loose texture of the Dixieland ensemble with the ever-changing patterns of a kaleidoscope, and concluded with a ringing endorsement of the Bob Cats, Spanier and Red Nichols.

So, to return to Seymour Wyse's handy classification, we can say that his two central categories – "jump music" and Dixieland – represent the preferences of the average British jazz lover at the end of the war. This was the *status quo* which was about to be upset, as the two extremes, his "new jazz" and "phantom jazz", captured the attention of the post-war generation. Since they travelled in entirely opposite directions, and seemed almost to inhabit separate planets, it will be necessary to chart their initial courses separately.

3 Austerity Stomp

Among some wartime teenagers, the age-group just after Lyttelton's, a new infatuation was making itself felt. It took the form of an obsession, not simply with jazz, but specifically with early jazz, the music's origins in New Orleans at the turn of the century and its first great flowering in Chicago during the 1920s. The genesis of this passion is maddeningly difficult to pin down, but its symptoms were exuberantly recalled by George Melly in his book, *Owning Up*:

> All over wartime Britain, at every class level, the same thing was happening. Throughout the thirties a mere handful of people had remained interested in early jazz. They corresponded with each other about the music, published transitory typewritten sheets, and spent their weekends junk-shopping for rare records among the scratched and dusty piles of Harry Lauders. Suddenly, as if by some form of spontaneous combustion, the music exploded in all our heads.[1]

Melly's account of his jazz epiphany began, you may recall, with hearing Armstrong's 'Drop That Sack' coming through an open window at Stowe School. Freddy Legon (born 1925), later to become the guitarist in Humphrey Lyttelton's band, experienced his in somewhat different circumstances. A teenaged apprentice draughtsman, he was mooching around Petticoat Lane market, in London's East End, one Sunday morning when his ear was caught by a record being played on a wind-up gramophone. "To my ears at the time it was a complete jumble. I couldn't make head or tail of it, but somehow it appealed to me and I bought it on the spur of the moment."[2] The record was Muggsy Spanier's 'At The Jazz Band Ball'.

After the first revelation came initiation. Melly: "Slowly I learnt something about the music and its history, most of it inaccurate, all of it romantic. I heard my first Bessie Smith record. It was 'Gimme a Pigfoot and a Bottle of

Beer'."[3] Legon: "On the radio I heard a programme called something like *A Visit to New Orleans*, describing the dance halls, the street parades, even a funeral – all illustrated by Jelly Roll Morton records. That really was it. That's when I realised what jazz was about."[4]

In 1944, at the age of eighteen, Melly was conscripted into the Royal Navy as an ordinary seaman aboard *HMS Dido*:

> I took my gramophone and records with me, and on my ship I found two or three people with the same obsession . . . In the *Dido*, in the chain locker, I and a few friends gathered like early Christians in the catacombs to listen to our records. One of them told me that he had heard there was a live revivalist band which played in a pub on the outskirts of London. Actually it was George Webb's Dixielanders, but I never got to hear them. I didn't really believe it was possible to play this music any more. I imagined that the secret had been lost, like early Cubism. I knew intellectually that the Spanier Ragtime sides had been recorded in the early forties [*actually 1939*], but I didn't believe it emotionally. All real jazz existed in a golden age before big bands and riffs and saxophones and commercialism had driven the jazzmen out of the garden.[5]

George Webb's Dixielanders did indeed play "revivalist" jazz in the unlikely surroundings of the downstairs bar at the Red Barn in Barnehust, Kent, a stretch of inter-war suburb between Bexleyheath and Dartford, and the clue to what made them noteworthy lies in that word "revivalist". Like Melly, they passionately loved old jazz, but, unlike him, they did not think it impossible to bring it back to life by learning how to play it. No one has ever seriously challenged their claim to have been the first British revivalist jazz band, and they came together in the first place only through a historical and geographical quirk of fate. They were all young men and, this being wartime, they would in the normal course of events have been called up into the forces. But the industrialized south bank of the Thames, from the Medway to the Pool of London, was lined with munitions factories and other war-related establishments, and jobs in them were deemed "reserved occupations". It was dangerous work and they were a sitting target for German bombers – people used to joke that it would be a quieter life in the army – but they stayed put.

George Webb (1917–2010) worked as a machine gun fitter in the Vickers-Armstrong factory at Crayford. The son of a former music hall artiste turned fishmonger, he was a keen jazz enthusiast and self-taught amateur pianist. He took it upon himself to organize lunchtime entertainment at the factory, assembling scratch bands from among the workers. A number of the players were jazz-minded, like himself, and soon became bored with playing endless sing-along versions of 'We'll Meet Again' and 'Oh, Johnny, Oh!' Webb looked around for somewhere they could get together to play in their spare time.

The Red Barn, a couple of miles from the factory, turned out to be the place. "A perfect position in a cellar bar below the main pub, safe from air raids, and any noise the bands might make could not annoy the customers. The room had a beautiful Chappell piano – in tune!"[6] They were offered the room free for a month's trial period. Webb decided to do the thing properly and make it official. "It was named the Bexleyheath and District Rhythm Club and allotted a club number by the *Melody Maker*." Strict punctilio, it seems, was maintained, even in a corner of England which, under heavy bombardment, had become known as "Bomb Alley". Monday evenings at the rhythm club followed the customary pattern. The first hour would be devoted to a record recital, followed by a discussion. After that there would be a jam session by local musicians, where the musical fare was the usual selection of familiar standards. During the worst of the bombing dance halls and suchlike venues were closed, leaving even the best local musicians at a loose end and eager to play. The Red Barn offered the perfect opportunity, and had the added attraction of taking an unusually free and easy attitude to licensing hours: "Being below the pub and out of sight and mind, we could carry on playing and drinking, sometimes until after midnight."

Things might have continued like this indefinitely, had it not been for the arrival of one Owen Bryce (born 1920). It was unusual at a rhythm club for a musician to give a record recital, but Bryce was one of these rare birds. A semi-professional musician from the age of fifteen, he played trumpet in the band at the local Palais and was an avid collector of jazz records, which he also occasionally bought and sold. As a conscientious objector, he worked in the Rescue Service, an often grim job. He first appeared at the Red Barn in the role of recitalist, playing records by Red Nichols. He and Webb struck up a friendship. Visiting Bryce's home, Webb was astonished by the breadth of his collection. "He had dozens of American records which included many names familiar to us – Clarence Williams, Bessie Smith, McKinney's Cotton Pickers, Eddie Lang and Joe Venuti – but which we had never actually heard."[7] Inspired by these vintage recordings, Webb and Bryce began playing duets together. They gathered a few more musicians around them, with the aim of doing something more interesting than tramping the well-trodden paths of 'Honeysuckle Rose' and 'Lady Be Good'. After trying several models, they settled on emulating the dense texture and powerful drive of the pioneer New Orleans bands, in particular King Oliver's Creole Jazz Band of 1922–23. They rehearsed in the Webb family's front room. Players came and went. By 1943, conditions on the Home Front had quietened considerably. Places of entertainment were open again and musicians who had been glad of having the Red Barn as a place to go for a weekly blow found themselves in demand once more for paid gigs. "On some Mondays," Webb wrote later, "there were only a few players available, and we were reduced mainly to record recitals. We were left wondering how we could survive."[8] This was the moment for the front-room band, hastily christened (rather confusingly, in view of their chosen style) "George Webb's Dixielanders", to step into the breach.

> The reaction to the sound we created as we kicked off with 'At A Georgia Camp Meeting' was dramatic. God knows what we sounded like – nervous, ragged, out of tune – but by the time we completed the tune we were playing to about ten members. The other fifty or so had fled to the saloon bar upstairs. But we stuck it out and carried on regardless.[9]

It must have been a shock. No one in England, evidently not even members of the Bexleyheath and District Rhythm Club, would have heard anything like it before. Back in the early 1920s, the only way to record music had been by the acoustic method, involving an enormous horn which funnelled the sound to a cutting needle. The result was never particularly true to life and, with the eight members of King Oliver's band squeezed together around this contraption, it is surprising that there were any coherent results at all. If you close your eyes and concentrate hard you can hear enough to tell what a truly wonderful band it was, but it is like listening to a radio playing in the house next door, with one ear pressed to the wall. We know from the recollections of those who experienced it in person that the effect of the two cornets (Oliver and the young Louis Armstrong), clarinet, trombone, piano, banjo and drums was overwhelming. George Webb's Dixielanders never achieved anything like the force and intensity of that, but they used the same instrumentation (with the addition of sousaphone, playing a bass part) and clearly captured enough of the original ferocity to scare the living daylights out of the unwary, especially in a confined space. Recordings made by the Dixielanders in 1945 and '46 sound unimpressive today, but music heard live is always more potent than the best recording, so we should bear in mind that these records convey reality at the Red Barn in 1945 no better than the old acoustic recordings convey the reality of King Oliver at the Lincoln Gardens, Chicago, in 1923. Another thing to bear in mind is the utter strangeness of this music to 1945 ears accustomed to the types of swing and small-band jazz described in the preceding chapter. This was essentially ensemble music. Occasional brief solos emerged, but the most distinctive feature of Oliver's music was the dynamic interweaving of separate improvised lines (dubbed "collective improvisation" by the first revivalist critics), all borne along on the irresistible, rolling beat of the rhythm section. It calls for alert ears, nimble technique and complete mutual understanding among the players. Having two cornets playing the lead, instead of just one, adds to the difficulty, since much of the time they will have to be playing in something like unison or close harmony. The Dixielanders were rarely well in tune and their rhythm, hampered by the laborious sousaphone, never once got off the ground. On the other hand, Eddie Harvey's firm trombone and Wally Fawkes's clarinet, with its wild, skirling vibrato, catch the style very well. No one in Britain had made a sound on a clarinet remotely like that since Sidney Bechet's brief visit in 1919.

The distinction between real jazz and dance music, which had so preoccupied British jazz lovers before the war, now settled down into a clear ideology, its most common expression being the use of "commercial" as a term of general abuse. Among revivalists, the reasoning went something like this: "Jazz is music of sincerity, self-expression and the free spirit. It is not entertainment for sale, and does not pander to fashion and popular taste. We decide what we play and how we play it. (Lyttelton's first volume of autobiography, it may be recalled, was entitled *I Play as I Please.*) Professional musicians, even the best of them, are under orders to play what the public wants, and what bandleaders tell them to play. That is commercialism and we reject it." Although revivalist bands were usually paid something for their performances, their members all had other jobs, or were students, and were therefore able to hang on to their ideals in relative security. Modernists had a different anti-commercial rationale, which will appear in due course. The ideology was entirely self-generated. There was no trace of anything remotely like it among the pioneers whose work the revivalists were emulating – quite the reverse, in fact. Rather like primitive religion, it was a mechanism for explaining a phenomenon that was real to them but which they could not account for. They had found this music which moved and excited them, which they had come to value highly, amid the puerile trivialities of early twentieth-century popular music. This was a way of extracting it, bringing it to light and according it the status of an art. Looked at from one point of view it was absurd, but from another it made perfect sense. Other aspects of the anti-commercial ideology made no sense at all. Along with their status as wage-slaves, dance-band musicians had acquired professional skills of a high order – instrumental dexterity, the ability to read music, a memory stored with popular tunes from several decades. All this was denounced. Indeed, it was common for revivalists to reject all conventional musical knowledge, for fear of commercial pollution. As a result, revivalist jazz was often badly played, out of tune and, because the players could only manage to get around in a limited number of easy keys, monotonous.

As the years passed and a more rounded picture gradually emerged of the musical upbringing of leading New Orleans-born figures in early jazz, this cock-eyed primitivism became increasingly untenable. In particular, it was understood that the interaction between working-class African-Americans, like Armstrong, and sophisticated, mixed-race Creole musicians, with names such as Picou, Baquet and Bigard, schooled in the French tradition, had been sustained and intense, and valuable to both.

Once the first shock had passed, Monday nights at the Red Barn changed radically. Although wartime conditions kept the lid on it to a certain extent, the speed with which news of the Webb band spread is proof enough that there was an audience ready and waiting. Within a few weeks people were making long and difficult journeys by public transport, through the wartime blackout, to the Red Barn to experience the brassy, stomping revivalist jazz of the Dixielanders. "It was musically crude," recalled Freddy Legon, by now a Red Barn regular, "but in this pub basement, crowded with people, the atmosphere was absolutely electric."[10] Experienced musicians scoffed at the whole thing: the amateur technique, the wandering intonation, the antiquated tunes and, most of all, the collective improvisation. To them it was beyond a joke; it was an insult, especially since it seemed to be attracting all the attention. This only strengthened the resolve of the revivalists and converted their enthusiasm into a cause. Causes tend to breed fanaticism, which in turn breeds ideologues and commissars, as Eddie Harvey (1925–2012), the band's trombonist, discovered at first hand. Aged nineteen at the time, an engineering apprentice at Vickers-Armstrong, he was a naturally talented musician whose love of jazz ranged well beyond the boundaries of early New Orleans and 1920s Chicago. He listened enthusiastically to records by J. C. Higginbotham, Jack Teagarden and other trombonists of dubious provenance. His ability to read music, highly suspect in itself, had led him so far astray as to play on occasion in a local dance band. "I was called up in front of the Jazz Police," he recalled cheerfully, sixty-five years later. "George, Jim Godbolt, who was sort of the band's manager, and various others. I was well and truly ticked off and ordered to stick to the straight and narrow. It's funny when you look back on it. Pathetic, really."[11]

Jim Godbolt (1922–2013), the band's "sort of manager", went on to a varied career in jazz promotion and publishing. In the second volume of his *History of Jazz in Britain*,[12] published forty years after these events, he agrees good-naturedly with Harvey, before going on to present an admirably impartial assessment of the band which had once inspired him to so much fervour:

> It was pastiche; it *was* artistically futile; the performance *was* far below the technical standards of the musicians who had inspired it. But, contradiction that it is, Webb's Dixielanders were, in their time, a force and often tremendously exciting "live". They were to become the inspiration for many similarly styled bands throughout the country.

Beyond the charmed circle of revivalism, public reception for George Webb's Dixielanders remained patchy, to say the least. It was their rueful boast that they had played every hall in south-east London and north Kent – once. They did, however, receive the patronage of the Young Communist League (YCL). Moscow's line on jazz continued to fluctuate but, in their newspaper, *Challenge*, the British YCL constructed their own rationale, which may be summed up as "people's music played by young proletarian workers". Under the banner of the Challenge Jazz Club they put on a series of concerts in the tomb-like Memorial Hall in Farringdon Street, near the offices of the *Daily Worker*. The band even had the effrontery to enter for a local dance-band championship, sponsored by the *Melody Maker*, where they won third place (out of a field of five) and a silver cup. The judges' report was encouraging but guarded. The Dixielanders' first attempt at recording, for Decca in May 1945, proved a disaster. Accounts vary, but it seems that the intonation was even worse than usual, and the Decca engineers spent most of the session attempting to isolate the "tune" from the melee of collective improvisation. A second attempt, privately recorded in Derby in December, produced two numbers, 'New Orleans Hop Scop Blues' and 'Come Back Sweet Papa', which were issued on the Jazz label (Jazz 001), specially set up for the purpose. It was priced at an eye-watering fifteen shillings, but all copies were eventually sold. Over the next couple of years the Dixielanders made a number of broadcasts on BBC radio, and several more recording sessions.

Once the war was over, and despite the surrounding devastation and grinding austerity, much more movement and general activity became possible. Webb began branching out. Leaving the comrades and their mausoleum in Farringdon Street, he and Godbolt began putting on their own monthly concerts at St George's Hall in the West End, under the title of the Hot Club of London. These were run rather along the lines of an extra-large rhythm club, with a record recital before the live music. Now, however, this included at least one guest band in addition to the Dixielanders. It soon became obvious that bands and individual musicians were popping up everywhere. The Christie brothers, Keith (trombone) and Ian (clarinet), came from Blackpool; a phenomenal young Welsh pianist, Dill Jones, turned up from Newcastle Emlyn; a team glorying in the name The Gut Bucket Six arrived from Birmingham; Freddie Legon made an early appearance with his Original London Blues Blowers (guitar, washboard, comb-and-paper and vocals). Most notable of all, in January 1947, Humphrey Lyttelton arrived on the scene, released from the Army and enjoying a kind of postponed late adolescence.

Having failed to impress anyone with his suitability for respectable employment, Lyttelton had taken stock of his prospects and decided that his only hope lay in exploiting his talent for drawing. With the aid of an ex-serviceman's study grant, he had enrolled as a student at Camberwell School of Art, his sights set on a vaguely defined career as an illustrator. In order to look the part he bought a roll-neck sweater, which he wore with his old battledress dyed navy-blue and, to complete the effect, grew a beard. The idea of becoming a professional musician seemed quite out of the question. Under the aegis of Carlo Krahmer, he had been taking part in jam sessions around London, including at the Feldman Swing Club in Oxford Street, and on Sunday lunchtimes at the Orange Tree, a pub in Friern Barnet. Word had got around about a tall art-student type who played hot trumpet and, as part of the quest for new faces to present at the Hot Club, an expedition was dispatched to Friern Barnet to seek him out.

He related in *I Play as I Please,*

> One day a delegation from George Webb's band came out to the Orange Tree – Jim Godbolt, manager of the band, and Wally Fawkes the clarinetist. They asked me to visit the Red Barn with my trumpet and suggested that I might appear as a guest in one of the Hot Club of London concerts. I felt a terrible new-boy when I first went off to rehearsal on a Sunday morning at the Red Barn. I wore my dyed battledress and my beard and sandals – the full art-student's uniform – and I think they thought me an odd fish. My nervousness arose chiefly from the fact that I was not at that time an Accredited Revivalist.

He later admitted that what really made him nervous was crippling shyness: "I was as shy as anything. I just didn't know how to talk to people."[13] But it is true that his few years' head-start as a jazz convert, his absence during the war and subsequent involvement in the latter-day jam-session milieu around Carlo Krahmer had conspired to isolate him from revivalism. "The beginnings of the movement – the critical cryings in the wilderness and attacks on current taste – went right over my head, so that by the time I reached Camberwell and began to look around the jazz world I was by no means a purist."[14] He had, in fact, heard the Webb band already, while on leave in 1944, at a concert at Toynbee Hall. "I sat three rows back in the stalls and wallowed in the great flood of brassy sound from the two cornets and trombone, but I didn't really attach any particular significance to it."[15]

Soon after his Hot Club appearance Lyttelton became a member of George Webb's Dixielanders. He took over when Reg Rigden, who played first cornet (cornet and trumpet being more or less interchangeable), left. Owen Bryce, the second cornet, found he could not re-establish the close rapport he had developed with Rigden and left shortly afterwards. Lyttelton remained with the band, the sole cornettist, until the end of 1947. Although the band made no official recordings, six privately recorded numbers do survive from the nine months during which Lyttelton was effectively leader of the Dixielanders and they contain a number of small revelations. In the first place, the band is now reasonably in tune, with the exception of the new trombonist, Tony Finnis. (Eddie Harvey, having abandoned his apprenticeship through lack of interest, was now serving in the Royal Air Force.) The sousaphone has been replaced by a string bass, to the great improvement of the rhythm section. The presence of Lyttelton himself, the easy authority of his playing, even at this early stage, with its confident phrasing and rhythmic flexibility, simply lifts the whole affair onto a new level. One can detect, too, the beginnings of a lifelong friendship with Wally Fawkes and a close musical partnership which was to continue for the best part of a decade. They are both sophisticated musicians, with an instinctive taste well beyond the grasp of the others. They had much in common. Fawkes, too, was an art student, soon destined to become one of Britain's most successful cartoonists, under the pen-name "Trog". They shared a sense of humour, and even a murky ancestral past. The last member of the Lyttelton family to be christened Humphrey had been hung, drawn and quartered in 1606, for his part in the Gunpowder Plot. The Fawkes family at that time had contained one Guido, or "Guy", who is still burned in effigy every fifth of November, the anniversary of the foiling of the Plot.

One thing is especially noticeable in this first recording of Lyttelton's, and that is his rapid and pronounced vibrato. This was characteristic of a number of early New Orleans cornet players, in particular Mutt Carey, who first recorded in 1921 (or it may have been 1922) with Kid Ory's Sunshine Orchestra. As a latecomer to revivalism, whose guiding light had been the classic Armstrong, it seems that Lyttelton had set himself the task of absorbing the earlier idiom and, consciously or not, had adopted the vibrato along with the cornet. This is significant, since it reveals a sensitivity to nuance which enabled him to develop and to change stylistic direction throughout his life. He could, as it were, step into a style and quickly feel at home in it. A perfect early example of this can be found in six pieces recorded only a few months later than the one cited above, by a pickup band calling itself Carlo Krahmer's Chicagoans. Playing trumpet this time, Lyttelton adopts the slightly bumptious manner characteristic of the white Chicago school. The two-bar break that opens his solo on 'Who's Sorry Now?' – eager, bustling, reckless – captures it to perfection. Of the rapid vibrato there is not a trace.

George Webb's Dixielanders disbanded in January 1948, after a final Hot Club of London concert. "It had only happened because we were all thrown together while Britain was at war," Webb wrote in his memoirs.[16] Now, with the wartime industries closing down, they were scattering in pursuit of other work. In the same month Humphrey Lyttelton and his Band came into existence, with Wally Fawkes firmly on board. As an institution, it was to remain in being for the next sixty years. Lyttelton's timing was exactly right, as it turned out. Webb's revivalist jazz had filled the downstairs bar of the Red Barn every Monday night. Other bands had begun to draw similar crowds in other places. The more ambitious Hot Club of London concerts had filled St George's Hall once a month. That seemed to be about the limit of the audience which revivalist jazz could reach, if presented according to the rhythm-club formula established in the early 1930s – record recital, discussion, concert. No one, apparently, had ever thought to question this. Then, in 1947, Australia's version of George Webb arrived out of the blue and proceeded to stir everything up. His name was Graeme Bell (1914–2012). He and his band turned up in England, unannounced, broke and stranded. Invited to play at a socialist youth festival in Prague, they had given up their jobs, cashed in their savings and headed for Czechoslovakia. There had been vague promises of appearances in Britain once that engagement was over. The promises had fallen through but they had come anyway. They were taken on to play at a new venture, the Leicester Square Jazz Club, held on Monday nights in a hired hall above the Café de l'Europe. The Bell band had no interest in recitals or discussions. They advertised themselves as playing jazz for dancing.

Because, in Britain, jazz had for years defined itself as the opposite of "dance music", and because England favoured a particularly formal and buttoned-up variety of social dancing, the announcement caused some consternation. But this was the West End, where people traditionally came to enjoy themselves, even in a post-war London sadly short of fun and sensation. Everybody knows that, given half a chance, most young people enjoy jumping about to loud music, and with art colleges, medical schools, a large university and miles of suburbs close at hand, the place was soon stuffed to capacity. When Graeme Bell and his Australian Jazz Band eventually returned home, and Humphrey Lyttelton and his Band took over, Leicester Square was well on its way to becoming the youth capital of London, on Monday nights at any rate. To begin with, nobody had the faintest idea of what dancing to revivalist jazz might entail. As Lyttelton recalls in *I Play as I Please*:

> The sort of jiving that was done in the ballrooms smacked too much of swing music and "jitterbugging" to be countenanced at all (for the youngsters were as purist as the old-timers in their tastes), and of course no-one knew anything about the dances which were originally danced to the music in New Orleans at the beginning of the century. So the dancers at the Leicester Square Jazz Club just invented steps of their own. Led by the art school contingent – the least inhibited of those present – they flung themselves onto the floor and just did the first thing that came into their heads. No doubt it was a terrifying spectacle and there were moments when the band began to look anxiously towards the fire escape. What the diners in the Café de l'Europe below thought about it has never been ascertained.

All this was a gift from heaven to the popular press, and after one particularly graphic account, in *The Leader* (". . . shirt tails fly, feet stamp, hands flutter, hair-do's tumble in ruins, a bearded artist hurls his partner half-way across the room. . ."), the revellers were evicted. They moved to a new club, the London Jazz Club, held two nights a week in a Soho basement, and carried on as before. In the years around 1950, revivalist jazz came to occupy a position in the public mind very similar to that held by flappers and the Charleston a quarter-century earlier and punk rock a quarter-century later – simultaneously fashionable and shocking, seductive and outrageous. In London, at least, there was a distinct touch of chic in the air, too. Regulars at the Lyttelton band's sessions included the young Mary Quant, then studying design at Goldsmiths' College, and Joan Collins, a teenage film starlet, fresh from her debut appearance in *Lady Godiva Rides Again*.

Humphrey Lyttelton generally disliked talking about himself, except in the lightest and most self-deprecating terms, so when he roundly declared, in a television documentary towards the end of his life, "Youth culture began with us," we may be sure that he meant it. By the early 1950s, revivalist jazz had become the focus of what we would now recognize as a fully developed subculture. It defined itself not only by music, but by appearance, demeanour and, to a certain extent, social class. Mere youth, curiously enough, was not a strongly determining factor, perhaps because, for many, youth had been interrupted either by war service or post-war conscription. The "art school look", a sort of contrived scruffiness, provided a sartorial basis which could be enlivened with whatever exotic bits and pieces came to hand. It was not necessary, of course, to be a student of any kind, as Lyttelton noted: "Young people came too from shops and offices, seizing the opportunity to assert themselves by dressing up in bright, highly original fashions."[17] In its more extreme forms the outfit bore a strong hint of *la vie bohème*, suggestive of picturesque squalor and "free love" – a commodity eagerly sought but not readily available in Britain at the beginning of the 1950s. A pipe-smoking bookishness remained popular among some of the men. This type was immortalized in the person of George, eldest son of the Giles family in the *Daily Express* cartoons of the period. George was always pictured smoking an enormous pipe, with his head stuck in a book. It is a fair bet that George took an interest in revivalist jazz. As for demeanour, the easiest way to characterize it is to say that it was the exact opposite of the way young people were expected to behave at tennis-club or youth-club dances. "My violent enthusiasm, frequent drunkenness and personal manner of dancing attracted a lot of not entirely kindly amusement," recalled George Melly. "Much later I discovered that Humph had christened me 'Bunny-Bum'."[18] No social activity in Britain, England especially, is ever without implications of class, but revivalist jazz did at least succeed in causing a fair amount of confusion in the matter. It appealed to rebellious instincts, still chafing at the constrictions of post-war daily life and, although it thrived in the suburbs, it was the natural enemy of pursed suburban rectitude. In short, revivalist jazz plus dancing caught the mood of the times and it was fun. By a strange irony, the music which had defined itself as not being "dance music" now gained its success by actually *becoming* dance music.

Bands sprang up all around the United Kingdom: Sandy Brown and his Band (Edinburgh), the Yorkshire Jazz Band (Leeds), the Saints (Manchester), Mick Gill's Band (Nottingham), the Second City Jazzmen and Ray Foxley's splendidly-named Levee Loungers (Birmingham); the Riverside Stompers (Bedford), the Merseysippi Jazz Band (Liverpool), the Avon Cities Jazz Band (Bristol), the Clyde Valley Stompers (Glasgow). In the fullness of time, there was scarcely a major waterway in the Kingdom without its eponymous jazz band, and when the major ones were all spoken for, the merest trickle might be adopted – as happened in the case of the Crane River Jazz Band (see Chapter 5). Nor did the ancient universities remain aloof. Oxford boasted the Salty Dogs, while Cambridge, in a display of recondite learning, fielded Tony Short's Varsity Sackdroppers. Around each of these grew up a "scene", a loose-knit community of like-minded young people. Trumpeter Dickie Hawdon (1927—2009), who was *de facto* leader of the Yorkshire Jazz Band at this time, recalled their sessions at the Adelphi, in central Leeds, as "a very big deal – packed out every Wednesday night."[19] Typically, Leeds College of Art provided many of the leading lights, including musicians such as guitarist Diz Disley, clarinetist Alan Cooper, trombonist Eddie O'Donnell and an aspiring vocalist, Frank Abelson, who later achieved fame under the name Frankie Vaughan.

Performances almost always took place in hired rooms or halls, the vast majority of them attached to pubs, inns or hostelries of various kinds. This was the way social events had been arranged in Britain for generations and it suited everyone quite well. To a large extent it still does. It is only when we look around the world and see where jazz is performed in other countries that we realize how untypical it is. The promotion of jazz at grassroots level, the process of actually getting bands up in front of audiences, advertising events and dealing with the money (if any), has been mostly a labour of love in Britain – until recently, at any rate. A large Victorian city pub, with its "function room", made an ideal venue, at the same time removing from the promoter all responsibility for the catering and hospitality side of things. Even the décor, blowsy and a little faded, chimed nicely with the gusto and bonhomie of revivalist jazz. When veteran American musicians began touring widely in Britain in the 1960s, many of them were quite charmed by the whole set-up.

There is no way of avoiding the fact that the majority of dedicated jazz lovers were and are male. Probably it starts with that predilection, often found among intelligent teenage boys, for attaching themselves to arcane fields of interest. Add the attraction of jazz purely as music, the general influence of the zeitgeist, and the phenomenal ability of the growing mind, when aroused, to absorb information, and you have the perfect recipe for a lifelong attachment. Or, if you prefer, for the creation of a lifelong jazz bore. That is why jazz would never have caught on as it did if it had been left to the efforts of the rhythm clubs. It was the dancing that did it. Dancing to jazz in a free-and-easy atmosphere was more fun for both sexes than the tennis-club and youth-club stuff. Even so, for young male devotees, record collecting still constituted an important part of life.

Records have always played a pivotal role in British jazz. The original rhythm clubs functioned largely as opportunities for jazz record collectors to meet, exchange information and opinions and – no doubt like collectors of anything the world over – show off to one another about their acquisitions.

The recording and manufacture of gramophone records was a fairly elaborate industrial process, confined mainly to a few large firms with international connections. The two principal British companies, EMI and Decca, controlled all the major labels – HMV, Parlophone, Columbia, Decca, Brunswick and Capitol. These regularly included jazz records in their lists and some even established sub-catalogues, along the lines of Parlophone's Super Rhythm Style Series and Columbia's Swing Series. HMV, as a result of its long-standing connection with RCA Victor in the States, had access to a particularly rich store of well-recorded US jazz, stretching back to the 1920s and even before. Using these resources, British record companies had managed to keep pretty well in step with the tastes of the broad majority of jazz lovers. Their prices in the post-war years ranged from under 3/6 (16.5p) to more than five shillings (25p) for a ten-inch disc.

However, with the advent of the revival, and bebop a little later, the match between demand and available supply became increasingly unsatisfactory. Revivalists wanted copies of antique rarities, while modernists wanted the latest bebop recordings on small US labels which had no connections in Britain. With the country in the grip of a dollar crisis, large-scale importation of US discs was out of the question. The inevitable result was small-scale importation, by devious and irregular means and at black-market prices. Freddy Legon recalled buying ten-inch 78s by Kid Ory, on a US west-coast label, Crescent, around 1950 at the incredible price of £1:7:6 (£1.375) each. This would be the equivalent of £35 at 2010 prices. The average weekly wage in 1950 was less than eight pounds – approximately £190 in 2010. ("My father went mad!" Legon recalled, "but other people spent just as much on their motor bikes.")[20] Enthusiasts would travel long distances in pursuit of a prized item, even just to see and hear it if they couldn't buy it. The pianist Stan Tracey remembered acquiring a copy of an American Blue Note disc by Art Hodes, even though he had no means of playing it, and of keeping it with him, as a kind of talisman, throughout his two years' National Service. Such devotion was not uncommon. By the early 1950s a scattering of small local record companies had set themselves up, both to release their own editions of American originals and to record British bands. To reissue obscure vintage material it was simply a case of getting hold of the cleanest copy available, re-recording it through a mechanical process called "dubbing", and pressing multiple copies. For current material, licensing deals of various kinds were arranged. The resultant discs were not readily available in high street shops, but every city and many large towns had at least one dealer who carried a stock. The shops were easy to spot because the actual labels on the records in the window were more boldly designed and coloured than the sober magentas and dark blues of the major companies – the influence, no doubt, of all those art students. Leading labels included Esquire (operated by the ubiquitous Carlo Krahmer), Melodisc (with its startling purple-and-yellow design), Tempo, Jazz Parade and Vogue (franchised by the French company of the same name). Some tiny minnows managed to share the same small pool, a good example being Delta, whose entire operation, complete with disc-cutting equipment, occupied the back room of Pete Payne's record shop in Catford, south-east London.

Through the post-war period and the 1950s, especially on Saturday afternoons, these shops acted as informal jazz colleges. A crowd of teens and twenties flicked through boxes of new, second-hand and imported records or just hung about, talking learnedly, while what amounted to a non-stop request programme revolved on the shop's turntable. Newcomers were absorbed into the group, beginning as silent outsiders, hanging around on the periphery, and gradually proceeding, via a sagely nodding apprenticeship, to the dignity of full pundit. One read the reviews and articles in *Melody Maker*, listened to a couple of hours' jazz on Saturday afternoons, while receiving miscellaneous bits of information, and in quite a short time acquired a kind of aural map of the subject. Success could be measured by being able to pick out, say, Jimmy Noone, from a parade of records featuring him and other clarinetists – Barney Bigard, Albert Nicholas or the young Benny Goodman.

Interestingly, the most authentic and convincing tribute to the educative power of a jazz record shop is the work not of an ex-teenage boy, but an ex-teenage girl, Val Wilmer, in her memoir, *Mama Said There'd be Days Like This*:

> I began going to the Swing Shop regularly and, with Bert Bradfield's help, found out how the music sounded. I came home with *Dippermouth Blues*, where Armstrong and Oliver's cornets dovetailed in classic virtuosity – albeit a little hard to hear over the decades – and played it and other records to death. I discovered Morton, Keppard and other New Orleans key figures, such as Bechet and my particular hero, clarinetist Johnny Dodds. And, of course, the blues.[21]

The early influence of the Swing Shop, Streatham, makes several appearances in this engaging account of a life in and around the jazz world.

All this learning was entirely informal and non-official. In fact, that was a large part of the attraction. As Larkin noted: "This was something we had found for ourselves, that wasn't taught at school (what a prerequisite that is of nearly everything worthwhile!)."[22] In a generation heartily sick of being told what was good for it this is hardly surprising. On the other hand, there was the old British instinct towards formalizing interests through clubs and societies which had led to the formation of the rhythm clubs before the war. This, it was still generally agreed, was the way to get things done. Accordingly, in 1948, an ambitious body bearing the worthy title National Federation of Jazz Organisations (NFJO) was founded. Elected officials included musicians such as Webb, Lyttelton and Harry Gold, the editors of *Melody Maker* and the fledgling *Jazz Journal*, broadcasters, club organizers, record shop proprietors and so on. On the principle that every letterhead needs to be graced by at least one title, the position of Patron was accepted by the Marquis of Donegal, a genial old party who might have stepped from the pages of P. G. Wodehouse. In fact, the title was all he had left. The rolling acres that went with it were now part of the Irish Republic, although he appeared not to have noticed.

The NFJO, under its down-to-earth, not to say earthy, Secretary, James Asman, achieved many of the things it set out to do, in the way of putting on concerts and band contests, badgering the BBC into auditioning jazz bands and getting major companies to release a few more jazz records. It is a measure of how much the following for jazz grew in a few years that the NFJO Blue Book, its guide to jazz clubs in Britain, published in 1952, listed more than thirty venues featuring live jazz in the London area alone, and in the same year its annual Jazz Band Ball, having outgrown Hammersmith Palais, was held in the vast Empress Hall (later renamed Earl's Court Arena).

Over one matter, however, the NFJO struggled in vain. All attempts to arrange appearances in Britain by American musicians were blocked by officialdom. The gatekeeper was the Ministry of Labour, but the Minister looked for advice to the Musicians' Union, which refused to countenance the idea. The cause was an ancient row between the British and American unions, dating back to 1935. The view expressed by the Union was that Britain had players just as good as any in the US, and to import American musicians would be to deny work to Britons. The Union, a body formed in 1893 to protect the rights of professional instrumentalists in the days of music hall, was out of its depth in a changing world and increasingly impervious to reason. The louder the complaints grew, the more entrenched the positions became, but the Union had all the power and the jazz lobby had no leverage. The shouting match reached its climax in 1951, the year widely accepted as marking the end of the fagged-out post-war era and the beginning of the optimistic fifties, the year of the Festival of Britain. The Festival celebrations included the opening concert series at the brand new Royal Festival Hall, in which, after much lobbying, it was agreed that jazz should be represented. Who should top the bill at such a momentous event? Why not the man revered almost as a living god by most British jazz lovers? Why not Louis himself? As soon as the idea became public, the Union, in the person of its General Secretary, Hardie Radcliffe, spoke: "Why do we need Louis Armstrong when we've got Kenny Baker?" he was reported as demanding. And that was that.

And so the first-ever jazz concert at the Royal Festival Hall was an all-British affair, although the NFJO did succeed in scoring at least one publicity triumph. A second title had now been added to the letterhead, namely that of the Hon. Gerald Lascelles, younger son of the Princess Royal and therefore first cousin to HRH Princess Elizabeth, the future Queen. It was at his invitation that the Princess attended the concert. This turned the occasion into a newsworthy event, and helped to foster the idea of jazz as a harmless, if eccentric, addition to the cultural landscape. Humphrey Lyttelton topped the bill, followed by the Saints, Manchester's favourite band, Joe Daniels and his Jazz Group, Freddy Randall and his Band, Mick Mulligan's Magnolia Jazz Band with George Melly, the Crane River Jazz Band, boogie-woogie pianist Cyril Scutt, and Graeme Bell's Australian Jazz Band, making a return visit and conveniently representing the Commonwealth. "Revivalist" jazz now began to be called "traditional" jazz, which avoided the problem of explaining exactly what it was that was being revived, while at the same time marking a clear distinction from "modern".

Traditional jazz had not yet become "trad", but a tiny straw-in-the-wind floated by at this concert. The Saints were the unexpected hit of the evening, with a rendition of the old music-hall song 'I Want A Girl (Just Like The Girl That Married Dear Old Dad)' – the precursor of many similar jolly makeovers a decade or so later. The traditional jazz concert, on Saturday 14 July, was followed by a further concert two days later, devoted to modern jazz. It would have been unthinkable to combine the two. Even the weekly Jazz Club broadcast on the BBC Light Programme came in two segments, the second, and smaller, bearing the title Jazz for Moderns. Like hostile tribes, the two factions kept themselves apart, hurling occasional insults at one another from a safe distance. This may be an opportune moment to meet the opposing team.

4 Welcome to Club Eleven!

There was no Royal presence at the modern jazz concert, on Monday 16 July 1951, but the Royal Festival Hall was full nevertheless. The music mostly reflected the styles of currently fashionable American models. As a gesture towards sophistication, or perhaps in an effort to push the budget to its limit, two of the bands appeared with small string sections added. Heading the programme was the Johnny Dankworth Seven, whose twenty-four-year-old leader had recently topped three categories in the *Melody Maker* readers' poll, including "Musician of the Year". By 1951, Dankworth was Lyttelton's opposite number, the figurehead of British modern jazz. The two came from wildly different backgrounds and seemed superficially to have almost nothing in common, but in one respect they were the same: each had begun his jazz career as something of an outsider – as, in Lyttelton's words, "an odd fish".

John Philip William Dankworth was born on 20 September 1927 in Hyams Park, Essex. His parents were Methodists; his father was the sales manager of an electrical insulation firm and his mother trained and conducted amateur choirs. He was educated at Sir George Monoux Grammar School for Boys, Walthamstow, where, during the war, he fell in with a clique of schoolboy jazz fanatics. In his memoirs, *Jazz in Revolution*, he mentions listening to Armstrong's 'Weatherbird' and Ellington's 'Harlem Airshaft' as the shrapnel from anti-aircraft shells pattered onto the roof. As a well-behaved and dutiful son, in the years before teenagers were invented, he felt diffident about confessing his interest in jazz to his parents. "There was no real embargo . . . but the general parental message was that the only 'quality' music was the classical variety. This was the edict tacitly understood and until now rigidly observed by all."[1] His decision, at the age of sixteen, to take up the clarinet was largely determined by the fact that it was used in both jazz and classical music, and hence least likely to cause offence. The fact that Benny Goodman was known to have performed the Mozart concerto also proved useful. Later, however, when news that Dankworth was playing occasional gigs with local dance bands reached the ears of his Headmaster, a letter was despatched, summoning his father for an urgent conference. When Dankworth eventually gained a place at the Royal Academy of Music, the fact was entered in his school record with a note of relief. He was now someone else's problem. Dankworth eventually graduated LRAM from the Academy, and this fact alone made him not merely an "odd fish" but almost unique in the British jazz world he was soon to enter.

Roughly between the years 1940 and 1945 a new and revolutionary style of jazz, known as bebop, came into being in the United States. Its leading figures were young African-American musicians, many of them junior members of regular swing bands, and their revolution embraced not only music, but racial politics, a critique of the economic basis of the entertainment business and, by implication, shifting definitions of art and culture.[2] From the musical point of view, bebop was harmonically more complex than previous forms of jazz and its improvised lines more convoluted, while its typical mode of address to the listener was one of studied indifference. By 1945 bebop had acquired a small but growing cult following, especially around New York City, whereas Britain, isolated by almost six years of war, was unaware of its existence.

Ronnie Scott recalled hearing, in 1945, at the age of eighteen, the American alto saxophonist Art Pepper, sitting in at the Feldman Club. Pepper was then aged twenty and serving in the US Military Police. When Scott congratulated him on his playing, Pepper replied, "Wait till you hear Charlie Parker!" It was the first time Scott had heard the name. We do not know when the first recorded example of the music itself was imported. Various London musicians have claimed that the first bebop record they heard was Gillespie's 'Groovin' High',[3] at the Fullado, a club in New Compton Street frequented by musicians. The disc itself was the property of the cloakroom attendant, named Horace, who played it repeatedly to anyone who would listen.[4] The date is presumed to have been late 1945 or early '46. Another, perhaps stronger, possibility is that bebop was first heard in Manchester, with 20,000 GIs at nearby Burtonwood, the biggest US base in Britain. One of their favourite haunts was the Astoria Ballroom in Plymouth Grove, where the bandleader, Tony Stuart, was unusually keen on jazz and had a "jazz quintet" inside his fourteen-piece band. "The GIs regularly brought Tony the latest US pressings of 78 rpm jazz records, which he played for the teenagers, so creating greater interest in his burgeoning jazz policy."[5] These records almost certainly contained some early examples of bebop. As early as 1945–46, we are told, the young jivers referred to themselves as "boppers".[6] "Although the band was semi-professional, it contained musicians clever enough to figure out the harmonic complexities of the new sound through listening to these records, then transcribing and playing them. Lead-trumpet player Ken Radcliffe was particularly adept in this department."[7] We know that bebop was broached as a topic to spark controversy by Seymour Wyse in his *Melody Maker* article of 11 March 1946 (quoted in Chapter 2). This was continued in a Radio Rhythm

Club discussion between Wyse and Denis Preston, broadcast on 4 May, on the subject of "the future of jazz". In *Melody Maker* of 31 August, a further article by Wyse appeared, under the strapline and heading "During the past few months more and more people have been asking: '*What Is Bebop?*'" There followed an enthusiastic introductory piece, concentrating almost exclusively on Dizzy Gillespie, "whose importance in jazz today is tremendous", with Charley (*sic*) Parker cast in a supporting role. We can therefore fix 1946, with reasonable confidence, as the starting date of the post-war modern movement in British jazz.

Compared with revivalism, bebop was a late arrival and, at first glance, the contrast between them is total. There were, however, similarities. Both revivalism and British bebop began with eager novices learning a new musical language. The crucial difference was that, whereas revivalism originated among non-playing enthusiasts, interest in bebop began primarily among musicians. As far as the vast majority of the population was concerned, the two would have come about equal in the Unholy Row stakes. In place of the boisterous cacophony of six or seven fervent revivalists, all blowing and banging at once, bebop offered a parade of frowning young men taking it in turns to utter streams of notes as fast as possible – most of them wilfully discordant, or so it seemed. Not surprisingly, bebop's earliest British audience occupied not so much a niche as the merest crevice. For musicians, the fascination lay not in the music's background, with all its social, cultural and racial entanglements, but in the music itself. Bebop, in its pristine state, was a soloist's music and the new harmonic language offered exciting new possibilities to the improviser. These had first been glimpsed in the late 1930s. Certain recordings from this period by established artists, such as Coleman Hawkins, the King Cole Trio and the John Kirby Sextet, are remarkably "advanced" in their harmonic content and general configuration. These ideas were picked up and more thoroughly explored by Gillespie, Parker, Thelonious Monk and others. The melodic shapes these pioneers delineated, and the phrases they coined, formed the basis of a musical idiom, known as bebop (or "rebop"), which some British musicians found irresistible – even though at first they barely understood any of it.

Musicians captivated by the new music were typically very young members of professional or semi-professional dance bands. To join a band called for no formal qualification and there was no systematic training to provide a route into the job, apart, perhaps, from early lessons in actually playing an instrument. Novices underwent a process of hit-or-miss selection, followed – if they were lucky – by a kind of casual apprenticeship overseen by older players. Many were completely self-taught and very few had any grounding at all in musical theory. How could they come to grips with this new music, which had excited their passion yet sounded so strange and unapproachable? Some began by lifting common phrases, or "licks", from records and dropping them into their solos more or less at random, or inserted "weird" notes in an arbitrary kind of way. Others were smart enough, or lucky enough, to find a mentor who knew how the thing worked – someone, for instance, like Denis Rose.

In the reminiscences of the first generation of London's post-war modern jazz musicians, Rose's name, like that of Carlo Krahmer, is bound to crop up sooner or later. A Londoner, Denis David Rose (1922–1984) possessed an excellent ear (trained, he always insisted, by daily lessons in tonic sol-fa at elementary school) and a systematic, analytical turn of mind. Conscripted into the army in the later stages of the war, he had soon deserted. As a result, he had no permanent address or telephone number. A veteran of the wartime bottle-party scene, he played trumpet, piano and, occasionally, tenor horn. By dint of close listening to the few available bebop records, Rose isolated the distinctive elements in bebop harmonic practice. These were not particularly new in Western music. Anyone familiar with the work of Debussy and Ravel would have heard similar combinations of notes a thousand times. They were, however, new to jazz, which hitherto had not strayed far beyond the harmonic palette of, say, Sousa marches or Viennese operetta. And it was one thing to *compose* music incorporating these devices and quite another to improvise coherent melodic lines. These new lines turned out to be disconcertingly jagged and tortuous to ears accustomed to the shapes of older jazz. But there was a musical logic at the heart of bebop which it did not require mighty brains or superhuman ears to understand, once it had been teased out and demonstrated. It only remained then to become fluent in the grammar and vocabulary of this new musical language.

The earliest stirrings of revivalist jazz in Britain took place in suburban front rooms and the back rooms of pubs. Those of British bebop are to be traced to the peripheries of the dance-band world and long-defunct musicians' hangouts. Not only is the Fullado Club itself long-defunct, its very site, at 6 New Compton Street, London WC2, has vanished under redevelopment. Between the years 1945 and 1950 it went under at least five names: La Bouillabaise, the Fullado, the Metropolitan Bopera House, the Downbeat and the Zanzibar. It wasn't much of a place, by all accounts, just a basement bar with a few tables and chairs and a serviceable upright piano. It was open from around 3pm until midnight and was a popular meeting place for African-American servicemen. Musicians at a loose end would often drop in and there was usually a jam session of some kind in progress. Taking part might be members of London's first wave of bebop pioneers, which included saxophonists Ronnie Scott, Don Rendell, Johnny Rogers and Tommy Whittle, trumpeter Hank Shaw, drummer Laurie Morgan, drummer and pianist Tony Crombie, pianist and vibraphonist Tommy Pollard, guitarists Pete Chilver and Dave Goldberg, bassist Lennie Bush – and Denis Rose, the guru to whom they all deferred. "I remember him teaching Laurie Morgan simple ways of making tunes sound nice on the piano," Don Rendell recalled. "Laurie would plonk out, say, 'All The Things You Are' with Denis's voicing, using just about three fingers to get the essential notes of those chords. In turn, I learned a lot from Laurie".[8]

The tiny London bebop scene was centred in the West End. It was close-knit, and very intense. Don Rendell, for example, was a member of Duncan Whyte's band at the Astoria Ballroom, Charing Cross Road and spent most of his spare hours at the Fullado. Ronnie Scott had first met Denis Rose in 1944, at the age of seventeen, when they were both members of the Claypigeons, a jazz-oriented dance band led by the Belgian-born trumpeter Johnny Claes. Hank Shaw, too, began as a teenaged professional and by his early 20s had played in the bands of Jack Jackson, Teddy Foster, Oscar Rabin, Tommy Sampson and Basil Kirchin. Most of the others had similar musical beginnings, and many moved around the various bands resident in West End restaurants and nightclubs. With very few exceptions they were all in their early twenties and imbued with the energy and impatience of youth. They found the shortage of new recordings, and the impossibility of hearing masters of the style, live and at close quarters, highly frustrating. In 1947, the very idea of travelling to New York to hear Gillespie, Parker and co. was, for most Britons, like contemplating a journey to the moon. This failed to deter Laurie Morgan, who sold his drums to help raise the fare, or Ronnie Scott and Tony Crombie, who scraped together just enough to buy one-way tickets on Icelandic Airways, for a journey which proceeded by a series of hops between refuelling points and lasted twenty-two hours. (The return journey would be by sea, aboard a converted corvette, named the *Ernie Pyle*.) New York proved a life-changing experience for them all. The contrast with post-war London was, in itself, breathtaking, and the effect of the music almost unbearable in its intensity.

The adventurers returned full of zeal, bearing records which were played endlessly among the initiated. Musicians' flats served as salons to this tiny but intense milieu, in particular the one in Charing Cross Road shared by the guitarists Dave Goldberg and Pete Chilver, and the already much-frequented premises of Carlo Krahmer in Bedford Avenue.

Archer Street, an unprepossessing back street joining Windmill and Wardour Streets, had for many years been the scene of an open-air labour exchange where, on Mondays, dance musicians could pick up casual gigs from bandleaders and fixers. It worked rather like a Victorian rural "hiring fair", although its spirit was more Damon Runyan than Thomas Hardy. The main meeting place was a café, the Harmony Inn, whose Czech proprietor, George Siptac, endeared himself to all, partly by providing cups of tea and snacks on credit, and partly because his name, spelt backwards, was pronounced "cat piss". Other resident characters included the showgirls appearing at the Windmill Theatre and a barber known as "Yossel the Executioner". Many would turn up, even if they weren't in immediate need of work, simply to meet one another, have a laugh and keep up to date with the business. It was via Archer Street that John Dankworth edged his way into the world of West End music.

During his period at the Royal Academy Dankworth lived an energetic double life. He continued playing in dance bands, as he had while still at school. Just a week before his seventeenth birthday he made his first recording. This was with Freddie Mirfield and his Garbage Men, a Dixieland-style band which had won second place in the National Dance Band Championship at Belle Vue, Manchester. Their recording of 'Good Old Wagon Blues'[9] reveals a tentative but clearly competent young clarinetist. He had also taken up the alto saxophone, a fact which had to be kept from the college authorities, who regarded the saxophone as an instrument of the Devil because of its identification with American popular music and jazz. As Alistair Cooke noted, "English magistrates rarely missed an opportunity to ascribe petty thieving and illegitimate birth to the fearful influence of the saxophone".[10] One of the instrument's rare appearances in the conventional symphony orchestra is in Bizet's suite *L'Arlésienne*. Dankworth actually played the saxophone part in a performance of this work with the Royal Academy orchestra, but pretended he had borrowed the instrument for the occasion. He later rejoined the Garbage Men for an engagement in variety at the Grand Theatre, Clapham. They had now transformed themselves into a comedy outfit, after the style of Spike Jones and his City Slickers, in which his part entailed, among other indignities, having joke instruments smashed over his head twice nightly. In search, perhaps, of some relief from the assault and battery, he gravitated to Archer Street. There he met Ronnie Scott and others, along with the inevitable Carlo Krahmer, who, taking account of Dankworth's tiny budding reputation as a Dixieland clarinetist, booked him to appear at the Feldman Club. The *Melody Maker* of 25 April 1946 carries an advertisement for a forthcoming "Dixieland Session" there, featuring Johnny Dankworth (clarinet) and Humphrey Littleton (*sic*) (trumpet). They would have been aged eighteen and twenty-five respectively.

But Dankworth's days as a Dixieland clarinetist were numbered. From July 1946 to June 1947 he was away on National Service, most of it agreeably spent playing in an unofficial dance band at an Army depot near Cirencester. On being released he made directly for Archer Street. There he encountered Ronnie Scott, who, having only recently returned from his epic trip to New York, was helping the drummer Bobby Kevin assemble a dance band to audition for a job that would take him back there again. It was to be aboard the liner *Queen Mary*, then preparing to leave on her maiden post-war transatlantic voyage. They duly auditioned before Geraldo, the über-bandleader of the Cunard fleet, and, having passed, were enrolled as members of the corps known jocularly among musicians as "Geraldo's Navy".

It was an extraordinary life, coming and going every two weeks between Austerity Britain and what Dankworth called the "dream world" of America. The attraction, of course, was the brief stop-over in New York. As luck would have it, the ship docked at Pier 92, right at the end of 52nd Street. From the mid-1930s until the early 1950s, the stretch of 52nd Street between Fifth and Seventh Avenues contained more jazz talent per square inch than anywhere else on the planet, all packed into tiny basement clubs where its full force could be experienced at close quarters. On each visit they were in port for two days, and spent the night between listening to music for as long as they could manage to stay awake. In particular they were transfixed by Parker, the young Miles Davis, the drumming of Max Roach, Gillespie's big band, and the sheer ubiquity of this new form of jazz. The brief time with Geraldo's Navy remained perhaps the most vivid and exciting moment of their lives for Scott, Dankworth and the others. They certainly never stopped talking about it.

When their Cunard engagement ended, it was back to dance-band work. There was now a fair sprinkling of budding beboppers among the nation's dance bands, especially in London. The new music was catching on among jazz-minded young players just as swing had caught on a few years before. With dancing so popular, there were bands everywhere. Routine British dance music of the immediate post-war years was just as dreary as that of pre-war times, being largely confined to "strict tempo" ballroom numbers and party dances, such as the Paul Jones, and the Palais Glide. The taste for swingy music revealed in the regular radio output found precious little echo in the repertoire of the average dance band. There had always been a tendency among dance musicians to look with disdain upon the musical taste of the public. Their attitude contributed to the general camaraderie of the bandstand and was, on the whole, good natured. A novice could not have helped picking some of it up, along with the implicit values that came with it, such as respect for instrumental technique and a keen interest in the latest developments. Almost without exception, the post-war generation of modern jazz musicians came from this background. They were the direct descendants of those pre-war professionals and semi-professionals who made jazz their speciality while remaining members of regular dance bands. However, the music to which the new generation was dedicated sat even less comfortably than swing alongside the dance music which they were called upon to play. The resulting combination of boredom, disaffection and youthful devilment often led to trouble. An air of desperation can be detected in the two words sometimes appended to job advertisements in the musical press of the day: "No Characters".

But there was one successful band, founded in late 1946, which turned out to be the Trojan Horse of British bebop, not to mention a veritable haven for characters. It was led by Tito Burns, who played that most unlikely of jazz instruments, the piano-accordion. The accordion was the most popular instrument in Britain at that time. One or two accordionists, plus a drummer, constituted the full band at many a village hall hop, and the accordions advertised for sale in the pages of *Melody Maker* and *Exchange and Mart* outnumbered most other instruments. Burns had devised a unique approach to the accordion. Concentrating on the piano keyboard, largely ignoring the left-hand bass buttons, and playing close to a microphone, he was able to approximate the sound of the trumpet section in a big band. It was probably this unusual technique which gained his sextet a spot on the Light Programme show *Accordion Club*. Having appeared on all six programmes in the series, no doubt to the bafflement of listening accordion buffs, he was surprised to be invited back as a permanent fixture for subsequent series. In the meantime, as he recalled, "Bebop had got hold of me".[11] By the summer of 1947 the members of his sextet included Denis Rose, Ronnie Scott and Pete Chilver. When Chilver left in March 1948, Scott suggested he replaced the guitar with an alto saxophone, and produced young Johnny Dankworth. "He looked like a kid," Burns remembered. "I said, 'You'll get me had up for kidnapping, bringing children in here!'"[12] When the popular broadcasting singer Terry Devon joined them soon afterwards, Burns had all the ingredients for creating a popular band with a carefully modulated bebop slant. The Tito Burns Sextet soon became a stage and ballroom attraction. They took as their model an American band led by saxophonist Charlie Ventura, which advertised itself with the motto, "Bop for the People!" It featured two singers, Jackie Cain and Roy Kral, in cleverly harmonised, bebop-styled versions of old favourites, such as 'I'm Forever Blowing Bubbles'. Tito Burns and Terry Devon (who eventually became Mrs Tito Burns) developed a very similar act and presented a slick and entertaining show.

In terms of British entertainment, the Tito Burns Sextet was positively avant garde, but its timing was just right. In the US, 1948 saw the beginning

Tito Burns & his Sextet, Wimbledon Palais, London, 1949. From left: Derek Price (drums), Frank Donnison (bass), Jimmie Chester (alto), Rex Morris (tenor), Albert Hall (trumpet), Ronnie Price (piano), Terry Devon (vocalist), Tito Burns (accordion) (Photo: Walter Hanlon, courtesy Peter Vacher Collection)

of a mini-craze for what might be called pop-bebop. Its main features were scat vocals, fast tempos and wild, screaming brass. In a year that saw the death of most of the big bands which had ruled the swing era, the ones that managed to remain viable were those, such as Woody Herman's and Stan Kenton's, that embraced pop-bebop. It took a while for the ripples to reach Britain, and they were never very pronounced, but Tito Burns caught and defined the moment. By 1949 he had signed a recording contract with Decca, was regularly featured on radio and, when not touring, held a residency at Wimbledon Palais.

Almost as quick off the mark with pop-bebop, and much more long-lasting in its popularity, was the Ray Ellington Quartet. Ellington (1916–1985), a drummer-vocalist whose father was African-American and his mother Russian, was born in London. He had played with Harry Roy's dance band in the 1930s, as well as in many of the capital's swingier pre-war night-spots. In 1946 he played in a remarkable quintet led by Stéphane Grappelli, the other three members being George Shearing on piano, Dave Goldberg on guitar and the Jamaican bassist Coleridge Goode (born 1914). A fourteen-minute film of this band exists, in which fragmentary but distinct traces of bebop phraseology can be detected. Ellington formed his quartet towards the end of 1947, its other members being Coleridge Goode, the Trinidadian guitarist Lauderic Caton (1910–1999) and pianist Dick Katz (1916–1981), who was a German Jewish refugee. Their style effectively combined tight, tricky arrangements, performed with pinpoint accuracy, in the style of the King Cole Trio, and zany humour, after the manner of Louis Jordan. Indeed, the quartet scored one of its biggest early successes with a version of Jordan's 'Five Guys Named Moe'. So well did the Ray Ellington Quartet conceal the skill and ingenuity that went into its snappy little numbers that the musicianship involved was consistently under-rated. Listening to its recordings nowadays, especially the early ones from 1948 and '49 can be quite an eye-opener, particularly when you compare them with some of the more laboured efforts of their contemporaries. The lightness of touch, the rhythmic poise and harmonic sophistication are remarkable and almost unique for the time. The Ray Ellington Quartet went on to be a fixture in the *Goon Show* on BBC radio, starring in every edition throughout the 1950s and sharing in the offbeat celebrity of Goon culture.[13] Although the guitarist and bassist changed from time to time, Ellington and Katz ensured that the quartet's style remained constant and that the playing retained its edge. Ellington occasionally joined the show's cast, too, playing various parts, including Chief Ellinga, Sergeant Throat and the much-feared Red Bladder.

Meanwhile, the bebop devotees carried on with their informal sessions. They sometimes hired Mac's, one of several rehearsal rooms in the West End used mainly during the day by dance troupes and variety acts. It occupied a basement at 41 Great Windmill Street, next door to Phil Rabin's celebrated salt-beef bar. Laurie Morgan recalled the excitement of those days:

The Ray Ellington Quartet, c.1950. From left: Coleridge Goode, Dick Katz, Lauderic Caton, Ray Ellington (Photo: © Val Wilmer Collection)

> We were *boiling* with music. Go down Archer Street, Mondays, meet the guys – of course, we always considered ourselves different from other musicians – say out of the corner of your mouth, "Fancy a blow, then?" Secret. It had to be secret. Go to Mac's, book the room, get out the drums, start to play, and in minutes these curious faces would poke round the door. "What are they doing?"[14]

There are some people who can spot a business opportunity in the most unpromising circumstance, and such a man was Harry Morris – whose suit and clip-on bow tie declared him to be one of nature's go-getters. They must be crazy, he told them, shelling out money for rehearsal rooms and giving free concerts to every idler in Soho. They should advertise their sessions and sell tickets at the door. And the place itself, when they were in residence, should have a name. There were eleven of them gathered at the Harmony Inn on this occasion,[15] so they decided to call it "Club Eleven".

The club opened for business shortly before Christmas 1948 and immediately became a focus of interest to the expanding bebop audience around London. The original eleven were soon joined by Denis Rose, Don Rendell and others,

Club Eleven, Mack's Rehearsal Room, Great Windmill Street, London, 1949.
From left: Jack Parnell (drums), Lennie Bush (bass), Denis Rose (trumpet),
Tommy Pollard (piano) (Photo: Courtesy Peter Vacher Collection)

including the exuberant Flash Winston, who made the announcements, filled in on drums when required and generally kept everyone's spirits up. (He called himself "Flash" for the good and sufficient reason that his parents had named him "Cecil".) Club Eleven operated on Thursday and Saturday nights, and the musicians gradually settled down into two bands – the Johnny Dankworth Quartet (later Quintet) and the Ronnie Scott Sextet – although these formats were far from stable as players came and went. Admission was set at three-and-six (17.5p). There was a decidedly louche atmosphere at Club Eleven sessions, unlike the Feldman Club, which was family-run and quite decorous. The more night-time elements gravitated to 41 Windmill Street – showbiz types, Soho characters, dealers in this and that, military absconders. If devotees of revivalist jazz liked to picture themselves in old New Orleans or Roaring Twenties Chicago, London's beboppers were more inclined to fancy the shadowy world of *The Blue Dahlia*, in the company of Alan Ladd and Veronica Lake. After 1949, when clothes rationing was abolished, this tendency acquired a sartorial dimension, too. Colin MacInnes, looking back ten years later, recalled the "American Drape" look:

> This hit Charing Cross Road in the late 1940s and constituted ... the first underground revolt against wartime uniforms and sackcloth, and the whole "men's wear" conception of English male attire. Padded shoulders, straight, waistless coat hanging well below what tailors call the "seat". Material flannel or gabardine.[16]

MacInnes fails to mention the most prominent feature of this get-up, namely the garish tie, loosely knotted beneath an extravagantly rolled shirt-collar. Throughout most of the ensuing decade it would easily have been possible to distinguish, purely by their appearance, gabardine-suited modernists from arty-scruffy traditionalists. The former gradually mutated into proto-Mods, while the latter's scruffiness grew increasingly stylised, as we shall see.

Encouraged by growing excitement in the music press and echoes from across the Atlantic, interest in bebop burgeoned. At some point, early in 1949, came the moment when a significant minority of the public "got" bebop. The sound of it chimed with the restless frustration felt by many young people, and its status as an embattled underground cult added to the attraction. "The people didn't seem baffled at all by the new music we were playing", recalled Don Rendell. "It seemed to be so obviously right. We just fell naturally into it, and the audience lapped it up."[17] The kind of bush-telegraph which had drawn revivalist crowds to the Red Barn a few years earlier now drew modernists to Club Eleven, until Harry Morris's cashbox was overflowing with three-and-sixes, and conditions at 41 Windmill Street threatened to become unbearable. Within a few months the club moved to bigger premises at 50 Carnaby Street, with sessions on six nights of the week.

In Manchester, where any form of public dancing was banned on Sundays, Tony Stuart (the bebop-loving dance-band leader) got round the prohibition by creating the Manchester Modern Music Club, a "private" club which just happened to meet at the Astoria Ballroom on Sunday nights. Annual membership was two shillings (10p), which even in 1948 was absurdly cheap. Within six months it had a thousand members, and Stuart could afford to bring bands up from London to play there.

Whereas revivalist jazz had begun to acquire a public reputation for unconventionality and youthful over-exuberance, and was viewed on the whole with a kind of baffled indulgence, bebop (or "bop") was not so kindly received. In the first place, there was what once might have been called "the inferiority of its connections". It had no adherents among the gentry and few among the conventionally educated classes. Many of its leading musicians, the London ones at least, came from the East End Jewish community, from families of craftsmen, small businessmen and, quite often, entertainers. Then there were bebop's "night-and-the-city" associations (its jagged phrasing is regularly hinted at in *film noir* soundtracks of the time), the clothes (see above), the strange and elaborate haircuts, the wearing of sunglasses when there was no sun, the language ("part jazz argot, part Marx Brothers and part Goons")[18] and a general air of cultivated insouciance. Worse, alarming tales had begun to appear in the tabloid press concerning an epidemic of drug addiction in the US, often linked to this new style of music. The fact that the American phenomenon involved heroin, and that drug use in Britain was confined almost exclusively to cannabis,[19] posed a distinction far too subtle to be considered. Almost inevitably, Club Eleven received a visit from the Vice Squad. It happened on 15 April 1950.

According to Ronnie Scott,

> There are various theories about what happened, but the probability is that somebody had told the police – out of spite. They found me with a tiny packet of cocaine. That was very rare, cocaine. Maybe I got lucky. I told them I had it for my toothache. We spent the night in Saville Row police station. Then – fined twelve pounds, fined fifteen pounds, and so on. And that was the collapse of the club.[20]

In the four years between their first encounter with bebop and the demise of Club Eleven, London musicians had made remarkable progress in absorbing the new idiom. Indeed, in some respects they were the equals of their American contemporaries. Naturally, one leaves out the great figures – Parker, Gillespie, Powell, Monk – but on recorded evidence the young Ronnie Scott, Hank Shaw and Johnny Dankworth stand comparison with, say, Ernie Henry, Little Benny Harris or Frank Socolow. The earliest examples reveal weaknesses, particularly in rhythm and phrasing, but the speed with which these were overcome is truly amazing.

Players' styles evolved from different starting points, at different rates and in varying directions. Ronnie Scott's earliest recordings, for example, reveal him following the path of full-toned, late-swing tenors such as Don Byas and Lucky Thompson.[21] By January 1948, with the Esquire Five, his curious, ballad-tempo opening of 'Lady Be Good' still sounds that way, although with more harmonic colouring in the actual notes. The tone lightens when the tempo doubles, in keeping with the greater mobility of line, but he is obviously still feeling around for a way into the new idiom.

In March of the same year, Carlo Krahmer led a mixed band of young boppers and established swing players in a concert at Birmingham Town Hall, some of which he recorded. The recordings provide a glimpse into a jazz culture on the cusp of change. It seems likely that a few early live recordings of the American touring show *Jazz At The Philharmonic* (JATP) had found their way across the Atlantic, since the format is identical and it generates some of the same heated, competitive atmosphere. The trumpeter, Reg Arnold, aged twenty-nine at the time, was a hugely accomplished player, with great technique and range. He was able to move effortlessly from Dixieland to latter-day swing and had picked up a good general idea of bebop. Also present was the tenor saxophonist Jimmy Skidmore, a popular figure of the wartime jazz scene whose expansive style was essentially pre-bebop. The others were Scott, Dankworth and Denis Rose, all Club Eleven habitués, plus the Canadian bassist Jack Fallon and Krahmer on drums. As in JATP concerts, the most forceful and extrovert players, in this case Arnold and Skidmore, tend to set the tone. Scott reverts somewhat to his earlier, heavily accented approach while Dankworth seems to be playing flat-out and as loudly as possible. (To be fair, it should be pointed out that this is his very first recorded appearance playing the alto saxophone, all his previous recordings being on clarinet.) Denis Rose, on piano, plays efficiently and idiomatically, while Jack Fallon emulates Slam Stewart's singing-and-bowing routine in his solos. Carlo Krahmer's laudable openness to new influences never really transferred to his drumming. He remained a somewhat stolid player, whose attempts at bebop here sound rushed and awkward.

Perhaps even more than notes and harmonies, it was the difference in articulation, accent and rhythmic attack which marked the divide between bebop and what went before. During the period of transition this proved to be the stumbling block for even some of the most accomplished older players. Strings of heavily accented "swing quavers", particularly when applied to a sequence of descending phrases, often gave the game away. Even Coleman Hawkins ("Hawk", born 1904), the great harbinger of the harmonic expansion which led to bebop, was pronounced "square" in this regard by players of the next generation. It was another tenor saxophonist, Lester Young (known as "Prez", born 1909), eschewing harmonic complication but playing with a lighter tone and less emphatic phrasing, who set the pattern here. Dexter Gordon put the matter succinctly: "Hawk was a master of the horn, a musician who did everything possible with it, the right way. But when Prez appeared we all started listening to him alone. Prez had an entirely new sound, one that we seemed to have been waiting for."[22] It was this difference in sensibility, between the "hot" of Hawkins and the "cool" represented by Lester Young, that divided the musical generations, a divide which few older players could successfully cross, no matter how earnestly they tried. This was as true in Britain as it was in the US, and it is quite touchingly revealed in some recordings made in April 1948 by a semi-regular band called the All-Star Sextet. The two instinctive beboppers are Tommy Pollard, playing vibraphone, and pianist Ralph Sharon. Reg Owen fits in very well, as before, and the bass-and-drums team of Jack Fallon and Norman Burns manage well enough. It is Aubrey Frank, the tenor saxophonist, a jazz specialist in the dance-band world since

1936, who sounds unconvincing. His musical tone of voice is not quite right, despite studious and intelligent use of the bebop vocabulary. On the other hand, the scat singing of Alan Dean, in numbers such as 'Galaxy' and 'My Baby Likes To Bebop', is faultlessly idiomatic. It would be easy to assume that he had been studying the young American bebop vocalist Buddy Stewart, except that Stewart's most characteristic recordings were made at almost exactly the same time (spring 1948) as the All-Star Sextet sessions, or even slightly later.

The following year, on 9 April 1949, Club Eleven put on a concert at King George's Hall, previously the venue of the Hot Club of London's regular shows. Both Club Eleven's resident bands were featured and the proceedings were, once again, recorded by Carlo Krahmer. The Ronnie Scott Boptet's set opens with a manic cry of "Welcome to Club Eleven!" from Flash Winston, followed by a furious version of J. J. Johnson's 'Wee Dot'. The ensemble unison is excellent, the tempo (driven by Lennie Bush's bass and Tony Crombie's drums) never falters and the solos are, in the main, fluent and stylistically consistent. This is especially so in the case of Ronnie Scott and Tommy Pollard, with Johnny Rogers not far behind. Denis Rose's trumpet technique is not really up to the demands of performance at this level, but strategic simplicity keeps disaster at bay, while Ginger Johnson patters away harmlessly on the bongos. At first hearing this might easily be a live recording from a US concert of the period.

Bebop (or "rebop" or "bop") began to creep into BBC jazz radio programmes in 1947. Its first appearance seems to have been in Jazz Club on 24 May. Among those taking part were Reg Arnold, Denis Rose (this time playing the tenor horn),[23] Pete Chilver, and pianist Ralph Sharon. Also included were the programme's regular musical director, pianist Billy Munn, Ray Ellington as vocalist and Harry Parry acting as master of ceremonies – presumably to cushion the Shock of the New for listeners of a nervous disposition. One particularly interesting broadcast, on 30 August, featured Harry Hayes and his band. Always open to new ideas, Hayes had recently heard Parker for the first time and was greatly impressed. This programme included Gillespie's 'Ol' Man Rebop' and two presumed Hayes originals – 'The Rebop' and 'King Parker'. A meticulous man, Harry Hayes often worked his solos out in advance and wrote them down.

It is worth mentioning at this point that jazz received some early exposure on post-war television. A limited BBC service reopened, for the London area at first, on 7 June 1946, and a month later, on 11 July, the *Radio Times* announced an appearance by "Leslie 'Jiver' Hutchinson and his Coloured Orchestra". On 23 September, and again on 8 October, there were appearances by the duo of tenor saxophonist Kathleen Stobart and her then-husband, the Canadian pianist Art Thompson. Kathy Stobart was an impressive player, and destined to become a considerable figure in British jazz, but the fact that she was then aged twenty-two and blonde may have helped. She was back again on 6 January 1947, in the first of a short-lived series, *Jazz Is Where You Find It*, along with some leading musicians of the day, such as Duncan Whyte, Nat Temple, Frank Deniz and Coleridge Goode. In light of the above, one cannot help noticing that, in those few months, BBC Television broadcast more jazz on its single channel, operating for a few hours daily, than it could manage sixty-five years later with four channels, two of them broadcasting round the clock.

Just as revivalist jazz renamed itself "traditional jazz", so the term "modern jazz" began to supplant "bebop" at quite an early stage. This was partly the result of a deliberate policy on the part of critics and commentators who thought it more dignified, and partly because it was a more useful label for the broad variety of styles and sub-genres that had come to comprise contemporary jazz around 1950. As has been pointed out, most of Britain's pioneer bebop players were constantly moving in and out of established bands. Some of them may have been a source of irritation to the bandleaders, but they were good players and their solo spots often counted among the high points of a band's performance. Via them, elements of bebop phraseology spread by a kind of osmosis through the fabric of professional and semi-professional popular music making. A glance at the personnel of the Ted Heath orchestra shows, in 1946, Kenny Baker, Norman Stenfalt and Jack Parnell – all seasoned swing players, alongside Ronnie Scott and Dave Goldberg. A year later Scott left, to be replaced by another modernist, the brilliant young Scotsman Tommy Whittle, while Pete Chilver took the place of his flatmate, Goldberg. The trumpet section acquired Dave Wilkins (born 1914), a survivor of the 1941 Café de Paris bombing. By such mixing of musical generations, "modern jazz", while undoubtedly still something of an exclusive cult at its sharp end, became an active ingredient of current British jazz and, increasingly, of popular music in general.

Something similar was also taking place in the US and, in matters of style, Britain continued to follow American models. The position was neatly summed up in the choice of programme for the modern jazz concert at the Royal Festival Hall in July 1951. The show opened with a set by the Toni Anton Orchestra, a twenty-piece band of professional and semi-professional players, created in frank imitation of Stan Kenton's orchestra. Although he had started out leading a dance band, Kenton's music was increasingly tailored for the concert platform. He cultivated a studiously avant-garde air, intended to convey the impression that his music was a cut above mere jazz. The very titles of his numbers – 'Artistry In Rhythm', 'Opus In Pastels', 'Collaboration' – reinforced the notion that here was something serious and challenging, a new kind of big-band music. His successive bands were certainly very big (the biggest numbered forty players), and they were very loud. As the swing era came to an end and long-established big bands broke up, Kenton triumphantly survived. He had many admirers in Britain, and Toni Anton attracted their loyalty.

Similarly, Norman Burns was a disciple of George Shearing. Indeed, before Shearing emigrated to the States, Burns had been his regular drummer. The unique, light sound of the George Shearing Quintet – blending piano, guitar, vibraphone, bass and drums – caught the ear of the American public and, in 1949, its record of 'September In The Rain' sold 900,000 copies in the US alone, to be followed by many others. The Norman Burns Quintet faithfully reproduced the "Shearing Sound", and in young Victor Feldman, who had now taken up the vibraphone, it had a rising star. But as the tag-line "Nearing Shearing" in the band's publicity openly admitted, it remained what would nowadays be called a "tribute band".

This was followed by the Tito Burns Sextet, augmented by a small string section. Burns (no relation to Norman) presented a polished show, influenced by Ventura's "Bop for the People" band, as described earlier. What the strings could have contributed it is hard to tell.

The open-ended, Club Eleven side of things managed to get a look-in only once, with an "All-Star Sextet" of well-known players: Leon Calvert (trumpet), Harry Klein (alto saxophone), Kenny Graham (tenor saxophone), Dill Jones (piano), Joe Muddell (bass) and Martin Aston (drums). The surprise here is Dill Jones, whose first London appearance had been at the Hot Club of London in 1946. He was one of the few jazz musicians, then or at any other time, to seem equally at home in any style. He also shared with Dankworth the rare distinction of having studied music formally to diploma level – in his case at Trinity College of Music.

The oddest item on the bill was the Vic Lewis Orchestra (plus eight strings). Lewis first appeared on the London jazz scene in 1938, playing guitar. Through a friendship with the New York-based British music journalist Leonard Feather, he visited New York and sat in there with some of the greatest names in jazz, including Armstrong. While serving with the RAF during the war, he and Jack Parnell formed the Lewis-Parnell Jazzmen, an excellent small swing band which recorded regularly for Parlophone. He changed direction completely after the war and assembled a big band on the Kenton pattern. At this concert, though, he appears to have been overwhelmed by the splendour of the occasion and veered in the direction of popular light music. Even the *Melody Maker* commentary, by his old friend and supporter Leonard Feather, was moved to terms like "watered-down Kostelanetz". The worst decision of all was to close the evening with a version of Gershwin's 'Rhapsody In Blue', composed in 1924. It is quite possible that Lewis was seizing the opportunity of a high-profile event to set out a new stall as a purveyor of light music, which was, after all, the most ubiquitous form of music in Britain in 1951. Or maybe those strings just went to his head.

The undoubted triumph of the concert, however, was the preceding set by the Johnny Dankworth Seven. Although clearly influenced by the Miles Davis nine-piece band of 1949–50, this was by no means an attempted clone of any American model. The arrangements, many of them original compositions by Dankworth himself, were full of changing textures and clever devices. The hand-picked band was minutely rehearsed, the improvised solos poised and assured, and the twenty-three-year-old leader stylish and handsome in a boyish, Sinatra-like way. To cap it all, he was playing an alto saxophone with a white plastic body, a British innovation known as the Grafton Acrylic. On the stage of the ultra-modern Royal Festival Hall, centrepiece of the bright, forward-looking Festival of Britain, the Johnny Dankworth Seven both sounded and looked like the future.

5 New Orleans to London

When Seymour Wyse came up with his four categories of jazz, you may recall, he consigned revivalism to the dustbin of history under the heading "Phantom Jazz". It was, he maintained, more a case of antiquarian myth-making than of serious musical endeavour. This was the general view among adherents of modern jazz, if they bothered to consider the topic at all. Ronnie Scott's dismissive question – "Why do they want to play like old men?" – settled the matter as far as most were concerned. But it was more complicated than that and, at the start of the 1950s, about to get more complicated still.

With hindsight, beginnings of the complication can be spotted in the line-up for the first 1951 Royal Festival Hall concert. Basic revivalism was represented by Lyttelton, Mick Mulligan, Graeme Bell and the Saints, while the bands of Freddy Randall and Joe Daniels represented Dixieland. The two idioms are recognizably distinct (a result, in part, of the professional polish displayed by the latter) although they inhabit the same musical universe. So does the Crane River Jazz Band, but there is a rough-hewn doggedness about this band's whole approach that sets it somewhat apart. Its members were pioneers in Britain of New Orleans purism, a cause which inspired one of the band's two trumpeters, Ken Colyer (1928–1988), with particular zeal. His uncompromising passion was to lead to undreamt-of consequences, not merely for jazz in Britain but for popular music and culture generally.

Like bebop, New Orleans purism began in the United States towards the close of the 1930s. From the outside, it seemed like a radical variant of revivalism, but to its devotees it was more a matter of nurturing an obscure but still living art. The revivalists looked upon turn-of-the-century New Orleans as the fountainhead, but found their main inspiration in the music of King Oliver, Jelly Roll Morton, Sidney Bechet and, above all, Louis Armstrong. Born and bred in New Orleans, these pioneers had left the city during the great northward migration of African-Americans to Chicago in the years following the end of World War I. It was there that they found success and where the great recordings of the 1920s (sometimes characterized as "classic" jazz) were made. In the process, they converted the music of the New Orleans streets and dance halls from a kind of urban folk-art into a branch of the nascent entertainment industry. But, demanded the purists, what of the musicians who had *not* left – those who had stayed behind in New Orleans? Surely, among them, if anywhere, could be found living vestiges of the original jazz? Up to a point this was true. The old red-light district of Storyville, with its brothels and honky-tonks, had been abolished by decree in 1917, but New Orleans still had its parades, its picnics, its elaborate funeral processions, in which music played a vital role. No social gathering was without its attendant band, whose style may not have changed much in half a century.

The idea was first articulated in a book entitled *Jazzmen* (Ramsey and Smith, eds, 1939), a pioneering collection of essays dealing with the history of jazz and its early masters. Among the authors was William ("Bill") Russell (1905–1992). A classically trained violinist, composer of avant-garde classical music, friend of John Cage and Henry Cowell, Russell had studied various forms of non-Western music, to the extent of becoming an acknowledged performer on several traditional Chinese instruments. He was particularly interested in percussion and had composed a number of large-scale works for percussion ensembles. In 1939, an interest in jazz led him to collaborate with another enthusiast, Frederick Ramsey Jr, on research for chapters in *Jazzmen*. In particular, they were keen to make contact with members of the founding generation, contemporaries of the legendary "first jazz musician", Buddy Bolden. They met with little success at first. Most of these men seemed either to have died or disappeared into unreachable obscurity. Bolden himself had gone mad and ended his days in a mental institution. However, during their enquiries one name occasionally cropped up as possibly still being alive and *compos mentis* – the trumpeter, William Geary ("Bunk") Johnson (born c.1889). Louis Armstrong was reported as enthusing: "What a man! . . . I used to hear him in Frankie Dusen's Eagle Band in 1911. Did that band swing! I used to follow him around. He could play funeral marches that made me cry."[1] Johnson had last been heard of driving a truck in the rice fields around New Iberia, Louisiana. To their amazement, a letter from Russell and Ramsey, addressed to him care of the New Iberia postmaster, elicited a reply from Bunk himself. He had not played for many years, he wrote. He was almost penniless and had lost all his teeth. Russell and Ramsey sent money and a new trumpet, and arranged for Sidney Bechet's brother, who was a dentist in New Orleans, to make Bunk a set of dentures.

In 1942, in a room above a New Orleans music shop, Bunk Johnson made his recording debut at the age of fifty-three with a specially assembled band. The results were so rough that when the discs were sent for processing the factory called back, wondering if there was some mistake. Nevertheless, it was a project to fire the imagination and it attracted a small but fervent band of devotees. Bunk gradually regained some of his old skill, and in his recordings it is possible to catch fleeting hints of how he might have sounded in his youth, at the birth of jazz, when Louis Armstrong was a boy. Other musicians came to light, some of Bunk's generation, some younger, but all steeped in the traditions of New Orleans music. Prominent among them were the clarinetist George Lewis and trombonist Jim Robinson, both soon to become members of Bunk's band. Russell eventually started his own record label, American Music, to record these and other New Orleans musicians, and a distinct subculture took root. With this, just as with bebop, huge (although very different) aesthetic questions were broached: Is the concept of "progress" applicable to any form of art? How important is authenticity? If simple music sounds naïve, is that because the ear has been corrupted by over-sophistication? It later emerged that Bunk was not entirely happy with his status as a kind of living exhibit. He could be cantankerous in the extreme, was frequently drunk and wont to enliven his reminiscences with inventions and tall tales. He had also lied about his age, making out that he was older than he actually was. He wasn't even the first New Orleans rediscovery to record; that distinction belongs to his close contemporary, the trumpeter Kid Rena (1898–1949). But the romantic legend – Armstrong's boyhood memory, the descent into obscurity, the remarkable rediscovery, even the false teeth – all this was too powerful to be dismissed. And there was, after all, something noticeably different about the music that surfaced in the wake of Bunk's rediscovery, a simple, springy, look-on-the-bright-side tunefulness, with a touch of melancholy at the edges.

Bunk died in July 1949. Late in his career he made some records for two major labels, Decca and RCA Victor. These received international distribution, appearing in Britain on Brunswick and HMV in the late 1940s and captivating, among others, Ken Colyer, who was to emerge as purism's leading spirit in Europe.

Kenneth Edward Colyer was born the son of parents "in service", his father being a chauffeur and his mother a cook. His early life was one of deprivation, constant removal and sometimes extreme squalor. He recalled some of the family's lodgings as being "bug-infested". At one point Ken and his two brothers were discovered fending for themselves in a derelict railway carriage and taken to a Dr Barnardo's institution for their own protection. Ken caught his enthusiasm for jazz from his elder brother, Bill. At age seventeen, after a period working as a milkman, he joined the Merchant Navy. After many voyages – South America, Australia, New Zealand, South Africa – his ship docked at New York, where he was able to experience jazz played live. This was at around the same time as the future founders of Club Eleven were making their transatlantic excursions. It is somehow emblematic of the difference in their expectations of life that, whereas Scott, Dankworth and co. travelled as musicians aboard a luxury liner, Colyer did so as second cook on a tramp steamer. The clubs Colyer visited in New York, and the musicians he heard there, were quite different, too. At Eddie Condon's he recalled Pee Wee

Russell, Wild Bill Davison, George Brunis and other veterans of the white Chicago school, while at Nick's none other than Muggsy Spanier was holding forth.

Throughout his time at sea, Colyer had with him both a trumpet and a guitar, which he had learned to play by ear, mainly by listening to his brother Bill's jazz and blues records. Although he had gained a fair facility on trumpet, he had never played with a proper band. Towards the end of 1948 he left the Merchant Navy, took a job cleaning Underground carriages for London Transport and set about finding a band to play with. Auditions and attempts at sitting-in came to nothing, largely because of his complete lack of experience: "Having played at sea, from memory, I used to make up bits to fit. I would change key without realising it."[2] Bill Colyer was now working at the International Bookshop, a left-wing establishment in Charing Cross Road with a stock of records consisting largely of jazz, blues and Russian folksong. It was he who introduced Ken to the music of Bunk Johnson. "When I first cottoned on to Bunk," Ken wrote later, "I admit I slavishly followed him. Bunk was a wonderful teacher".[3]

There was, in those early post-war years, a spontaneous desire among many young people (mostly young men) to make music. It was often unfocused, but amounted in some cases almost to a compulsion. The music could take various forms but had to be lively and rhythmic and, most important of all, informal, the whole idea of "taking lessons" being anathema. They were ready to adopt any style which appealed, or to follow a leader with a particular vision, allied to a strong personality. The group which eventually gathered around Ken Colyer was in precisely this position, and Colyer, freshly enthused by the revelation of Bunk Johnson, was the man. They were all as inexperienced as himself and mostly lived in or near the west London suburb of Cranford, Middlesex. They began by paying to rehearse in an annexe, little more than a shed, in the backyard of the White Hart pub. The White Hart (now much altered) stands on the northern perimeter of what is now London Heathrow Airport. A modest stream, a tributary of the Thames called the Crane, flows nearby. Perhaps inevitably, they named themselves the Crane River Jazz Band.

An archetypal recruit was the clarinetist, Monty Sunshine (1928–2010). Son of an East-End tailor, he won a scholarship to Camberwell School of Art, where he became caught up in the general passion for jazz among both students and younger staff. The first jazz he heard in person was at a concert by George Webb's Dixielanders in nearby Peckham. "The very next day," he recalled, "students from the art school were going round local junk shops, looking for instruments to buy."[4] He himself had been especially impressed by Wally Fawkes's playing and managed to borrow an ancient clarinet, which he taught himself to play as best he could. Hearing that a band in west London might be looking for a clarinet player, and having ascertained the time and place of rehearsals, he turned up at the White Hart one Friday evening.

The Crane River Jazz Band, unknown location, London, 1949. From left: Sonny Morris (cornet), Pat Hawes (piano), Julian Davies (bass), Ken Colyer (cornet), Ben Marshall (banjo), Monty Sunshine (clarinet), John R. T. Davies (trombone) (Photo: Courtesy Peter Vacher Collection)

> I sat in the pub garden, listening to the sounds coming from this green hut with a tin roof, but they seemed to have a clarinet player, so I didn't go in. Then a chap came out carrying a tray of empty glasses, and came back again with a tray of full glasses. He asked if I was listening to the band, and I said, "I'm a clarinet player!" – came out with it, just like that! And he said, "Well, come in then and sit-in." I didn't know many tunes, but I joined in and blew quite loud – and they asked me to join. The chap with the beer was Bill Colyer and the band was the Crane River Jazz Band.[5]

Soon, developments at the White Hart exactly paralleled those at Mac's Rehearsal Rooms. A friend of the band offered to take money at the door. The result in Soho was London's bebop HQ, Club Eleven; in Cranford it was New Orleans in Middlesex – the Crane River Jazz Club.

From the musical point of view, the main features distinguishing the Crane River band from the usual revivalists were its emphasis on ensemble playing, with few solos, and its choice of material from outside the normal repertoire of classic jazz. This was in line with the idea that, as a living idiom, the New Orleans style could be applied to any suitable tune. As Monty Sunshine explained it, "We were emulating the style of contemporary New Orleans music, the kind you might have heard if you'd gone to New Orleans in the early 1950s – popular songs of the day being incorporated into the music."[6] New Orleans bands on records certainly played a marvellous rag-bag assortment of stuff: 'Won't You Come Home Bill Bailey', 'Little Red Wing', 'Linger Awhile', 'When You Wore A Tulip' – and at least one spirited rendition of 'I Saw Mommy Kissing Santa Claus'.

The very fact that the Crane River Jazz Band was included in the Festival Hall programme is testimony to the progress it had made, and the status it had achieved by 1951. Almost immediately after that concert, however, Colyer left to join a newly projected band, the Christie Brothers' Stompers, co-led by trombonist Keith and clarinetist Ian Christie, from the Lyttelton band. During its brief period of existence the Christie Brothers' Stompers fizzed with energy and ideas but was never able to shake down into a solid entity, mainly because its principal members were all pulling in different directions – Ian towards the loose-knit New York Dixieland style, his brother intent on going over to full-blown modern jazz, and Colyer resolutely sticking to the pure New Orleans path. After a few months Colyer left, to be replaced by Dickie Hawdon, late of the Yorkshire Jazz Band, who was also becoming interested in modern jazz. With Keith and Dickie amusing each other by inserting outrageous snatches of bebop, against a rhythm section dominated by a stolid, clanging banjo, this later incarnation of the Stompers really must have been something to experience live. Not surprisingly, stability remained as elusive as ever and the whole affair self-destructed in little more than a year. Ken Colyer was not around to witness the death-throes. He had by then embarked upon the adventure which was to bestow upon him the aura of a seer or prophet among the ranks of European jazz purists.

In November 1952 he rejoined the Merchant Navy with the sole purpose of getting to New Orleans, no matter how long it might take. "I thought, these men were still playing in New Orleans. They weren't that old. They must still be playing, so the logical thing was to get there while they *were* still playing."[7] It took him the best part of a year, working on various ships and visiting some of the most remote spots on earth, including St Helena and Pitcairn, before reaching Mobile, Alabama aboard a "stinking little tub" called the *Empire Patrai*. Taking advantage of his seaman's papers, which allowed him twenty-nine days ashore, he took a Greyhound bus the 160 miles to New Orleans. There he met and played with men whose music he had long revered, and related the whole story in a series of long letters home to Bill. ("The band eventually kicked off on *Weary Blues*, the Kid damped down and muted all the time – probably just as well, else I might have died of happiness.")[8] It seems that the New Orleans musicians were, in turn, astonished by Colyer. Sitting-in with the George Lewis band, he wrote, "I took the first break. I heard Lawrence (banjoist Lawrence Marrero) say to George, 'Ain't that Bunk, George? That's Bunk, man!'"[9] This was, of course, the segregated Deep South, where white and black musicians playing together had to remain constantly alert for signs of trouble, as the letters made clear. In the end, Colyer was arrested for overstaying his twenty-nine days' shore leave, held in the parish prison and deported back to England via Ellis Island.

Excerpts from his letters to Bill appeared in *Melody Maker* while Colyer was away, setting off a surge of interest in New Orleans music in general and Ken Colyer in particular. There was an epic quality to the whole extraordinary tale which simply could not be denied: the year-long voyage, through many hardships, to reach the fabled city; acceptance by his heroes as one of their own; conflict with the forces of darkness in the shape of Southern racism; imprisonment and expulsion. He may not have set out to do it, but by the time Ken Colyer arrived back in England on 12 March 1953, he had made himself into a hero.

In the meantime, Monty Sunshine and trombonist Chris Barber (born 1930) had got together with the aim of forming a New Orleans-style band of their own, but were short of a trumpet player. With Colyer expected to return any day soon, trailing clouds of glory, they sent a message, via Bill, inviting him to join them. Barber recalled,

> Our group had no name as yet, and we could imagine that Ken's name would bring people to hear what his sojourn in New Orleans had brought. We were a co-operative group – i.e. nobody owned it and we would share any income equally – but we wanted Ken to be the leader in musical terms.[10]

Colyer said he would "give it a go", and the result was everything Barber had hoped for. "Ken's lead was, as always, the best lead I ever played with in a band of that instrumentation."[11] Public expectation was built up by keeping Ken Colyer's Jazzmen under wraps while they rehearsed. The band played itself in with a brief tour in Denmark and made its British debut at the London Jazz Club, Bryanston Street, in May. Then, most important of all, in February 1954, came the release on Decca of a ten-inch long-playing record, *New Orleans to London*.

The band on the album consists of Colyer on trumpet, Barber (trombone), Sunshine (clarinet), Lonnie Donegan (banjo), Jim Bray (bass) and Ron Bowden (drums). This was to become the standard instrumentation for bands of this style, although the absence of a piano from the rhythm section caused some comment to begin with. As a demonstration of Colyer's formula for the playing of New Orleans jazz, the performance is impressive. Full-ensemble playing predominates, but the variations in volume, balance, texture and intensity are truly remarkable. They followed the practice of several New Orleans bands of having derby mutes (metal mutes, shaped like bowler hats) on stands for the two brass instruments, so that the player had only to turn slightly to one side to produce an uncanny, hollow sound. Sunshine's fluid line and singing tone is a delight and Barber plays immaculately. (He was, at the time, studying trombone at the Guildhall School of Music, with double bass as his second study.) Colyer himself is rather self-effacing, contenting himself with taking a simple lead part. His playing has a distinct New Orleans accent, including the characteristic rapid, shallow vibrato. Among the best pieces are the rags ('Harlem Rag', 'Cataract Rag', 'Tuxedo Rag'), appropriately arranged and delicately played.

Even after the passage of six decades, the eight tracks of *New Orleans to London* make delightful and entertaining listening. Whatever the aural equivalent of "brightly lit" might be, that is the effect which the Decca engineers managed to produce. This is so different from the cavernous echo or soggy obscurity that characterizes many authentic New Orleans and early British revivalist recordings, that the music itself is subtly transformed. The record stands as an artefact in its own right, rather than a captured sample of music performed live. This was to become one of the defining characteristics of pop records. One track from the album, 'The Isle of Capri', was released as a single and did actually receive substantial airplay on popular BBC record programmes. The album itself sold far better than expected, too, and over quite a long period.

Certainly, the popular audience for revivalist and traditional jazz had been growing rapidly since Graeme Bell and Humphrey Lyttelton had introduced dancing in 1948. The number of bands, mostly amateur or semi-professional, had grown enormously too. By the early 1950s the phenomenon was big enough to attract the attention of entrepreneurs unconnected with the jazz world. Among these were Harold Fielding, the future West End impresario, and Maurice Kinn, proprietor of the newly launched *New Musical Express*. Each hired large halls, including the Royal Albert Hall, on several occasions in 1952, mounting shows featuring up to as many as seventeen bands. The fact that each band barely had time to get on stage and deliver a couple of numbers in a frantic burst before being ushered off again raised howls of protest from the bands concerned, but didn't bother the young crowd, who, by all accounts, enjoyed themselves hugely. Reviewing one of Fielding's concerts in *Melody Maker*[12] Ernest Borneman noted that there was "barely a vacant seat", and that the audience was made up of "non-initiates" – by which he appeared to mean newcomers to jazz. Nowadays this would give cause for rejoicing, but the phenomenon made Borneman uneasy. He was not alone. Jazz had been an exclusive cult for so long that its devotees had built themselves a snug redoubt of shared tastes and arcane knowledge, which this new army of "non-initiates" threatened to invade and upset. It was a portent of the way things were to develop.

In 'Festival!', his much-quoted essay on the Festival of Britain, Michael Frayn personifies British approaches to the arts, business and public affairs generally at the time in terms of two species. First, there were the Herbivores, or gentle ruminants ("the do-gooders . . . the signers of petitions"). Opposed to them came the Carnivores ("who believe that if God had not wished them to prey on all smaller and weaker creatures without scruple He would not have made them as they are").[13] In jazz, the cosy, Herbivorous, argumentative world of rhythm clubs and Collectors' Corner was gradually slipping away, to be replaced by something less benign. The fate of that supremely Herbivorous body the NFJO provides a perfect example of what happens when modest success attracts the attention of a Carnivore. Harold Pendleton, a young chartered accountant and jazz fan from Merseyside, had been living and working in London since 1948. He was elected onto the NFJO committee and, in 1952, in the fading afterglow of the Royal Festival Hall concerts, he became its Secretary, having ousted the clubbable and easy-going James Asman. In February 1953, with committee members amiably absorbed in the perennial argument about what was jazz and what wasn't, he found it easy to organize support for a series of canny motions which caused the committee effectively to abolish itself. In his own words:

> To cut a long story short, I threw the lot of them out and took the damned thing over. First thing I did was to shorten the name to the National Jazz Federation, NJF. My intention? A career. Number one, I thought, this thing has got to be run properly – and, two, profitably.[14]

It was against this background that the brief career of the first Ken Colyer's Jazzmen was played out. The explanation for its brevity depends on who is doing the explaining. Whether Ken sacked the band or the band sacked Ken scarcely matters now. Colyer – self-taught, stubborn, doctrinaire and firm in the belief that his dedication and experience gave him a unique inwardness with New Orleans music – was never going to be a mere figurehead. Barber – musically trained and literate, more catholic in his jazz tastes, aware of the changing environment, but equally stubborn – was never going to be anyone's sideman. A co-operative band with those two in it was a contradiction in terms. So they parted company, Colyer to recruit the next in a long line of Jazzmen, Barber to persuade Pat Halcox, trumpet player with the Albemarle Jazz Band, to give up his day-job as a research chemist and join the new Chris Barber Jazz Band, a job which he was to hold for more than half a century.

Chris Barber's Jazz Band was formed in May 1954 but its remarkable career began in earnest in July, with the recording of its first ten-inch LP, *New Orleans Joys*. In some respects this is the direct successor to *New Orleans to London*; the instrumentation is identical, the recording has the same bright, sharply defined quality and the rhythm section produces the same light, springy beat. The points of difference, however, are more apparent. In place of the continuous ebb and flow of the full ensemble, each number features brief solos by several players, often backed by pre-arranged harmonies or riff figures, and various orchestral devices, such as the bell-effect in 'Chimes Blues'. Great attention has been paid to getting some variation into the rhythm, with breaks, stop-time passages and, particularly effective, the *habañera* pattern with which they spice up Jelly Roll Morton's 'New Orleans Blues'. If this is what Barber had in mind all the time, it is quite obvious that he and Colyer could never have worked together for long. On the other hand, the lesson of 'The Isle of Capri' had been taken on board: a catchy tune, simply played, makes the perfect start to an album. This one starts with the jaunty traditional ditty, 'Bobby Shaftoe'. All the elements which were to ensure the Barber band's long and immensely successful career are present in this first record – careful presentation and a lively sense of the audience, originality in choice of material and attention to detail. Over the first year *New Orleans Joys* sold in excess of 60,000 copies.

And who bought those copies? It certainly wasn't the broad popular record-buying public, judging by the kind of thing that caught on in 1954–55. A random sample from that list might include: 'The Happy Wanderer', sung by a children's choir, Eddie Calvert and his Golden Trumpet with 'Cherry Pink And Apple Blossom White', Norman Wisdom singing 'Don't Laugh At Me ('Cos I'm A Fool)', and the 'Dambusters' March' played by the Central Band of the Royal Air Force. One short answer to the question was offered by Monty Sunshine: "Fifth and sixth formers in grammar schools all seemed to have our records."[15] Presumably, there would have been a fair number of these among the lively young people who had caused Ernest Borneman such disquiet at the Royal Albert Hall. The 1944 Education Act had now been in operation for the greater part of a decade, providing secondary education for all, with grammar schools as the élite division of the system. Admission to them was by examination, regardless of family circumstances, and the pupils often found, as they matured, that they had more in common with each other than with their families and neighbours. They tended to stick together out of school, enjoying the same pastimes and entertainments, sharing the same jokes and generally constituting a recognizable tribe. Traditional jazz came high among their enthusiasms. The bass player, Bill Reid, recalling his schooldays in the very early fifties, observed:

> You know, school-kids didn't know much about music except for the Hammersmith Palais and listening to Joe Loss, and so we were onto the in thing – grammar school and art school types, you know, we all got into it – New Orleans jazz. It was a fresh, invigorating sort of folk music.[16]

There was an element of mild revolt, or at least of resistance, involved here, too. Grammar schools were bent on raising their pupils from the Other Ranks of society to become Officers in adult life, a process which usually involved learning to conduct themselves as though they were products of a minor public school. Some took to it and some didn't, and the latter tended to be the ones who took to jazz.

The same crowd fell with equal enthusiasm for *The Goon Show* on the radio, which appealed to the same rebellious instincts. To understand the power of this appeal, it helps to have some notion of how suffocatingly smug and pompous the voice of official culture was at the time. A glance at a contemporary copy of the *Radio Times*, for instance, will reveal an endless parade of programmes with titles such as *We, The British* and *Our Island Fortress*. The British seemed forever to be telling each other how much better they were than anyone else – the bravest fighters, the cleverest inventors, the most intrepid explorers. *The Goon Show* blew a loud and sustained raspberry at all this. Prominent among its cast of characters were Major Bloodnok, a dedicated coward with exploding bowels, Neddy Seagoon, the intrepid hero, easily deflected from his purpose by specious argument, and the knobbly-kneed and ineffectual Boy Scout, Bluebottle. There was an affinity, too, between jazz and Goon humour. It appeared in the use of minutely timed sound effects, plots that were improvisations on well-worn tabloid newspaper themes (*Rommel's Treasure, The Dreaded Batter-Pudding Hurler of Bexhill-on-Sea*) and, most of all, conversations whose twists and turns pulled logic inside-out. For instance, the celebrated exchange between Eccles and Bluebottle which begins, "What time is it, Eccles?" in *The Mysterious Punch-Up-The-Conker*, unfolds like a good jazz solo – or duet.[17] *The Goon Show* ran from 1951 to 1960, and gradually gained a mass audience, but its first and truest adherents were teenage grammar-school pupils and those who were, like the Goons themselves, ex-servicemen.

And, as Monty Sunshine had noticed, young people bought records. With post-war austerity now a fading memory and the supply of luxury goods increasing, most teenagers could afford to buy the occasional record, even if it meant saving up. Advancing technology gave them a bewildering choice of formats. Long-playing records (LPs) came in two sizes, ten-inch (each side playing for about fifteen minutes) and twelve-inch (twenty-four minutes a side), revolving thirty-three times a minute (33 rpm). Like most jazz LPs, *New Orleans Joys* was a ten-inch, retailing at £1.0.4d (£1.02). Then came seven-inch "extended play" discs, playing for around seven minutes a side, each side normally bearing two items, and revolving at 45 rpm. Finally, there were seven-inch 45 rpm discs with one item per side, called "singles". All the above were plastic "microgroove" discs, requiring special new machines on which to play them. It was expected that the new 45 singles would quickly replace the old-style 78 rpm records, but things didn't quite work out that way. Manufacturers desperately wanted to abandon the 78 and rationalize production. Dealers longed to clear their shelves of the bulky, fragile discs in their brown-paper wrappers, but families clung on to their treasured radiograms and wind-up portable gramophones and demand simply refused to die away. As a result, record companies were reduced to releasing singles in both formats simultaneously. In 1954 a popular ten-inch 78 from HMV sold for 5/- (25p) and its seven-inch counterpart for 5/8 (28.5p). This crazy state of affairs continued until the end of the decade.

Initially, members of the Barber band really had no idea of how quickly their popularity was growing. They were young, single and dedicated, and the last thing they expected was any kind of pop success. According to Monty Sunshine, the first intimation of their new celebrity came one night at Keighley Baths, where they were appearing out of their normal habitat, as a kind of novelty support band to the Hedley Ward Trio, stars of radio, television and the variety stage: "When they were announced the crowd all headed for the bar. They'd only come to hear us!"[18] Their following had now spread far beyond the grammar-school, art-school crowd to take in young people of all classes. Traditional, Revivalist, New Orleans, Dixieland – to this burgeoning audience such distinctions meant little. The appeal of the music lay in its lively informality, and the fact that it didn't entail a "right way" to dance or to dress. A large part of the attraction lay in the similarity in age and appearance between audience and band. The musicians were not seen as "entertainers", an alien corps of specialist professionals, but as young people very much like themselves, sharing their values and attitudes. John Osborne hit the nail on the head when he made Jimmy Porter, the emblematic mid-1950s youth hero of his play *Look Back in Anger*, not only angry and young, but also a would-be jazz trumpeter.

A fascinating short film, *Momma Don't Allow*, depicts a night with the Chris Barber band at a typical London suburban jazz club. Shot in the winter of 1954–55, over the course of nine Saturday nights, at the Fishmongers' Arms, Wood Green, this semi-documentary concentrates mainly on the audience. Three of its members are specifically identified – a railway carriage cleaner, a butcher's apprentice and a dentist's assistant – and the camera returns to them repeatedly throughout the film's twenty-two minutes. There is no dialogue, only the music of the band and the general buzz of the crowd. The atmosphere is so vividly conveyed that anyone who ever spent an evening at a fifties jazz club will recognize the scene, the music, the clothes and the styles of dancing. They will recall, too, the pungent blast of hot air that greeted one at the door, a miasma of smoke, sweat, cheap scent and old beer. Nothing renders this youthful 1950s world "at once immediately recognizable and impossibly distant"[19] more powerfully than the smoke. Everyone present smokes constantly, even the band. The historian Eric Hobsbawm (writing under his jazz-critic *nom de plume* of "Francis Newton"), contemplating a similar jazz crowd, noted: "By aficionado standards, few of these were serious jazz fans. It was simply that for them jazz had become what Viennese waltzes were for their grandparents, and shimmies or foxtrots for their parents: the normal kind of music for dancing and a good time."[20]

Momma Don't Allow was made under the auspices of the British Film Institute's Experimental Film Fund and directed by Karel Reisz and Tony Richardson, soon to be leading figures in British cinema's "New Wave". It is noteworthy for having no narrator and maintaining a friendly but neutral point of view, unlike contemporary newsreel items on youth and jazz, with their condescending, amused-uncle commentary.

This was essentially a culture based on live music. All over the country, in pubs, hotels, social clubs, Co-op halls and rooms above the premises of Messrs Montague Burton, the "Tailor of Taste", young local bands were doing their stuff. Almost all the players were self-taught, and standards varied, but one thing was certain – they were enjoying themselves as much as the audience, if not more so. Increasingly, they were taking as their models neither the giants of classic jazz, nor latter-day New Orleans idols, but the British bands which they knew, especially Barber and, to a certain extent, Colyer. (Lyttelton was becoming altogether too mercurial to copy.) The instrumentation was standard, give or take a piano, the music simple in form and relatively undemanding technically. By sticking to the easiest keys for the trumpet, clarinet and trombone to negotiate, and not requiring the banjo to do more than bang out simple chords four times a bar, an amateur band might get itself started. Drummers could be a problem, because, having bought a drum-kit, they wanted to use all of it, all the time. Would-be bass players were hard to find, the role of the double bass being unspectacular, and the instrument itself unwieldy and apt to attract cries of "How do you get it under your chin?" and suchlike witticisms. Although many failed to get far beyond 'When The Saints Go Marching In', in the key of F, a kind of primitive meritocracy evolved, by which players with a bit of talent would move from hopeless bands to less hopeless ones, replacing more talented ones who had moved up, and so on. This presented the perfect opportunity for club promoters, local newspapers, cinema managers, and so on, to stage jazz-band competitions. The panel of judges usually included a minor celebrity and each band would bring along its own claque of followers, thus ensuring a lively audience. The end result of all this activity was a thriving scene and some efficient bands, although they did all tend to sound the same.

To be fair, sameness was what most of them were aiming at. The six-piece traditional jazz band, after the Barber/Colyer pattern, proved perfect for the kind of small-to-medium-sized event epitomised in *Momma Don't Allow*. It was the right size, made the right noises, and was loud enough to fill the room without elaborate amplification. The sound of the banjo, in particular, cut through the other instruments and all the ambient noise, where a piano would have been overwhelmed. In short, like its precursor, the small dance band of the 1930s, it was an organism ideally adapted to its environment. This was when the word "trad" began to be used as the generic term for this standard type of popular jazz.[21] Understandably, there was an instant rush by independent-minded musicians, Colyer among them, to disown the trad label. Barber, who had started the whole thing, made no objection, but neither would he confine himself to the straitjacket which his imitators had made for themselves. With the band's first album, *New Orleans Joys*, he had demonstrated ingenuity in the use of limited resources, and this continued to be one of his strong points. He also had a penchant for springing surprises. The first of these came at the Royal Festival Hall on 9 January 1955, when Ottilie Patterson made her debut. It was not unusual for bands to feature singers (George Melly had, after all, been a fixture with Mick Mulligan's Magnolia Jazz Band for some time), but this demure twenty-four-year-old art teacher from Newtownards, County Down, scarcely looked the part. The real surprise, though, came when she opened her mouth and out came a rich, dark, soulful sound startlingly reminiscent of the late "Empress of the Blues", Bessie Smith. A recording of that concert also reveals Barber's skills of arrangement and presentation. Ottilie's first song is 'St Louis Blues', taken at Bessie Smith's original slow, dragging tempo. Anyone acquainted with classic jazz would know Bessie's version, in which the accompaniment consists only of trumpet and harmonium. Barber hints at this by restricting the band's accompaniment to trumpet, trombone, banjo and bowed bass. The effect is both subtle and evocative. Barber continued to spring surprises, presenting unlikely and stimulating guest soloists and tunes from well outside the New Orleans and classic jazz repertoire. They were often introduced at the band's regular concerts, held in the Recital Room, a smaller venue (later replaced by the Purcell Room) attached to the Royal Festival Hall. These shows attracted dedicated jazz lovers and were inevitably sold out well in advance. Indeed, this committed audience continued to grow, a by-product of the growing general popularity of traditional jazz, and it was the less formulaic, more adventurous bands which attracted and retained its interest.

Originality revealed itself, in most cases, by the way in which a musician, having begun by imitating an admired model, succeeded in building an unmistakably personal style. Take, for instance, two clarinetists, Cy Laurie (1926–2002) and Sandy Brown (1929–1975). Both began as devotees of Johnny Dodds (1892–1940), whose passionate, blues-inflected playing with King Oliver, Louis Armstrong and others is one of the dominant sounds in recorded classic jazz of the Chicago era. Laurie, a Londoner, and Brown, born in India and brought up in Edinburgh, began playing at about the same time. On their first recordings there is little to choose between them. Each affects the heavy Dodds vibrato and simulates his characteristic tone and phraseology quite convincingly. Over the course of the 1950s, however, Laurie succeeded only in becoming a better Dodds imitator. Brown, on the other hand, grew in stature. His musical sphere of reference broadened to include an increasingly idiosyncratic collection of jazz influences, yet the influence of Dodds on Brown's clarinet playing remained as strong as ever. In 1951 Cy Laurie, leading his band, the Cy Laurie Four, opened his own jazz club at Mac's Rehearsal Rooms, 41 Windmill Street – the premises previously occupied by Club Eleven. It came complete with the same Stygian lighting and decrepit furniture. The club became noted for its "Bohemian" atmosphere and "all-nite raves". As one of Laurie's obituaries recalled: "The very words 'Cy Laurie's' were said to raise nameless fears in the minds of suspicious parents."[22]

The vigorous growth of standardized trad as social dance music tended to obscure the fact that the broadly "traditional" jazz scene embraced a vast assortment of styles. Birmingham's Second City Jazzmen made adventurous use of unusual instruments, such as bass clarinet, valve trombone and electric guitar, in their treatment of material ranging from New Orleans to late-1930s Duke Ellington. Liverpool's Merseysippi Jazz Band actually surpassed their original model, the early American revivalist Lu Watters and his Yerba Buena Band. They were technically more accomplished, their attack was brisker and they swung more effectively; their clarinetist, Don Lydiatt, being particularly impressive. In London and the Home Counties, Mike Daniels and his Delta Jazzmen stuck with distinct flair and intelligence to the original revivalist line of interpreting classic jazz, their main rivals in this being the somewhat solemn and scholarly Steve Lane's Southern Stompers. The superb Alex Welsh Band adopted the mantle of the white Chicagoans, while there could be little doubt about the allegiance of Bobby Mickleburgh's Bobcats (see Chapter 7). Towards the end of the decade, guitarist Diz Disley's Soho String Quintet gave birth to a whole new sub-genre by reincarnating the pre-war Quintette du Hot Club de France. These were all excellent bands. They had keen followers and drew sizeable crowds of both listeners and dancers. The majority remained semi-professional throughout the 1950s, although some turned professional as the years passed. Sometimes a conflict of careers would force a painful choice. Sandy Brown, for instance, handed the leadership of his band to Al Fairweather in 1957, when his work as an acoustic architect became more demanding. The art-school contingent often managed to keep both activities on the go. Monty Sunshine designed LP covers for Decca and Vogue, Diz Disley drew cartoons for *Melody Maker* and other publications, and Wally Fawkes created the hugely popular strip *Rufus and Flook* for the *Daily Mail*; Humphrey Lyttelton, and later George Melly, collaborated on the story and wrote the copy for the speech bubbles. Others succeeded in combining music with more regular jobs. Freddy Legon played guitar in the Lyttelton band from 1951 to 1956 while continuing to work as sales manager for a catering equipment firm, but it was touch-and-go at times.

The parallel but separate world of modern jazz had its enthusiastic semi-pros too, but its dominant ethos remained staunchly professional. No one harboured the illusion that this music was easy to play, nor did its devotees identify with the players in the way trad fans did.

6 Couth, Kempt and Shevelled

John Dankworth's development as a player reflected his development as a composer-arranger, bandleader and all-round musician. At first, like all young bebop players of his generation, he was mesmerised by the overwhelming force of Charlie Parker. He had heard him in New York, in person and at close quarters, during his time with Geraldo's Navy, and again at the Paris Jazz Fair in 1949, where Parker had actually borrowed Dankworth's saxophone at a jam session. It would have been difficult to avoid falling under Parker's spell in any case. The phenomenal technique, the commanding tone, the sure-footedness with which he skipped through complex harmonic substitutions while at the same time playing mischievous tricks with the beat, the sheer abundance of the man's creativity – these set up a powerful magnetic field which it seemed impossible to escape. This was especially the case if one's instrument happened to be the alto saxophone. Yet escape was essential if one were to produce anything other than inferior imitations of Parker. Furthermore, there was a vehemence about Parker's music which was unique to him, a kind of despairing savagery which no amount of virtuosity or expertise could ever supply. The dilemma was neatly expressed by a close contemporary of Dankworth, the Swedish saxophonist Ingmar Glanzelius: "We were well brought-up lads," he said, "and lacked Parker's fury."[1] A timely new development in America, labelled "cool jazz", suggested a possible solution. Cool jazz incorporated much of the harmonic and melodic language of bebop but deployed it in a less intense, more considered form. Its leading exponents were as much white (Stan Getz, Gerry Mulligan, Lee Konitz) as black (Miles Davis, John Lewis, J. J. Johnson) and its acknowledged founder was the super-cool Lester Young. Most attractive of all to John Dankworth was the fact that cool jazz paid attention to aspects of music for which bebop had little regard, such as form, texture, orchestration and dynamics. Dankworth, as he often insisted in later years, never really enjoyed jam sessions because they produced music that was essentially shapeless. His instinct was always to turn a random musical event into a performance by imposing a shape upon it – even if that was merely to determine the order and length of improvised solos. In the winter of 1949 he put together a seven-piece band, composed of Club Eleven regulars, and wrote material for it to perform at the club. It was generally understood that this was part of a plan to launch himself as a bandleader.

The perfect exemplar of what he was after materialized in New York at around the same time, in the shape of a nine-piece band under the leadership of Miles Davis. Consisting of trumpet, trombone, French horn, alto and baritone saxophones, tuba and rhythm section, and scored mainly by Gerry Mulligan, Gil Evans and John Lewis, it recorded six 78s (twelve sides) for Capitol. Some of these were released in Britain in 1950, treated as Holy Writ by a few musicians and ignored by almost everyone else. All twelve came out some years later on a twelve-inch LP entitled *Birth of the Cool* and have been regarded as significant classics ever since. Miles Davis's band lasted a matter of weeks before falling apart for lack of work.

The Johnny Dankworth Seven was publicly launched on 5 March 1950. Its members were: Dankworth (alto saxophone), Jimmy Deuchar (trumpet), Don Rendell (tenor saxophone), Eddie Harvey (trombone), Bill LeSage (piano), Joe Muddell (bass) and Tony Kinsey (drums). Its debut was at the London Palladium, as part of a popular series of Sunday concerts called Ted Heath Swing Sessions. According to Mike Nevard's review in *Melody Maker*, "Many of the fans were baffled, confounded and unable to grasp the music they heard." It was beautifully scored, he wrote, "in the manner of the recently issued Miles Davis discs", but members of the band seemed tense – as well they might. The reviewer did get the main point, by praising the general concept of "playing MUSIC – and not merely a handful of clichés and rough unison passages", but warned that the Seven would "certainly have to bring a good proportion of 'commercials' into its repertoire to make any kind of country-wide tour possible."[2] Here Nevard was pointing to the undeniable fact that no fully professional band could hope to stay afloat in 1950 by playing unalloyed jazz of any sort, let alone the kind that left a London audience baffled, confounded and unable to grasp it. The Seven made its first recordings[3] a few weeks after that concert and, listening to them now, it seems impossible that anyone could have been perplexed by so clear, mellifluous and unthreatening a sound. The method of orchestration is obviously based on that of the Miles Davis band, with shifting combinations of the four front-line instruments, highly mobile inner parts, bridge passages linking improvised solos and accompanying figures behind them. But there are signs, even at this early stage, of what would soon develop into a characteristic Dankworth style.

The dilemma foreseen by Mike Nevard soon arose: the available audience was too small to support the band. Playing at the few existing modern jazz clubs and occasional concerts did not bring in enough money and Dankworth's own resources were soon exhausted. They were all in their early twenties, except for Joe Muddell, who was rising thirty and married with a small child. Unable to make ends meet, he reluctantly left, to be replaced by Eric Dawson. The others resigned themselves to adding "commercials" to the repertoire. Dankworth later wrote,

> We dealt with complaints from dance promoters by producing a clutch of versions of popular tunes and standards with reference to the style of Victor Sylvester's Ballroom Orchestra, placing these at strategic points in the programme . . . We added showmanship – waving instruments in unison, lighting effects concealed inside the drums, marches through the audience, long, spectacular Latin-American epics with all of us on percussion instruments, and even comedy routines.[4]

Some of this was copied from the Seven's Swiss counterpart, a similar-sized band led by Hazy Osterwald. Dankworth added singers, too – first Marion Williams and then Frank Holder, a born showman who also played bongos and proved a big asset.

Despite its rocky start, and the concessions that had to be made, the Johnny Dankworth Seven made remarkable headway in its first year. The number of venues presenting modern jazz was growing, although most of these were weekly one-night affairs with a house rhythm section and one or two star guests. To maintain the Seven's high standard and keep its jazz repertoire fresh, he established his own club night in the West End. It began on Wednesdays at 100 Oxford Street (the weekend venue of the Feldman Club), moving soon afterwards to Studio 51 in Great Newport Street, a rehearsal room in the daytime. There were a few broadcasts, including at least one in the BBC's French Service, concerts around the country and a number of brief overseas trips. In July 1950 Dankworth signed a recording contract for the Seven with Carlo Krahmer's Esquire label, the results being enthusiastically reviewed in the music press. That first year culminated with Dankworth gaining an unprecedented three first places in the *Melody Maker* readers' poll, published on 3 February 1951. His name headed the sections for alto saxophone, small band and Musician of the Year. Professional, semi-professional and would-be musicians still constituted the backbone of the paper's readership, and many of them were alive to the distinctive modernity of Dankworth's ideas and the quality of the musicianship involved. Indeed, it is possible to make some fair generalizations about the tastes of the readership from such poll results. Names of leading revivalists, for example, tend to appear, if at all, at around fifth place on the 1951 poll, usually just below the names of established older players, such as Sid Phillips and Nat Temple. The prominence of figures such as Ted Heath and Kenny Baker remains unchallenged. On the day after the

The Johnny Dankworth Seven, c.1951. Dankworth (with Grafton Acrylic alto saxophone) centre; others clockwise from top right: Don Rendell, Jimmy Deuchar, Tony Kinsey, Eric Dawson, Bill LeSage, Eddie Harvey (Photo: Author's collection)

poll results were published, Carlo Krahmer gathered as many of the winners as he feasibly could at his Esquire studio. Dankworth, in his capacity as Musician of the Year, composed and arranged the two 78 sides – 'Brand's Essence' and 'Marshall's Plan'. (Puns and wordplay, especially on people's names, were for some reason very fashionable as tune titles in early modern jazz. These two, now deeply obscure, refer respectively to a popular condiment of the time and the US aid programme for post-war Europe, coupled with the names of *Melody Maker*'s editor, Pat Brand, and its chief photographer, Jack Marshall.) As in all such efforts, nobody gets to do much more than fire off a desultory half-chorus, but Dankworth's arrangements do manage to impose some shape on the proceedings. The discs were in the shops the following week, and the haste in which they had to be written provides evidence of his remarkable facility. He was notorious for leaving things to the last moment – writing scores over breakfast was quite common – and other musicians were in awe of his casual brilliance in such matters. Many years later, the saxophonist Peter King recalled Dankworth reharmonising a passage in rehearsal, leaning over each part in turn, writing upside-down and transposing as he went.

In April 1951, Marion Williams left the Seven and they cast around for a replacement. Almost by accident, they found a completely inexperienced and untypical young singer called Clementina Langridge (née Campbell). She had been trying desperately to get into a band – any band – and taking auditions without success. Although she had only vaguely heard of the Johnny Dankworth Seven, she followed a tip-off and turned up at Studio 51 on a Wednesday afternoon to audition for Dankworth and Bill LeSage. She chose to sing 'Stormy Weather'.

> I knew that something out of the ordinary was happening. The throaty, husky tones were already giving a new meaning to the well known words. By the time the girl had reached the middle section and was a mere twenty or so bars into the classic standard it was all too apparent: here was a very unusual talent indeed. Obviously inexperienced, she nevertheless already had a presence in her delivery which conveyed both maturity and style.[5]

That night she sang with the band, who voted unanimously to offer her the job. They proposed six pounds a week; she asked for seven and got it. The name "Clementina Langridge" didn't sound right, though, and would take up too much space on the posters in any case. A brainstorming session with the band's publicist, Les Perrin, held in the saloon bar of the Porcupine, Charing Cross Road, resulted in her new name – Cleo Laine.

The ease and fluency of the Seven's playing, both individually and as a band, grew along with their confidence. Dankworth's composition 'Seven Not Out', recorded in July 1950, bears a more than passing resemblance to Miles Davis's 'Boplicity'. The ensemble blend is warm and secure, but the solos sound slightly tentative, as though the players are not entirely at home with the chord sequence – all except Dankworth himself, that is. His attractively pale tone and graceful phrasing are the epitome of cool. A version of 'Cherokee', on the other hand, which was recorded at the same session, sounds astonishingly assured at the hair-raising tempo of approximately 82 bars (or 328 beats) per minute. Dankworth's solo break in the introduction, Don Rendell's half-chorus solo and Bill LeSage's half chorus which follows are all impressively poised and fluent. Dankworth's arrangements continued to grow in boldness and ingenuity over the life of the Seven. To extract a wealth of orchestral timbres and textures from a small mixed group of instruments is a particular challenge, greater in many ways than deploying the much larger forces of the conventional "big band". Pieces such as 'I Hear Music' (July 1951), with its two-bar, and later one-bar exchanges and its repeated phrases adding a new voice with each repetition, or 'Webb City' (from the same session), with its clarinet-led ensemble, are still a joy to listen to. His exceptionally acute ear no doubt picked up and analysed everything he heard which interested him, but in 1950 there was nothing like the amount of material available that there would be now. We have no idea, for instance, whether he had encountered Gil Evans's early arrangements for the Claude Thornhill orchestra – probably not, since the records had not then been released in Britain. In which case his arrangement of 'Allen's Alley' (November 1951) hits independently on one of Evans's happy discoveries, namely that a fast-moving bebop line gains in intensity from being played quietly in unison octaves.

No matter how good she or he might be, it was usually a vocalist's fate to be handed the "commercial" side of a band's repertoire – in other words, to represent the stuff the musicians didn't want to play. Even in the Johnny Dankworth Seven this tended to be the case, and it is with Cleo Laine's earliest recordings that one catches a glimpse of this other, necessary side of life. In a half-hearted attempt to break into the early-fifties pop market, Carlo Krahmer had launched Esquire's red-label "Popular Series". That was where Miss Laine made her debut, with a song in the then-popular "wanderer" genre called 'Mr and Mississippi', already successfully recorded by Patti Page and Tennessee Ernie Ford. This performance features heavy bass on first and third beats, some off-beat clapping and harmony vocal backing by the "Jay Birds" – alias Messrs Holder, Harvey, Rendell and LeSage. There was a similar one soon afterwards, entitled 'Sin', already recorded by the Four Knights, the Beverley Sisters, Joe Loss and several others. It is easy to see why records like this don't work. The performers look down on the material. They are insincere and it shows. It so happened that 1952 was the year when pop sensibility in Britain began to change. The singer, not the song; the record, not the song-sheet, was now listed in the charts. It was the year of Johnnie Ray, the "Cry Guy" – and, boy, was *he* sincere! Judgment seems to have deserted everyone when it came to Esquire's excursion into pop. The reverse side of 'Mr and Mississippi' was Billy Strayhorn's 'Lush Life', possibly the most difficult jazz ballad ever written. Dankworth's arrangement, full of dramatic chords and portentous pauses, does neither song nor singer any favours. Among the instrumental pieces were the theme from *The Haunted Ballroom*, featuring double-tracked alto saxophone, and swingy versions of 'Marching Through Georgia' and 'At the Wedding of the Painted Doll'. The last two are quite witty arrangements, but eminently forgettable.

The audience for modern jazz grew substantially after 1951, and the need for such antics diminished accordingly. At the beginning of 1953 Dankworth signed with Parlophone, a major label and part of the EMI empire. This entailed exchanging the Esquire studio (in reality the basement of Carlo Krahmer's flat, with the toilet serving as an echo chamber) for EMI's palatial facilities at Abbey Road, and putting the band's recording career in the hands of Parlophone's junior Artist and Repertoire manager, George Martin. The Seven managed to record very little for the new label, however, because in June of that year Dankworth announced that he was breaking it up and preparing to form a big band. Fans of the Seven could not believe that, after struggling for three years, topping the polls and becoming the undisputed figurehead of modern jazz in Britain, he was now killing off the band that had enabled him to do so. The general opinion was that no good would come of it. In the twenty-first century, big bands are associated either with jazz or with nostalgic recreations of Glenn Miller, and so on, and even these are thin on the ground. Things were different in the early 1950s. Bands then were at the heart of popular entertainment, for dancing to, listening to, accompanying popular singers, and providing a sizeable chunk of the background to daily life on the radio. The best-known – Ted Heath, Ken Mackintosh, the Squadronaires, Teddy Foster, Joe Loss, Cyril Stapleton – were household names. Two new bands had been launched in 1952 – led by Jack Parnell and Basil Kirchin respectively. This was the competition against which Dankworth was setting himself. "It was meant to compete with Ted Heath as a commercial big band", he later explained.

> Though the band would obviously have to do commercial things from time to time, I wanted there to be plenty of opportunities for good solo playing as well. I always thought Ted was too cautious with his jazz policy – like telling the soloists to play the same solos every night. With his following, he had a golden opportunity to make certain parts of his repertoire more exciting, and that's what I tried to do.[6]

It was true that Ted Heath told his musicians to play the same solos every night. He couldn't understand what was wrong with that, and why some found it so irksome that they eventually left the highest-paid job in the business because of it. In other words, big bands and jazz did not necessarily go together.

The first Johnny Dankworth Orchestra had the standard format: four trumpets, four trombones, five saxophones (two altos, two tenors, one baritone), piano, bass, drums – plus Dankworth himself and three singers, Tony Mansell, Frank Holder and Cleo Laine. It made its recording debut on 12 November 1953 with two pieces, Dankworth's arrangement of Gershwin's 'S'Wonderful' and his own composition, 'Younger Every Day'. He has sometimes been criticized for over-writing, and the orchestration in both pieces could scarcely be called sparse, but it comes from an abundance of original ideas. The very first eight bars of 'S'Wonderful', a cheerful, perky little phrase played twice and differently voiced each time, are archetypal Dankworth – bright, urbane, optimistic. They encapsulate a compositional tone of voice that was later, through film and television, to become a familiar part of Britain's soundscape. At other times there are distinct reminders of the ballroom. These come not so much in the writing as in a certain stiffness in the playing, especially among the brass. They were all good players, but somewhat out of their element. The Seven had been together from the beginning, with very few changes. They spoke the same musical language and shared a common purpose – and there were only seven of them. Those who

Debut appearance of the Johnny Dankworth Orchestra, Astoria Ballroom, Nottingham, 23 October 1953 (Photo: Raymond New Agency, courtesy Peter Vacher Collection)

stayed on into the big band lamented the loss, not only of musical empathy, but of camaraderie. "When things get big nobody really feels they are a part of it," said Eddie Harvey.[7] That was something that particularly got to Bill LeSage: "I couldn't get over people moaning about the showmanship angle, and wanting to be paid union rate for rehearsals. I couldn't understand this because it had never been this way before."[8] He left in March 1954, followed by Eddie Harvey in January 1955. Even so, despite its shortcomings, this was noticeably more of a jazz orchestra than its rivals.

Cleo Laine had made a big enough impression to come second to Heath's Lita Rosa in the 1954 *Melody Maker* poll. She was still confined to the role of "band singer", and it was another year before she was able to record under her own name. Her debut album, a modest ten-inch LP for Esquire, was actually quite adventurous for the time. Entitled *Cleo Sings British*, it consists of eight songs by British songwriters, ranging from William Shakespeare to Billy Reid. The settings, by Dankworth, are arranged for a quintet drawn from the orchestra. Since he was now under contract to EMI, the accompanying band is billed as the "Keith Christie Quintet". Almost certainly it was Dankworth's idea, but what other singer in 1955 would have grasped it so well? And what other partnership would have brought it off with such panache? Clever, restrained and good-humoured, *Cleo Sings British* is the first expression of an artistic and personal relationship that was to continue for more than half a century. It remains a minor classic of vocal jazz, British or otherwise.

After tinkering for some time with the personnel of the big band, in efforts to make it more agile and responsive, Dankworth eventually came up with a radical solution. In setting up his band he had, like everyone else, followed the conventional structure. The American dance orchestra had evolved over half a century into the familiar shape of brass, saxophone and rhythm sections, the trumpets, trombones and saxophones being deployed antiphonally in blocks. This was the format employed by all the great bands of the swing era, including Basie, Goodman, Herman and so on, and it had survived largely unchallenged into the 1950s. In 1956 Dankworth reorganized his band into a format which ingeniously combined the lightness and fluidity of a small band with the weight of a full orchestra. He replaced the saxophone section with a section of soloists, very much like the front-line of the original Seven: trumpet, trombone, alto and tenor saxophones, plus a baritone. Behind this was the full brass section. The idea, reminiscent of the baroque *concerto grosso*, succeeded brilliantly. The new front-line section, with its range of possible combinations, was capable of all the tonal variety which the Seven had produced, while the soloists were less confined. In pieces such as 'Firth of Fourths', 'Export Blues' and 'Adios', the new band ("Dankworth MkII") fulfils the promise that MkI only hinted at. Everything it played carried the characteristic Dankworth stamp, in the clarity of the voicings, the attention to dynamics and the integration of improvised solos with the full orchestra. It also swung more freely than MkI, largely because the whole musical design was less cluttered. The sound of the new band was so distinctive because it depended on Dankworth's unique style of orchestration and turn of phrase. It would have been physically impossible for him to write it all, but fortunately he had the perfect collaborator in Dave Lindup. The relationship between these two was remarkably similar to that between Duke Ellington and Billy Strayhorn. It had begun with Lindup doing odd bits of freelance writing – dance numbers and vocal accompaniments – and gradually getting a feel for Dankworth's style until it became virtually impossible to tell one from the other, especially when played by the same band. The new band received an enormous boost in April 1956, when its first single, 'Experiments With Mice', became a Top Ten hit. Essentially a superior kind of novelty record, this featured half a dozen versions of 'Three Blind Mice' as brief musical caricatures in the styles of well-known bands, including Glenn Miller, Billy May, Benny Goodman and Stan Kenton. It rose to fifth place at the end of April and remained in the chart for eight weeks.

After some early reshuffling, the personnel of the second Dankworth orchestra remained remarkably stable, especially the front-line which finally settled down to Dankworth himself (alto saxophone, clarinet), Danny Moss (tenor saxophone, clarinet, bass clarinet), Alex Leslie (baritone saxophone, clarinet, flute), Dickie Hawdon (trumpet, tenor horn) and Lawrie Monk (trombone). The only change in the actual instrumentation of the band was the addition of a tuba, played by Ron Snyder. This was the band which appeared at the 1959 Newport Jazz Festival in the US, and the live recording made at that event displays it at close to its best. The American critic Nat Hentoff discerned many of its virtues, chief among them:

> the fact that the band is an organic, cohesive instrument of one man – Dankworth himself. The soloists certainly have freedom, but there is no mistaking that the band has a distinctive personality and sound of its own that reflect the thoughtful and exacting goals of its leader.[9]

Something very similar has often been said of the Duke Ellington orchestra. The very crispness and polish which so distinguished the band sometimes led, if not to censure, then to reservations in some jazz circles. Its music was not soulful, rugged or overtly emotional enough for them. There is nothing new in such criticism. Charlotte Brontë said much the same about Jane Austen. It comes down finally to a matter of taste and personal disposition. The most apt and kindly-meant comment in this regard about Dankworth's music was one made by a London journalist, the late Kitty Grime, which has been quoted so widely over the past half-century that few can remember who first made it. The music was, she said, "couth, kempt and shevelled".

Readers may have noticed, in the above account of John Dankworth's early career, three names previously associated with traditional or revivalist jazz. Eddie Harvey's migration from the world of George Webb's Dixielanders to that of Club Eleven has already been described. We last heard of Keith Christie, having passed through Humphrey Lyttelton's band, co-leading an amiable shambles called the Christie Brothers' Stompers. On the strength of this he was voted number two trombonist in the 1952 *Melody Maker* readers' poll and managed to get himself onto that year's all-winners record, the very first Esquire LP (ten-inch, naturally). This was how he announced his apostasy to the world, with two choruses of a twelve-bar blues by Dankworth, called 'Up The Poll'. He kept on with the Stompers until their dissolution and then joined Dankworth's band. It will be recalled that the accompanying group on *Cleo Sings British* is the "Keith Christie Quintet". The third name is that of Dickie Hawdon (1927–2009), Keith's fellow-modernist cuckoo in the Stompers' nest. He moved to London in 1951, having been, to all intents and purposes, leader of the successful revivalist Yorkshire Jazz Band. He played in Chris Barber's first band while working in jazz record shops, where records of all types of jazz were constantly playing. He found himself paying more and more attention to the bebop discs, especially to crisp, precise players such as tenor saxophonist Wardell Gray and trumpeter Fats Navarro. He had always prided himself on his ability to pick up and reproduce the style of any player he liked, but bebop defeated him. He simply did not know where to start. One day Jimmy Deuchar, trumpeter with the Dankworth Seven, came into the shop and Hawdon confessed his difficulty. "Let's pick a tune we both know, like 'Indiana'", suggested Deuchar. "You write down the chords you use and I'll write the ones I use." By comparing the two and teasing out the harmonic implications, Hawdon claimed, he discovered a whole new world. "Jimmy Deuchar revolutionised my understanding of jazz as music."[10] Also a prominent member of the MkII Dankworth orchestra was tenor saxophonist Danny Moss (1927–2008), who moved some way in the opposite stylistic direction. His inclination had always been towards the broad-toned, spacious style of the swing era, typified by Ben Webster and Buddy Tate, but he had cultivated the light, fast-moving modern approach, to conform with the times. Dankworth, however, valued individuality in soloists and encouraged him to play as he wished. In 1959, when the orchestra visited the US, Count Basie complimented Moss, saying, "That's real Texas tenor! That's the way it should sound. I wish some of the young guys would play that way."

John Dankworth may have declared his aim of rivalling Ted Heath, but his real rival for the affections of British jazz lovers was Jack Parnell (1923–2010). Four years older than Dankworth, Parnell had been a professional drummer from the age of sixteen. His family roots were deep in show-business. Both his father and grandfather were ventriloquists and his uncle, Val Parnell, was general manager of Moss Empires, the nationwide chain of variety theatres, and ran its flagship venue, the London Palladium. Jack Parnell already had a long list of recording credits, reaching back to the war years, when he left Ted Heath in 1951 to set up his own big band. Its first year was spent in the West End, playing for the show *Fancy Free* at the Prince of Wales Theatre, before going on tour. Among its personnel were some of the most promising young musicians of the day. The impresario Leslie Grade, a family friend, gave Parnell a word of advice early in the band's career: "You can't lead a band sitting down at the drums, Jack. You're the star of the show, so you'll have to be standing up, right in the front. And you will have to have a high spot, something that people will remember and talk about afterwards."[11] Accordingly, Parnell hired another drummer – the phenomenal, if unpredictable, Phil Seamen – and for the "high spot" he devised a routine in which the two of them played a spectacular synchronized drum duet. "It wasn't anything like as difficult as it seemed", he later confessed, "but it looked terrific and very clever. That's when I realized that most of the public listen with their eyes. The band had been losing money, but the duet saved us. It caused a sensation and made our name."[12] The tendency among the top dance bands was increasingly towards becoming show bands, as this story suggests. Spectacular routines, star vocalists, "novelty" numbers of one kind or another – these were essential to success. A big band's bread-and-butter work still came from playing at ballrooms around the country, but when a star band was appearing, dancers found themselves displaced to the back of the hall, behind a phalanx of fans crowded in front of the stage. It is difficult to imagine anyone dancing in conventional ballroom style while, under the spotlights, Jack Parnell and Phil Seamen knocked the living daylights out of a pair of drum kits. Two of the band's records, strident, frantic versions of Dizzy Gillespie's 'The Champ'

(1952) and Louie Bellson's 'Skin Deep' (1952), both climaxing in brief drum duets, were big hits, especially with teenagers.

The Jack Parnell band at its peak was every bit as much a jazz orchestra as Dankworth's, although in a very different way. A brash, hard-swinging affair, it was more like its American counterparts, such as Harry James's, or even Woody Herman's. By a curious turn of events it also brought about the birth of one of the great (if short-lived) British bands of the mid-fifties, the fabled "Ronnie Scott nine-piece". Scott left Parnell's band in 1952, intent on a solo career with his own quartet, and his place in the saxophone section was taken by Pete King. At around the same time, Parnell was urgently seeking a glamorous girl singer to complete the band's show. Eventually, he spotted Marion Davis, whom he judged perfect for the role, and offered her the job. But she was married to the tenor saxophonist Ronnie Keene and would agree only on condition that he joined the band as well. On the principle of "last in, first out", Parnell gave notice to Pete King. The sacking of the reliable and well-liked King – especially at the behest of a band singer, regarded as the lowest form of life by many musicians – caused outrage among his colleagues. Five of Parnell's key players resigned in sympathy, which left them virtuous but unemployed. Ronnie Scott, who had already used some of them in ad hoc groups, proposed that, with the addition of a few more, they should form their own band. Scott would act as leader, but all profits would be shared equally – an arrangement which one of the newcomers, baritone saxophonist Benny Green, dubbed "syncopated Marxism". Pete King, considered the most level-headed among them, was appointed manager and guardian of the purse-strings. The line-up, when completed, comprised: Jimmy Deuchar (trumpet), Ken Wray (trombone), Derek Humble (alto), Ronnie Scott and Pete King (tenors), Benny Green (baritone), Norman Stenfalt (piano), Lennie Bush (bass) and Tony Crombie (drums).

The *New Musical Express* (*NME*) made a point of supporting the new band and, to build interest, arranged for some rehearsals to be open to the public. At its launch in February 1953, Scott made the ritual protestation that the new band would be "commercial", dedicated to pleasing the public and catering for dancers. It would indeed be obliged to follow the inevitable round of venues gruesomely itemised by Jim Godbolt (himself a former band agent) in the second volume of his *History of Jazz in Britain*: "ballrooms, drill halls, corn exchanges, working men's clubs, institutes, colleges and various improvised venues such as aircraft hangars".[13] Not forgetting, of course, the echoing municipal swimming baths, with a dance floor laid over the pool. But, whatever the stated intention, there was something decidedly uncompromising about the Ronnie Scott Orchestra. Its whole presentation was at odds with dance-band practice. They looked different, for a start, behind their low, light blue Plexiglas music stands, each one bearing the name of its occupant. They knew they were good and didn't try to conceal the fact. It was as though the band were passing judgment on the audience and not being terribly impressed. As Tony Crombie recalled: "It was a closed community. There was no room for anybody else, no room for the audience. If they liked it – fine. If they didn't – too bad!"[14] This refusal to ingratiate proved unexpectedly attractive to a new young audience for modern jazz which was growing, almost unnoticed. Socially, it was almost indistinguishable from the traditional and revivalist audience, except that perhaps it contained fewer art students and more engineering apprentices, it dressed more smartly, and its style of dancing was less wild. It might go along to the local Palais when a top band was billed, but disliked novelty numbers, corny comedy routines and slushy, sentimental songs. The Parnell–Seamen drum duet always went down well, because of the skill involved as much as anything, but the Ronnie Scott nine-piece was the no-nonsense business. It built up a keen following throughout the country, especially in Manchester and the north-west, which, long after the three-year life of the band itself had ended, continued to sing its praises.

The band's recordings reveal something of its character. The first session, from 13 April 1953, produced a version of 'Lover Come Back To Me', taken at the insane tempo of around 96 bars (384 beats) a minute. Halfway through, everything stops while Stenfalt plays sixteen bars in the flowery, Palm-Court manner, after which mayhem is again let loose. The message could not be clearer: The tune comes originally from *The New Moon*, a genteel operetta of the 1920s, composed by Sigmund Romberg. In brutally tearing it to bits, the band was making a defiant gesture, the kind of gesture that punk rock was later to make, the difference being that this was talent with attitude, whereas

Ronnie Scott Orchestra (the "Nine-Piece"), London 1953. Front-line as announced on music stands; rhythm section, from left: Norman Stenfalt (piano), Tony Crombie (drums), Lennie Bush (bass) (Photo: Courtesy Peter Vacher Collection)

punk rock was merely attitude. In the circumstances, it was probably just as well that Romberg was already dead. Hearing this might have finished him off.

Predictably, the Ronnie Scott Orchestra was turned down at its first BBC audition, as "unsuitable for broadcasting". By 1955, the band's last year, a few changes had taken place. Norman Stenfalt left at the end of 1953, to be replaced by Victor Feldman, playing both piano and vibraphone. Jimmy Deuchar and Tony Crombie both left in September 1954 to start their own bands. Their places were taken by Hank Shaw and Phil Seamen. By this time, the rawness had been replaced by poise and a kind of relaxed energy, epitomised by splendid pieces such as 'S'il Vous Plait' and 'Jordu', both recorded in April 1955.

Although it had grown considerably, the British audience for modern jazz in the mid-fifties was still fairly modest in size. Bands such as Dankworth's, Parnell's and even Scott's remained at least partly reliant on ballroom work. Smaller venues – the modern equivalent of the traditionalists' Fishmongers' Arms – could rarely afford to pay for more than a "star guest" to appear with a local trio or quartet. More often than not, the locals were themselves professional or good semi-professional players, who worked regularly with dance bands in the locality, at hotels, town halls and so on. In fact, they very often ran the club nights themselves. A typical example would be a club called "The Gearbox", held on Friday nights in the function room of the Railway Hotel, Dartford, Kent.

It was at the Gearbox, in the latter part of 1953, that Don Rendell (born 1926) first encountered Ronnie Ross (1933–1991), another tenor saxophonist, then serving in the band of the Grenadier Guards. Their meeting led to a partnership which, early in 1954, produced the Don Rendell Sextet, one of the finest small bands of the period. The two other permanent members were Dickie Hawdon (playing both trumpet and flugelhorn) and pianist Damian Robinson. The bassist and drummer changed a few times during the band's regrettably short life. Only a regularly constituted band could produce original music, in an individual style, at a high level of performance, but the audience, though enthusiastic, was too small and scattered to provide a viable income. This virtually insoluble dilemma bedevilled British modern jazz throughout the 1950s, as Don Rendell and others found to their cost. In order to keep a band of professional musicians together as a going concern it was necessary for it to be fully equipped, not only with instruments and a repertoire, but transport, uniforms, music stands and so on. (Amplification, in those days, was usually the responsibility of the venue.) It also had to be permanently available, so its members were not able to take other work, except casual gigs at short notice. Despite all this, some of these small, short-lived bands reached extraordinary heights of artistry, and the Don Rendell Sextet was notable among them. It made its first recording, for the Tempo label, in June 1954, after which it was decided that Ronnie Ross should switch from tenor to baritone saxophone, to create a more distinctive blend of the three front-line instruments. A four-track EP, *Don Rendell Sextet*, recorded in February 1955, contains some of the most spirited, melodic and at times witty music ever recorded by British jazz musicians. Damian Robinson's arrangement of the old Louis Armstrong Hot Five number, 'Muskrat Ramble', is particularly delicious. It is hard to believe that, less than three years earlier, Hawdon had been playing in the Christie Brothers' Stompers and seeking instruction in modern jazz from Jimmy Deuchar. He sounds here like a cross between Chet Baker and Art Farmer. That record came out in March 1955, by which time mounting debts had forced Rendell to disband the sextet. Along with Ronnie Ross and Damian Robinson, he joined Tony Crombie's new orchestra for a while, until a lucky vacancy occurred in Ted Heath's ranks and, within a few weeks, he had earned enough to settle all his debts. Undeterred, he continued until the end of the decade to alternate between leading (or co-leading) good small bands and working from time to time in commercial orchestras in order to recoup his losses.

A similar fate befell the Ken Moule Seven, whose pianist leader had been a close friend of John Dankworth since school days. Their writing styles were broadly similar, although there was an attractive quirkiness about Moule's work which marked him out. The Seven consisted of Moule himself, Dave Usden (trumpet), Keith Barr and Roy Sidwell (tenor saxophones), Don Cooper (baritone saxophone), Arthur Watts (bass) and Lennie Breslow (drums). It lasted barely a year, partly, it seems, because Moule himself was not cut out to lead a band. There were rumours of wrangling and dissention among the members and he walked away from it in May 1955. He reassembled the Seven to record two albums for Decca and played briefly in one of Don Rendell's later bands, the Jazz Six, but his career from the late fifties until his death in 1986 was as a composer, arranger and – beginning with Lionel Bart's stage musical *Fings Ain't Wot They Used T'Be* (1959) – musical director.

Perhaps the bravest, and oddest, of the short-lived bands was Kenny Graham's Afro-Cubists (motto: "Don't be a Square, be a Cubist!"), which married bebop with Caribbean rhythms. The idea was not entirely new – Dizzy Gillespie had been experimenting with it since 1947 – but Graham launched his band as early as 1950. In a country where the Johnny Dankworth Seven had recently caused bafflement and confusion, and where Latin American music meant the genial sounds of Edmundo Ros, it is amazing that he kept it going as long as he did. With Graham himself on tenor saxophone, Jo Hunter on trumpet and the usual jazz rhythm section augmented by up to four percussionists, it was an invigorating sound. Graham, who later went on to write arrangements for Ted Heath and others, did much more than merely stick bebop lines on top of clattering percussion. His compositions for the Afro-Cubists were often quite ambitious. 'Skylon', for instance, although less than three-and-a-half minutes long in its recorded form, passes from one solo to the next via a series of ambiguous bridge passages in which the rhythm could either be 6/8 or the basic 4/4 tempo in crotchet triplets.

Similarly, his 'Mango Walk' prefigures some of the ideas that Art Blakey and the Jazz Messengers would be employing ten years later, especially in the use of accompaniment patterns (later known as "grooves") behind soloists. The Afro-Cubists disbanded as a permanent band early in 1952, although it was revived from time to time for recordings and other occasions.

One of those occasions was the opening on 29 August 1952 of Jazz at the Flamingo, a venue beneath the Mapleton restaurant, in Coventry Street, just off Leicester Square. Described in *Jazz Journal* as "the most comfortable, de-luxe surroundings the average jazz fan has ever experienced",[15] this soon became the headquarters of modern jazz in London, and indeed Britain. A reported 1,500 fans turned up on opening night, requiring 40 policemen to maintain order. If Britain's enthusiasm for modern jazz throughout the 1950s was to be judged by the liveliness of the London scene – and to some extent those in Manchester, Birmingham and other major cities – jazz musicians would have been fully employed, bands would not have been going bust or struggling around the country playing dance music in repellent surroundings, and jazz would not have been consigned to odds and ends of airtime by the BBC. But these were hot spots, whose audiences were drawn from far and wide. The jazz lovers who crowded into the Flamingo, the Feldman Club, Studio 51 and more temporary set-ups such as the Florida, the Downbeat and the London Jazz Centre might have come from anywhere in the Home Counties, and even beyond.

Regular appearances at these clubs, and hence in the club columns of *Melody Maker*, conferred status on musicians. In the case of the drummer and bandleader Tony Kinsey (born 1927), his entire career in the 1950s was centred on two clubs. After leaving the Dankworth Seven in late 1951, he joined the trio of pianist Ronnie Ball, resident at the newly opened Studio 51. When, in the following year, Ball emigrated to the US, Kinsey took over leadership, with Dill Jones, and later Bill LeSage, as pianist. From this point onwards, the trio became the basis of a series of quartets and quintets containing many of the finest players of that generation. It began with tenor saxophonist Tommy Whittle (1926–2013), who had left Ted Heath in frustration at having to repeat the same solos night after night. He somehow managed to combine playing with Kinsey with being a full-time member of the BBC Show Band. Whittle was followed by, among others, Joe Harriott, Bob Efford, Les Condon, Ronnie Ross and, for a while in 1956, both Ronnie Ross and Don Rendell – thus briefly recreating their classic partnership. Taking in a switch from Studio 51 to the Flamingo in 1954, Tony Kinsey's name was more or less a permanent fixture in the club columns. Recordings by the various Kinsey groups are full of delightful moments. The amount of tonal variety they contain, especially with LeSage doubling on piano and vibraphone, is quite remarkable. The arrangements are often replete with witty counter-melodies which cast well-worn standards, such as 'Making Whoopee' and 'Hey There!', in a surprising new light. The long series from the mid-fifties featuring Ronnie Ross is particularly good, revealing him to have been among the few great exponents of the baritone saxophone in his time, the equal of the American masters Gerry Mulligan and Serge Chaloff.

No one pretended that playing modern jazz for a living in the 1950s was easy or lucrative, but there was a growing confidence and sense of achievement by the middle of the decade. Paradoxically, perhaps, the stubborn resistance of the Musicians' Union to the entry of American musicians, while it deprived British musicians of the inspiration they might have gained, also protected them from competition during a crucial period of growth. The audience may not have been large, but it was expanding and they had it all to themselves.

7 Let's Settle for Music

In May 1954 the BBC Light Programme launched a new series, under the title *British Jazz*. Although only a measly twenty minutes in length, it set out to reflect the current diversity of jazz taste in the country. It gave air-time to a few of the most distinctive small modern bands, notably the Tony Kinsey Trio, Don Rendell Sextet, Ken Moule Seven and Ronnie Scott's nine-piece (which had passed its audition at the second attempt), and programmed more traditional bands impartially among them. It is fairly obvious that the latter were those that (a) were able to pass the BBC audition and (b) might be considered acceptable as Light Programme fare. Unsurprisingly, they were the bands of Humphrey Lyttelton, Chris Barber, Alex Welsh, Bobby Mickleburgh's Bobcats and Harry Gold and his Pieces of Eight. The appearance of *British Jazz* in the schedules was significant not so much for its specific content as for its even-handed approach. It marks the beginning, if not of a rapprochement, at least of the recognition that a middle ground existed between the two extremes. The animosity among the various jazz factions – not just modernists and revivalists, but splinter groups within the main contending blocs – had grown so absurd that a large section of the audience, the older members especially, simply ignored the whole business and followed their own tastes. It began as early as 1952, when the Light Programme launched a weekly jazz show that cannily avoided using the word "jazz" in its title. It was called *Let's Settle for Music*, went out initially on Friday nights (later moving to Thursdays) and featured Kenny Baker with a specially formed band, Baker's Dozen.

As its name suggests, the Dozen was thirteen strong and it comprised musicians of several generations. Its regular members included figures such as George Chisholm, Harry Hayes and saxophonist and violinist Freddie Ballerini, whose reputations had been established in the late 1930s, alongside modernists like Harry Klein, Phil Seamen and Club Eleven founder-member Joe Muddell. There was also the indispensable E. O. ("Poggy") Pogson, an extreme multi-instrumentalist whose permanent job at the time was in

Victor Sylvester's Ballroom Orchestra. In addition to the complete range of saxophones and clarinets, he played flute, oboe, bassoon, ocarina, penny whistle, musical straw, "hot fountain-pen" and several more oddities. There was always a feature for Poggy on one of his instruments, the more outlandish the better. As well as being a trumpet virtuoso, Baker was a quick and resourceful arranger. He wrote the vast majority of the scores for the show, thus defining an agreeable personal style. There was nothing particularly startling about Baker's arrangements, but they were brisk and swinging, always kept the melody in sight and presented soloists to good advantage. *Let's Settle for Music* proved unexpectedly popular. Devised and produced by Pat Dixon (who had also launched *The Goon Show*), it found just the right approach. The presenter, Wilfred Thomas, had an easy-going manner which paid listeners the compliment of assuming they would be interested in the music and who was playing it, without either being lectured to or entertained with jokes and inconsequential chatter. Although it had been intended as a lightweight filler, and scheduled for one short series, public demand ensured that the show was brought back repeatedly for further series over a period of more than six years. Each series consisted of at least a dozen programmes, and some of the earlier ones ran to more than twenty. Individual programmes varied in length between thirty and forty minutes each. Altogether, it adds up to a considerable amount of airtime.

The lasting success of *Let's Settle for Music* suggests that the widespread taste for swingy music, which had been evident at the end of the war, still existed quite separately from the factional brouhaha of the jazz world. We find it, for instance, in the two musical interludes which were part of each episode of *The Goon Show* – one by the Ray Ellington Quartet and the other by the Dutch harmonica player Max Geldray, whose style was slightly reminiscent of Benny Goodman. Similarly, the off-beat comedy show *Bedtime with Braden*, launched in 1950, had Nat Temple's small swing band in attendance. These and other radio programmes incorporated some form of jazz because it suited the style of the show, but the term itself did not appear anywhere in the publicity, nor was it uttered on air. Even in the early 1950s it seems that the word "jazz" frightened people off, as it still tends to. Almost certainly this has something to do with the aura of exclusivity which the jazz world has cultivated around itself. It probably dates back to the early 1930s and the efforts of the first jazz commentators to get the music of Armstrong and his contemporaries taken seriously. Their discourse took on the clannish and exclusive tone typical of embattled minorities. It can be detected in Spike Hughes's *Melody Maker* pieces and persisted through the forties and fifties, even in the work of relatively straightforward writers, such as Max Jones and Albert McCarthy. The notion took root, among the public at large, that an "understanding" of jazz called for the acquisition of arcane knowledge – or, as Philip Larkin gloomily observed on more than one occasion, attendance at a series of lectures at the local Adult Education Institute. That arch ironist,

Kenny Baker and Norman Stenfalt, preparing to dub Key Kendall's trumpet solo in the 1953 film *Genevieve* (Photo: Walter Hanlon, courtesy Peter Vacher Collection)

Ronnie Scott, would occasionally send up this whole idea, by surveying the audience on a particularly cheerful night at his club and sternly demanding: "Quiet please! You're not here to enjoy yourselves!"

Although professionals of Kenny Baker's generation and before took little notice of critical dogma and the antagonism it bred, revivalists, purists, boppers, cool cats and the rest stuck resolutely to their positions. This was particularly true at the traditional end of the spectrum, where, at the beginning of the fifties, attitudes remained pretty well where they had been in 1945. Professional skill and polish were suspect, deviation from the set stylistic path was condemned, use of written music was virtually unheard of and the saxophone was an emblem of the enemy. Yet, in the centre of all this, and regarded by many as its standard bearer, stood Humphrey Lyttelton. Non-doctrinaire, inquisitive, disposed to experiment and hugely energetic, he was soon showing signs of becoming semi-detached from the revivalist jazz camp, exploring new avenues and unfrequented byways.

The first intimation that Lyttelton was not going to be George Webb Mark II came in his first year as a bandleader, when he had the temerity to start writing his own material. One of his early acts after starting the band was to set up a small label, "London Jazz", to record it. Among its first releases were two Lyttelton compositions, 'Blue For Waterloo' and 'Vox Humana Blues'.

Both sound as though they could have been created specifically for a recording session in 1926 Chicago and they are played with confidence and a degree of technical command unusual in revivalist jazz of the period. They are not the first Lyttelton compositions on record (that was a piece called 'Humph Meets Trog', from the session with Carlo Krahmer mentioned in Chapter 3) and they are certainly not the last. He must have written hundreds over the ensuing six decades. Towards the end of 1949 the band was signed up by Parlophone Records and for the next ten years scarcely a recording session took place without at least one Lyttelton number being included. The very first, from January 1950, is an unusual piece entitled 'Straight From The Wood'. The band at the time possessed two clarinet players, Wally Fawkes and Ian Christie, and the tune features the pair of them in mellow harmony – a literally "woody" sound. Ian Christie left about fifteen months later, but Lyttelton was so taken with the two-clarinet sound that he bought one and taught himself to play it to a reasonable standard. There are occasional appearances by the Humph clarinet throughout his recorded work, the most attractive being a couple of duets with Wally Fawkes, dating from 1951 – 'Suffolk Air' and 'Blues For An Unknown Gipsy'. From the same year comes a piece of fun called 'One Man Went To Blow', in which he plays trumpet, clarinet, piano and washboard in an early example of multi-track recording.

In 1951 Graeme Bell and his band made a return visit to Britain. The Bell family were staying in the flat above the Lytteltons and musicians were coming and going all the time. ("We had Australians like other people had mice," Lyttelton recalled.) In the course of numerous parties and jam sessions a plan was hatched to combine members of the two bands to recreate the line-up of the Luis Russell Orchestra of the late twenties, but instead of merely playing a few tunes taken from that band's records, their idea was to write new pieces in the same style. The result was the Bell-Lyttelton Jazz Nine (also Jazz Ten and Jazz Twelve), which recorded five pieces for Parlophone towards the end of the year.[1] This was the kind of task Lyttelton relished – absorbing an idiom, capturing its rhythms and cadences until he knew them by instinct. His concentration and attention to detail at such times was formidable. "I've never known a man so rapt in his creative work," Graeme Bell wrote in his autobiography.[2] The Bell-Lyttelton records are lively and well played, with notable solos not only by Lyttelton, Fawkes and Christie, but also by the Australian saxophonists "Lazy Ade" Monsbourgh and Don "Pixie" Roberts, Graeme Bell himself and his trumpet-playing brother, Roger Bell.

"There was a faintly conspiratorial air about the whole proceedings," Lyttelton wrote in *Second Chorus*, his second book of memoirs, published in 1958. "Nine men playing jazz together from written arrangements is not exactly a revolutionary notion – but at that time, with Revivalist ardour still burning high in local jazz club circles, it amounted to subversion . . . The record-buying fans . . . were enthusiastic, bewildered or incensed in direct ratio to their familiarity with the big-band music of the late twenties."[3] Indeed, the proto-big bands of the late twenties, before their instrumentation settled down and their idiom solidified into swing, are not only fascinating historically but great fun to listen to. To hear such music played live, or to dance to it, should have been a novel and delightful experience, but far too often it was met by suspicion and carping criticism. There is a note of exasperation in much of Lyttelton's writing from the fifties, carefully disguised beneath a veneer of urbane humour. Among friends and colleagues he could be less guarded and sometimes said he despaired of getting bone-headed audiences to drop their fixed ideas, even for a moment, and use their ears for a change.

Even so, he was quite unable to resist an enticing musical adventure, such as the one which presented itself in 1952, at a "Mardi Gras Ball" in London. Lyttelton's band shared the evening with one composed of West Indian musicians, Cyril Blake's Calypsonians. As the evening neared its climax the two became merged in "a wild jam session in which anyone who could shake a maraca or strike bottle and spoon together joined in."[4] Thinking back later on this enjoyable event, Lyttelton reflected on the strong connection between New Orleans music and that of the Caribbean, both in rhythm and melody – on New Orleans Creole culture with its French origins, on Jelly Roll Morton's famous dictum that all New Orleans music had a "Spanish tinge", on the supple, rolling beat common to the Caribbean and the Gulf of Mexico. Mainly, however, he remembered how well the two bands had played together and how much fun it had all been. Thus was born the Grant-Lyttelton Paseo Jazz Band, a joint venture with the Guyanese clarinetist and saxophonist Freddy Grant. When the two first got together they discovered that venerable New Orleans Creole melodies, such as 'Eh, la bas!' and 'Blanche Touquatoux', were familiar, under other names, all over the Caribbean. The Paseo Band, containing several of the most distinguished West Indian musicians in London, such as the pianist Mike McKenzie and guitarist Fitzroy Coleman, along with Freddy Grant himself, toured around Britain with the Lyttelton band for about six months in 1952, "until the money ran out". The sheer *joie de vivre* of it succeeded in keeping most of the curmudgeons at bay. The band also recorded eleven numbers for Parlophone, produced by Denis Preston (see below), the first in the field when it came to recognizing the talents of West Indian artists in Britain. The records sold reasonably well. In this the Paseo Band did better than its modern-jazz contemporary, the Afro-Cubists, possibly because Lyttelton and Grant had worked up a full evening's show in which to present it. Lyttelton briefly revived the Paseo Band for a recording session in 1957, adding three flutes, marimba and timbales to the original instrumentation.

The derogatory term for a dyed-in-the-wool jazz revivalist or New Orleans purist was – and may still be – "mouldy fig". The etymology is obscure, the best attempt at an explanation being that by Eliott Horne in the *New York Sunday Times* of 18 August 1957. A "fig", he says, "is a traditionalist, a cat for whom jazz sort of ended with the swing era." A *mouldy* fig (or mouldy figge) is more extreme: "The swing era was avant garde for this guy". Among the tenets of true mouldy figgery was denial of the legitimacy of the saxophone as a jazz instrument, daft though such a view seemed to most people at the time and to everyone nowadays. In Britain, its principal proponent was one Rex Harris, author of a book simply entitled *Jazz*, published in 1952 under the "Pelican" imprint of Penguin Books. Among other things, Harris solemnly assured his readers that Coleman Hawkins might have become a noteworthy jazz musician if he had played some other instrument, such as the clarinet. It was against such a background, in January 1953, that Bruce Turner joined Humphrey Lyttelton and his Band, playing alto saxophone.

Malcolm Bruce Turner (1922–1993) had been a professional musician since his discharge from the RAF in 1946. He had played in the Dixieland bands of Freddy Randall and Joe Daniels and done a stint with Geraldo's Navy in 1949 (spending his brief visits to New York studying with Lee Konitz). A non-smoking, teetotal, vegetarian, public school-educated communist, he carried about with him an air of bemused abstraction, which is scarcely surprising. All this, along with a tendency to speak in the argot of an Edwardian schoolboy ("Some fun, I'd say! This is the life for a chap!") and to address everyone as "Dad", made him an unusual figure in the jazz world, to say the least. His first appearance with the Lyttelton band was at Birmingham Town Hall, where, during the show, a bunch of mouldy-fig students unfurled a banner bearing the message, "Go Home Dirty Bopper". Undeterred by this welcome, Turner remained with the band for four years. His arrival brought about a distinct change in the sound and approach of Lyttelton's regular band. Since the departure of Keith Christie, the front line had consisted only of the leader's trumpet and Wally Fawkes's clarinet. Now, with the addition of Turner's alto and soprano saxophones and clarinet the scope for new ideas was far greater. This is evident in the records made during this time, which still consisted largely of singles. Few of these exceed three minutes in length and they are all put together in such a way that their very brevity works to their advantage. Pieces such as 'Breeze', 'Mezz's Tune', 'Coffee Grinder' and 'The Glory of Love' are little gems of unpretentious jazz artistry. As with many jazz recordings of the 78 era, everything is condensed and concentrated to make the most effective miniature performance. Lyttelton had very definite ideas in matters like this, and always had the last word. When, in 1955, Oscar Preuss, Parlophone's label manager, who had signed him up six years before, retired, there was a battle of wills between Lyttelton and his successor, the young George Martin – "a brief but explosive moment of readjustment", as Lyttelton characteristically described it.[5] It seems that he won: "I can say that, for better or worse, every note and notion . . . came from myself and my various colleagues."[6] By then, Humphrey Lyttelton and his Band could no longer feasibly be fitted into the "revivalist" category – or, indeed, into any category but its own.

Humphrey Lyttelton, aged thirty-four, playing at his club's 1955 Christmas Party, 100 Oxford Street, London (Photo: © Val Wilmer Collection)

Lyttelton was not alone in his frustration with the way "traditional" jazz had developed – or, rather, failed to develop. Its growing audience demanded a standardized product, signified by the clang of the banjo, the fruity tones of the "tailgate" trombone and simple, repetitive tunes played at bright, jolly tempos. The musician, as Bruce Turner observed, "is not there to express himself, in fact, but to submerge himself in an already cut-and-dried style".[7] This was all the more irksome because there was so much in the jazz tradition waiting to be explored and expanded upon, as Lyttelton and Bell had shown in 1951 with their brief Luis Russell project. The restlessness and frustration caused by this state of affairs gave rise to a small but significant movement, led by musicians and supported by some in the music press (among them Max Jones of *Melody Maker* and Albert McCarthy of *Jazz Monthly*), to bypass the whole "trad v. mod" business and seek inspiration wherever it might be found. In practice, this usually meant finding it in the small-band jazz of the swing era – or, as Seymour Wyse would have put it, in "jump music". No style or sub-style of jazz can exist for long without having a label attached to it, and this one came to be called "mainstream" – a term introduced in the US by the expatriate British writer, Stanley Dance, as part of his effort to revive the careers of living swing-era musicians.

The sudden outburst of mainstream jazz in the mid-fifties was unlike the British beginnings of either revivalist jazz or bebop. It was to a certain extent backward looking, but carried no ideological baggage, and, although it involved skilled and often professional musicians, they did not, unlike the early beboppers, have to acquire a whole new musical grammar and syntax. As a result, there were no faltering early steps. The recordings sound purposeful and assured from the start, often subtle and beautifully crafted, and sometimes startlingly original. The main difficulty lay in finding an audience. Both traditional and modern jazz had established and well-delineated followings, each with its energizing core of fanatics, but a fanatical mainstreamer was almost a contradiction in terms – like a fanatical liberal. Furthermore, since the whole point of the thing was to follow one's own personal leanings, there was no single, identifiable style around which a popular following could form. This was the predicament in which jazz increasingly found itself. Was it to remain a form of popular music, or was it to turn itself gradually into some kind of concert or art music? What was it to be – the Fishmonger's Arms or the Recital Room of the Royal Festival Hall? Neither seemed particularly enticing. On the other hand, it was an undeniable fact that the original followers of both camps were, like the musicians themselves, growing older and, in some cases at least, more discerning. Hard facts and figures are impossible to come by, but the impression one gains is that it was people in their late twenties and thirties who first took to mainstream jazz. In fact, as modern jazz calmed down somewhat from its frantic bebop youth, and the more adventurous traditionalists began branching out, a new common ground looked like opening up. The greatest division now was between these and the more dogged traditionalists.

Perhaps the most remarkable figure among the emergent mainstream players was Sandy Brown. As mentioned briefly in Chapter 5, he began as a disciple of Johnny Dodds, and retained in his clarinet style the characteristic broad vibrato and deep blues inflections of his first model, with the addition of a mellow throatiness that was all his own. Moving from Edinburgh to London in 1954, he formed a band with his lifelong friend and colleague Al Fairweather on trumpet. Sandy Brown's Jazz Band began as a good revivalist band with a refreshingly relaxed approach to the idiom and almost at once showed signs of developing into something more formidable. In 1955 Brown was appointed chief acoustic architect to the BBC, a job which took up so much of his time and energy that he passed the band over to Fairweather in 1957. Shortly before this the band recorded the album *McJazz*, consisting of ten pieces composed by either Brown or Fairweather. Not only are they startlingly original, most of them are irresistibly catchy, especially 'Go Ghana!', a collaboration between Brown and drummer-pianist Stan Greig, the first of several African-influenced numbers. The following year the pair formed a new band, the Fairweather-Brown All-Stars, whose recordings remain as fresh and surprising as when they were first released. Their principal influences make a bizarre list: African "Hi-Life", 1930s swing, various offshoots of the contemporary Woody Herman orchestra, Charles Mingus (the latest *enfant terrible* of modern jazz), rhythm-and-blues, plus various odds and ends that appealed to them. The All-Stars' three albums – *Al and Sandy* (1959), *Dr McJazz* (1960) and *The Incredible McJazz* (1962) – are among the most inventive jazz records made anywhere, in any style, during those years. Sandy

Brown is probably the only jazz musician ever to have designed the very fabric of the studios in which he himself recorded – in this case Lansdowne Studios in west London. He later founded Sandy Brown Associates, the international firm of acoustic architects which still bears his name.

Like Sandy Brown, Wally Fawkes found his career outside jazz increasingly demanding. Keeping up a daily narrative strip cartoon is an unremitting task, as Humphrey Lyttelton found during his period as Fawkes's balloon-filler: "There's a nightmare quality about turning out a strip cartoon, rather like the bad dream in which some indefinable Thing is chasing you and your feet turn to lead. However hard you work to build up a stockpile, the insatiable daily consumption by the newspaper wears it ruthlessly down."[8] It all got too much for Wally Fawkes in the summer of 1956 and, with great regret, he left the Lyttelton band. He had no intention, however, of giving up playing and within a year he had a band of his own, the Troglodytes. Its name, of course, was a reference to Fawkes's *nom de plume*, "Trog". It was by no means a full-time affair and confined its appearances almost entirely to the London area, most notably a pub in Chelsea called the Six Bells, where it played regularly. By 1957 the jazz scene in London and the major cities was thriving, with the Six Bells regarded as a stronghold of the mainstream tendency. (In fact, the Six Bells had a venerable jazz connection. Spike Hughes wrote a number entitled 'Six Bells Stampede', recorded by Benny Carter and his Orchestra for Columbia, in New York, in March 1933.) The Troglodytes recorded a ten-inch LP and several EPs for Decca.[9] Their appeal lies partly in their ease of manner. Everyone sounds completely at home with the material and with each other. Particularly revealing is the playing of Spike Mackintosh (1918–1986), who, perhaps more than any other trumpeter, catches the grave elegance of classic Armstrong. Mackintosh (who incidentally was the father of the impresario Sir Cameron Mackintosh) and Fawkes were the only permanent Troglodytes, although some superb players passed through the ranks in the late fifties. Among them was the pianist Lennie Felix, who was able to produce the rare authentic sparkle which is the mark of such players of the 1930s as Teddy Wilson and Earl Hines. Fawkes himself made no secret of his attachment to Sidney Bechet, especially in the matter of vibrato. As leader of his own band he was now able occasionally to adopt Bechet's practice of leading the ensemble. The Troglodytes' version of Cole Porter's 'Why Can't You Behave?' presents a beguiling example of this. He was always a wonderfully intuitive musician, as his work with Lyttelton and Mackintosh proves. There is also a superb session by an offshoot of the Lyttelton band, dating from 1954, called the Fawkes-Turner Sextet[10] which catches both of them at their best and most characteristic.

Among those mentioned above, Sandy Brown was a distinguished architect, Wally Fawkes a leading cartoonist and Spike Mackintosh a successful timber merchant. In other words, they were not dependent on music for a living. Humphrey Lyttelton always maintained that his only financial aim for his band was that it should earn enough to keep itself. He looked to his other activities – cartooning, composing, writing, broadcasting, and so on – for his own income. Judging by the results, this freedom yielded artistic dividends. Others did not enjoy the same advantage. Bruce Turner left Lyttelton in 1957 to launch his Jump Band, patterned broadly on the small-band swing of the thirties, as played by John Kirby, Pete Brown, Johnny Hodges, Benny Carter and others. This was the music he liked best, which was why he chose it, but he had a rationale to back him up. Traditional jazz had become standardized and stultifying, he said, while modern jazz was fixated on harmonic complication ("fine if you haven't heard Alban Berg or Debussy, who do it so much better"). By contrast, there was the "hot music" of the thirties. "There is absolutely nothing in the realms of straight music with which it can be compared. It is an entirely new musical expression."[11] The variety of tone, the importance of individual style, the spontaneity – all these are at their most potent in this music, he declared. Bruce Turner's Jump Band met with great critical acclaim the moment it was launched, but mainstream jazz was in a similar position to modern jazz a few years earlier. The audience for it, while enthusiastic, was limited and patchy. Traditional jazz, now building up a head of steam as "trad", was universally popular as music for dancing and general good times, and the same type of crowd often took happily to the Jump Band, once they experienced it, but standard trad was a known quantity and guaranteed to pull them in anyway. For this reason the Jump Band led a somewhat precarious, on-and-off existence. In its early years Turner was often under pressure from club promoters to dilute its repertoire with trad favourites. Later, when the ban on American musicians had been eased, the Jump Band enjoyed a new lease of life, touring Britain as accompanists to some of their, now ageing, idols of the thirties and forties, such as Ben Webster, Bill Coleman and Don Byas.

As "trad" grew increasingly stereotyped, other styles which might previously have come under the revivalist or traditional banner became subsumed into the mainstream category. This was the case with the genre vaguely referred to as "Dixieland". It included such established professional bands as Harry Gold's Pieces of Eight, Sid Phillips and his Band and Bobby Mickleburgh's Bobcats, who operated in the borderland between strictly jazz country and the territory of dance-cum-general entertainment. "Dixieland" also referred to dedicated jazz outfits who took their inspiration from the white Chicago school of the 1920s – from Muggsy Spanier and the feisty, loose-knit music of the bands associated with the guitarist, raconteur and larger-than-life character Eddie Condon. Supreme among its British representatives was the Alex Welsh Band.

Like many outstanding British jazz musicians, Alex Welsh (1929–1982) was Scottish. Born in Edinburgh, he learned to play the cornet in a local silver band and took to jazz at around age twenty, playing with Sandy Brown, among others. In May 1954 he moved to London and launched his own band the following month. It was actually a co-operative venture and he was voted leader, partly perhaps because he had briefly been a civil servant and was able to keep accounts, and because he was at the time a teetotaller. (He was to fall spectacularly off the wagon in later years.) For the remainder of the fifties and beyond, the first Alex Welsh Band set a unique standard. There were other extremely good Dixie bands, notably Freddie Randall's, but their music lacked the tough-tender quality of Welsh's, and the depth that came from a well-matched and musically like-minded personnel. Clarinetist Archie Semple (also from Edinburgh), trombonist Roy Crimmins and pianist Fred Hunt remained with the band well into the sixties, the individual style of each contributing to a fascinating and often moving discourse. Semple, originally a disciple of Pee-Wee Russell, had built on his influence, rather as Sandy Brown had built on Johnny Dodds, evolving his own hoarse, diffident lyricism. Crimmins had the rare ability to take a very ordinary old tune, such as 'Chinatown, My Chinatown', and, with the minimum of alteration or elaboration, turn it into something almost sublime. Hunt's harmonies delicately implied more than they stated, and Welsh's own cornet playing, while firm, robust and incisive, never turned florid or vulgar, as Freddie Randall's tended to. It was, in short, a magical combination. The charm of it is captured very well on three albums: *Dixieland to Duke* (1957), *The Melrose Folio* (1958) and *Music of the Mauve Decade* (1959). In 1957, after the easing of the ban on American musicians, the Alex Welsh Band supported an all-star group, co-led by Earl Hines and Jack Teagarden, on its brief British tour. At the end of it, Teagarden wanted to take Welsh with him, back to the States, to play in his own band. It was a serious and firm offer, but Welsh turned it down. He must have been tempted, though.

Ill health forced Archie Semple to give up playing in 1964, and there were other personnel changes in the sixties, which brought with them changes in the band's style. The Alex Welsh Band was never as popular as the post-Barber trad bands, with their banjos, but it built up a sizeable following which enabled Welsh to remain a bandleader for twenty-eight years. It even found an audience in the US. In 1968 it played at the Newport Jazz Festival, to great applause.

The reason mainstream jazz, and much other British jazz of the 1950s, exists on record today in reasonable quantities is largely due to the efforts of a single energetic individual, Denis Preston (1916–1979). He first turned up as a writer and occasional broadcaster on jazz in the immediate post-war years and was soon busy in various capacities amid the sprouting undergrowth of small, specialist record labels. As a freelance producer, he was the first to record music by the "Windrush generation" of West Indian artists in Britain, for both the major conglomerate EMI and the somewhat rickety but enterprising little Melodisc label. Among those he recorded were Lord Kitchener (Aldwyn Roberts) and Lord Beginner (Egbert Moore), the latter's 'Victory Test Match Calypso' ("Cricket, lovely cricket!") scoring a minor hit in 1950. The experience taught him that an alert and knowledgeable freelance could usually beat the big corporations when it came to spotting promising new or out-of-the-ordinary artists and styles. This was the basis upon which he built a formidable business, Record Supervision Ltd, contracting artists and licensing their work to big record companies. When it came to jazz, Preston's taste was as acute as his business acumen. Having made a deal in 1955 with Pye Records to supply them with jazz items for their Nixa label, he proceeded to amass a marvellous collection of bands and individual players. Among them were Kenny Baker, Chris Barber, Sandy Brown, Kenny Graham's Afro-Cubists, the Don Rendell Sextet and Cleo Laine. Preston was also the moving spirit behind an interesting project which turned up at the time, called the Jazz Today Unit. That word "unit" has a forbidding ring when applied to any kind of artistic endeavour, almost as ominous as the dread term "collective", but the Jazz Today effort was far livelier than its name suggests. Preston greatly admired Norman Granz, the American impresario and record producer, who had single-handedly altered the business basis of professional jazz in the US, vastly increasing its audience and improving its public status in the process. He did it by building concert packages around collections of jazz stars and touring them throughout the States, and later around the world. This was Preston's model for the Jazz Today Unit. Its personnel was not fixed, but at one time or another included most leading figures on the modern and mainstream jazz scenes, from prominent "modernists" such as Bill Le Sage and Tommy Whittle to mainstreamers like Bruce Turner, veterans such as George Chisholm and Jimmy Skidmore, and the ubiquitous Kenny Baker often in pole position. The recordings came out under the logo, "Pye-Nixa Jazz Today Series", as did those of the Melody Maker All-Stars, which Preston took over from Carlo Krahmer. To Preston we owe the existence of classic albums by the Fairweather-Brown All-Stars (it was for Preston that Sandy designed Lansdowne Studios), Kenny Baker's Dozen and Half-Dozen (preserving much of the material originally played on *Let's Settle for Music*) and the delectable, if little-known, *Jazz for Young Lovers* by the Archie Semple Trio. The list continues into the sixties and beyond with Stan Tracey's classic *Under Milk Wood*, the Rendell-Carr Quintet, Indo-Jazz Fusions and many more.

Preston even assumed production of Humphrey Lyttelton and his Band for Parlophone – obviating further "explosive readjustments" with George Martin. That was in 1956, and one of their first sessions resulted in 'Bad Penny Blues'. This little piece, featuring muted trumpet and heavy boogie piano, caught the public ear sufficiently to land it in the Top Twenty, where it remained for three weeks, peaking at number 17. 'Bad Penny Blues' was a very close relative to a couple of numbers recorded in 1937 by Harry James and his Boogie-Woogie Trio, a fact which Saturday-afternoon record shop pedants took delight in pointing out. The move was timely in other ways, too. When Bruce Turner left Lyttelton's band in March 1957, his departure sparked off a whole set of changes. Turner's replacement was Tony Coe (born 1930), a virtuoso on both alto saxophone and clarinet. He was joined by the veteran Jimmy Skidmore on tenor. There was already a trombonist, the excellent John Picard, in residence, which made a four-piece front line of trumpet, trombone and two saxophones. As a reservist, the drummer, Stan Greig, had been recalled to the army during the previous year's Suez crisis. He had been replaced by the modernist Eddie Taylor (late of the Tommy Whittle and Johnny Dankworth bands), which in turn brought about a wholesale change in the rhythm section. Ian Armit (late of Sandy Brown's band) came in on piano, Brian Brocklehurst on bass, and the guitar was dropped – the departure of Freddy Legon severing the last link with revivalist days. What Lyttelton had now was a pocket swing band. From a purely chronological point of view, this could be construed as a kind of neo-revivalism. In 1945, George Webb's Dixielanders had dedicated themselves to playing the classic jazz of twenty years before, and now here were Humphrey Lyttelton and his Band, in 1957, looking back twenty years to the swing era. There had been prefatory stirrings in America for some time. In 1952, Count Basie had succeeded in launching a new big band, updated in some respects, but propelled by the same deep, relaxed, four-in-a-bar heartbeat and equipped with a cast of stylish and distinctive soloists. Its albums, especially the 1953 *Dance Session*, had made a great impression on this side of the Atlantic. At around the same time, Stanley Dance's efforts on behalf of neglected swing-era musicians began to bear fruit, bringing back to the recording studio such magisterial figures as the trumpeters Buck Clayton and Harry "Sweets" Edison, pianist Earl Hines, trombonist Vic Dickenson and Coleman Hawkins, founding father of the jazz tenor saxophone – all under the new banner of "mainstream". Most of these were hale and hearty and in the prime of life; to speak of them and their music in terms of a "revival" would have been absurd. Nor was geography the near-insuperable problem it had been a few years before. Paris had now become established as the jazz capital of Europe, and British jazz lovers who could get themselves there, despite the continuing currency restrictions, had the chance to hear many of these idols in person. The Musicians' Union ban was being slowly and grudgingly eased, too. In 1957, Basie's band was finally able to make a brief British tour, to be greeted with packed houses and wild applause. In view of all this, far from considering his new band to be any kind of exercise in revivalism, Lyttelton spoke of it as "contemporary" in style. The foreshortened time-scale of jazz history, in which stylistic periods overlap and succeed each other with bewildering speed, caused many ambiguities of this kind. In the 1950s, major representatives of the entire history of jazz up to that point were alive and playing. It was as though J.S. Bach and Arnold Schoenberg were living at the same time, competing for the same audience, their supporters engaged in bitter exchanges via the music trade press. Towards the end of the decade, the more absurd animosities gradually melted away. There was so much more of everything, and in such variety, that being a purist involved effort and self-denial and came to seem increasingly pointless.

As if to symbolize this fresh, relaxed attitude, a new club opened in London's West End in April 1958, with a policy – unthinkable a few years earlier – of presenting a variety of differing jazz styles. The Marquee was operated by Harold Pendleton, under the banner of the National Jazz Federation (see Chapter 5). Its home, beneath the Academy Cinema at 165 Oxford Street, had been designed as a lavishly appointed ballroom, complete with sprung dance-floor, coffee bar and décor on a circus-inspired theme by the theatrical set designer Angus McBean. The ballroom had met with little success, and so had previous attempts to put on jazz events, but Pendleton's timing was good and his pockets deep enough to see him through the initial build-up period. Pendleton also acted as Chris Barber's manager, and Barber in turn served on the board of the NJF, an arrangement which provided the new club with an instant star attraction. To begin with, it operated only at weekends, but gradually increased to five nights a week. In 1960 it became the Sunday night residency of the Dankworth orchestra, the room by then regularly being filled to its capacity of six hundred, and sometimes beyond. In 1962, thanks largely to Chris Barber's influence, the Marquee became the headquarters of the British R&B movement, with the residency of Alexis Korner's Blues Incorporated and its various offshoots, including the fledgling Rolling Stones. The club moved to new premises in 1964.

Melody Maker now carried weekly lists of the best-selling records at jazz specialist shops in London, Manchester, Birmingham, Newcastle and Belfast. They reveal that London took far more interest than the rest of country in mainstream jazz (names such as Buck Clayton, Ruby Braff and Dicky Wells), and less in skiffle, even at the height of the boom. The provinces bought more trad, Barber especially, but this may reflect touring appearances by the bands in question. In May 1956, Louis Armstrong finally got to play in England, for the first time since 1933. With his All-Stars, he played on a slowly revolving stage in the middle of the vast Empress Hall. This bizarre arrangement gave the event the air less of a concert than of the display of a Holy Relic. The impression was reinforced by the wave of love and adoration that arose from the packed audience, twice a day for ten days. One result was a nationwide boom in Armstrong records, both new and old, duly reflected in the lists. In other respects the lists are similar, exhibiting a broad range of tastes, from King Oliver and Kid Ory to Miles Davis and the Modern Jazz Quartet. It is noticeable that British artists (Barber and Lyttelton excepted) figure only rarely. The most obvious reason for this would be that they could easily be heard live. This would apply more to leading trad bands, which were constantly touring, than to modern jazz, and more to London and the Home Counties than further afield. The underlying reason is probably that British jazz was still viewed as a kind of junior apprentice to American jazz. Thus, prudent record buyers chose to spend their hard-earned wages on Louis Armstrong rather than Alex Welsh, Stan Getz rather than Ronnie Scott. But the gap was quickly narrowing.

8 Skiffle

Once the bomb damage had been patched up, British towns and cities in the 1950s looked pretty much the same as they had in the 1930s. Away from the town centres, in the small streets, among the grocers and tobacconists and fish-and-chip shops, it was common to find a type of shop called an ironmonger's. This sold all manner of bits and pieces for use in the home, not the modern, labour-saving home but the old-fashioned, scrubbing-brush, working-class type of home: black lead for grates, blue bags for washing clothes, blocks of chalk for whitening the front step, oil for stoves and nails for boots. In the spring of 1956, ironmongers throughout the land stood scratching their heads in bewilderment. Why on earth, they asked themselves, had they all sold out of the same three items at the same time – namely thimbles, broom handles and corrugated zinc washboards? It turned out that they were being bought up by "youths" (as the press still tended to call teenage boys) and converted into musical instruments, essential equipment in a sudden craze for the do-it-yourself music called "skiffle". You scraped the washboard rhythmically with the thimbles to create a beat, and the broom handle acted as the neck of a primitive double bass, when combined with a tea chest and a length of string. The other essential instrument was a guitar, but that had to be bought ready-made.

The craze had its origin in the Chris Barber band's first album, *New Orleans Joys*.[1] It was common practice to follow the release of a successful LP with a series of singles drawn from it and this was eventually done with *New Orleans Joys*. Two of the eight tracks ('Rock Island Line' and 'John Henry') were not by the jazz band at all, but by the "Lonnie Donegan Skiffle Group". The two numbers were issued as a single, with 'Rock Island Line' as the A side, towards the end of 1955. In January 1956 it entered the pop charts, where, rising briefly to sixth place, it survived for seventeen weeks. Donegan (1931–2002) had previously led his own band and had joined Barber, on banjo and guitar, in the period before Colyer became the band's titular head. He had always sung the occasional blues or spiritual, and it was with Colyer that the idea of a contrasting band-within-a-band originally took shape. Colyer himself played the guitar (left-handed) and his enthusiasm for the blues and its associated styles was as great as his love of New Orleans jazz. Indeed, for him they were all parts of the same expressive language. A kind of casual, spur-of-the-moment performance involving guitars, kazoos, washboards, jugs, and so on, had been common in the rural South at least since the end of the Civil War. There were numerous recordings by such groups, both black and white, dating from the 1920s and '30s. They were variously known as "spasm bands", "skiffle bands" or "jug bands". Colyer usually referred to this style of music as "breakdown", and his group, which played a set halfway through a club session by the jazz band, as the "breakdown band", with himself, Donegan, Barber (on bass) and Bill Colyer drumming with a pair of brushes on a suitcase. It survived as Lonnie Donegan's Skiffle Group after Colyer's departure. On the record, a washboard, played by Beryl Bryden, replaced Bill's suitcase. At most other times it was drums, played by the band's regular drummer, Ron Bowden.

Neither 'Rock Island Line' nor 'John Henry' is a blues, or even an old jazz song. They both come under the vague heading of folk songs, in Donegan's case learned from records by the African-American songster Huddie Ledbetter (1889–1949), known as Leadbelly. Much of Leadbelly's repertoire was learned during long stretches in prison for murder, attempted homicide and assault, a history which contributed greatly to his eventual *réclame*. In his final years he was taken up by the folksong collectors John and Alan Lomax, recorded a great deal and became a prominent figure on the American folk scene. He accompanied his stentorian voice on the mighty twelve-string guitar and was, by all accounts, a magnetic performer. The songs he sang tended to feature picking cotton, gambling, mules, prisons and railroads. 'Rock Island Line' is a railroad song, and Lonnie Donegan copies Leadbelly's rendition closely, right down to the bits of spoken narrative.

The relationship between traditional jazz and folk music is a tangled one. The blues, one of the main ingredients of jazz, was originally a folk music. New Orleans jazz itself could be regarded as a form of urban or street folk music, in that it arose spontaneously among the community, its repertoire and skills being passed around aurally. But "folk music" is a slippery term. To the average person in England at that time it conjured up a number of vague notions – morris dancing, sea shanties, Kathleen Ferrier singing 'Blow the Wind Southerly', or even boy scouts singing 'Green Grow the Rushes-O' around the camp fire – none of which had any discernable connection to railroads or cotton picking. In the United States, however, the term had come to stand for something rather different. It was associated with what later came to be called "protest songs" and a kind of left-wing idealism that agitated in favour of workers against bosses, the homeless against landlords, black people against racial oppression and the small man against giant corporations.

Since this was the period of anti-communist witch hunts and Senator Joe McCarthy's Un-American Activities Committee, well-known folk singers, such as Pete Seeger and Woody Guthrie, were widely suspected of being communist dupes and subversives. Among them was Josh White (c.1915–1969), the first representative of this genre to visit Britain.

Bearing in mind how unremittingly drab and meagre life was in 1950, it is not difficult to imagine how Britons yearned for something – anything – to come along from somewhere else and prove that the whole world wasn't as dreary as this. American film stars, like Danny Kaye, were always greeted with huge enthusiasm for that very reason, on the rare occasions they appeared. But they didn't appear very often because the country couldn't afford the dollars to pay their Hollywood-style fees. So when, one damp July morning, a plane from Paris landed at Manchester airport and from it stepped an unbelievably handsome black man, with a Ronald Colman moustache, elegantly dressed and carrying a guitar case, he attracted a lot of attention. He wasn't famous, but his records had been played on the radio from time to time and he'd had a small singing and acting part in a recent film, *The Walking Hills*. That, combined with the fact that he was American and not too expensive, was enough to get him booked for a tour of variety theatres. Once he was on stage, his voice, his guitar playing and his pleasant, easy-going style brought him a following that grew every night. Josh White was a polished, sophisticated performer, but his origins were impeccably authentic. Born in South Carolina, he left home while still a child, to act as guide to wandering blind blues singers. This was where he learned his trade. In his early career he sometimes worked under different names, depending on the style of music he was called upon to perform. For sacred songs he was "Joshua – the Singing Christian", while for worldly blues he was "Pinewood Tom". The quality which set him apart from the general run of rural blues singers and eventually brought him wider success was his clear diction. This was the case with all the most successful African-American singers before the 1960s – Paul Robeson, Louis Jordan, Nat King Cole, Chuck Berry – if you could understand English you could understand every word. Josh White returned to Britain many times, no longer as a variety act but for concert tours and broadcasts on all three BBC radio networks, Home, Light and Third. He had his own Home Service series, *The Glory Road*, singing what were then still called "negro spirituals" with the George Mitchell Choir, and recorded the hit song 'On Top of Old Smokey' with Britain's top vocal group, the Stargazers. He also sang blues, such as 'Outskirts of Town' and 'Hard Times Blues', which were clearly the real thing, gently but persuasively. Thus, by small degrees, Josh White introduced the ordinary, uncommitted British public to the musical language of the blues. No one had done it before; he was the first.

Among dedicated blues followers (and there weren't many of them in Britain in the early fifties), Josh White was never quite accepted. Despite his origins and his artistry, there was something not quite right, they thought, about a man who could sing 'Hard Times Blues' one minute and 'Molly Malone' the next – and he sounded a bit too sophisticated. What they were looking for was primal innocence, someone uncorrupted, who sang the blues because that's all he *could* sing, all he had ever sung – a kind of blues-singing Bunk Johnson. Candidates were not forthcoming, until someone recalled a pre-war show at Carnegie Hall, called *Spirituals to Swing*, at which had appeared a singer announced as "a Mississippi sharecropper", whose name was Big Bill Broonzy. If he could be found, this was the man. He was located quite easily. He wasn't actually being a sharecropper at the time – in point of fact he was working as a janitor at the University of Illinois – but he was ready and willing to sing and play guitar whenever he was asked. This was not surprising, since until recently he had been a professional blues musician in Chicago.

Like most of the African-American population of Chicago, Big Bill (1893–1958) had been born in the rural South (Arkansas in his case), given up a life of hopeless toil and joined the great black migration north. He had been engaged in playing the urban, Chicago blues for many years and now had a quiet job at the university. Just as jazz had changed in the move from south to north, so had the blues. It was heavier and more strident. Cotton and mules no longer figured as subject matter, being replaced by drink, fighting with broken bottles and sexual exploits which made the Cities of the Plain look like Tunbridge Wells on a quiet Tuesday afternoon. In 1951 Big Bill jumped at the chance of visiting Europe in the role of folk singer. A man of keen intelligence, he grasped the essence of the situation at once and, being the complete professional, set about supplying the required article. He exchanged his electric guitar for an acoustic model and made sure he had a repertoire not only of rural blues but narrative ballads as well, prominent among which was 'John Henry', a ballad recounting the legend of a black labourer of superhuman strength and his exploits during the building of the Chesapeake and Ohio Railroad.

Broonzy was a tall, imposing man of enormous presence and immense personal charm. It was impossible to avoid falling under his spell. Even the experts, who knew something of his history, willingly suspended their disbelief as he rambled amiably on about mules and cotton-fields. With all the expertise of a seasoned performer, he was recreating the world of his youth and, as is often the case with youth recalled, it was an idealized picture that he conjured up, replete with ancient country jokes and sly country innuendo. Realizing that folk music, in the modern American sense, included songs of protest, although there was no such thing in his own tradition, Broonzy wrote one of his own, 'Black, Brown and White'. It was his most requested number. For all that, he was a wonderfully persuasive artist. His singing was candid and genuinely passionate and delivered with a sincerity that disarmed all criticism.

Along with this, he had two further advantages when it came to entertaining audiences outside his own culture. The first, clear diction, he shared with Josh White. Without his warm, slow, well-articulated delivery he could never have made people laugh at his jokes or hang onto his tall tales. ("Folk music?" he'd murmur, stroking his chin thoughtfully. "Well, I guess it must be. I ain't never heard a horse sing yet.") Secondly, there was his guitar style. He had a perfect technique – the rhythm never wavered, the simple bass lines moved unerringly, the treble phrases fitted snugly between the vocal lines. Just as important was the fact that he almost always played in straight four-four time, with which everyone feels at home and which most kinds of songs will fit – spirituals, ballads, blues. Superficially his rhythm was easy to imitate, and it *was* imitated. Skiffle was inspired by him as much as by anyone, even if at second hand via Donegan *et al.*, and some of his best known songs, especially 'John Henry', became part of the basic skiffle repertoire.

The visits of both Josh White and Big Bill Broonzy awakened an interest in blues and associated forms of music, well before the sudden eruption of skiffle. Further stimulus came from the presence in Britain of the American folklorist and song collector, Alan Lomax (1915–2002). Born in Austin, Texas, son of John A. Lomax, the acknowledged expert on American folk music, particularly western and cowboy songs, he joined in his father's song-hunting expeditions from boyhood. In 1932, the pair were commissioned by the Library of Congress to record African-American work-songs, a task which involved several months of travel through the Deep South, where they found their most fruitful source of material in penitentiaries and prison farms. It was at one of these that they encountered Leadbelly, with his phenomenal repertoire. They helped obtain his parole and employed him as their driver for the remainder of the trip. In a later expedition, this time alone, Alan Lomax found and recorded Muddy Waters (McKinley Morganfield), working as a field-hand on a Mississippi plantation. In 1938, again for the Library of Congress, he recorded a remarkable eight hours of spontaneous reminiscence, spoken, played and sung by Jelly Roll Morton, in which the great pianist and composer, now fallen on hard times, conjured an unforgettable portrait of New Orleans at the time of the birth of jazz. In 1950, his father having died two years previously, Lomax moved to London, which he made his base for research into folk music of the British Isles, Spain and Italy. *Mr Jelly Roll*, his biography of Jelly Roll Morton, based on the recordings, was published in Britain in 1952. He also made a number of memorable BBC broadcasts on Morton, the blues, and American folksong. Lomax's dynamic presence, with his affable Texan style, sparked a lively interest among people of wide musical tastes, including many jazz lovers. The library of the United States Information Service, attached to the US embassy in Grosvenor Square, London, suddenly found its small and sparsely visited collection of folk-song records in great demand, with long waiting lists, especially for the Lomax recordings.

These were some of the elements that went into the emergence of skiffle in Britain, and at first their influence remained strong. Ken Colyer recorded the first session with the "breakdown" group from his new band a matter of days before Donegan's. His approach to it, like his approach to jazz, was wholehearted and committed, if somewhat solemn and dogmatic. He stuck resolutely to a repertoire based on Broonzy, Leadbelly and the kind of material uncovered by Alan Lomax.[2] As for Donegan himself, once 'Rock Island Line' had taken off, and he had learned that Barber's contract with Decca did not allow for royalties to be paid to individual band members, he left to go solo and capitalize on his hit. He signed with Denis Preston, who in turn placed the Lonnie Donegan Skiffle Group with Pye-Nixa. Donegan, too, stuck to traditional material to begin with, including some western ballads, such as 'The Wreck of the Old 97' and 'The Ballad of Jesse James'. Perhaps still smarting from the non-receipt of royalties for 'Rock Island Line', he began to acquire a reputation for driving hard bargains. In 1957, the high-water mark of skiffle, he had several hit records, including 'Cumberland Gap' and 'Putting On The Style'. Skiffle arrived at the exact moment when the first wave of rock 'n' roll broke, when teenagers were emerging as a distinct segment of society and when the general mood was cheerful and optimistic. It is hardly surprising in such circumstances that youthful exuberance should take over. In no time at all skiffle groups were twanging and scraping everywhere. It became almost mandatory for every trad band to include a skiffle session in its performance, and record company release lists were full of such names as the Vipers, the City Ramblers, Bob Cort, Chas McDevitt and Nancy Whiskey, Bill Bailey and the 2.19 Skiffle Group. Alan Lomax good-naturedly joined in as Alan Lomax and the Ramblers. There were also opportunists, such as Don Lang – formerly Gordon Langhorn, trombonist with the Vic Lewis and Ken Mackintosh orchestras – who turned briefly to skiffle before finally settling for rock 'n' roll, with his Frantic Five. Chris Barber struck lucky. Having lost Lonnie Donegan, he found a genuine bluegrass singer virtually on his doorstep. Johnny Duncan (1932–2000), from Oliver Springs, Tennessee, had been stationed with the US forces in Cambridgeshire, married a local girl and had been working on her father's market stall. Not only was he a good and authentic singer, he played excellent guitar and phenomenal mandolin. He stayed with Barber for a year, imparting to the skiffle group a distinct flavour of white country music and more than compensating for the loss of Donegan. Eventually, he followed the usual path of forming his own band, the Blue Grass Boys. He signed on with Denis Preston and, through him, with Columbia. In July 1957 Duncan's 'Last Train to San Fernando' went into the charts, rising to third place and remaining for sixteen weeks.

By a stroke of luck, the perfect venues for amateur skiffle groups to perform in were appearing everywhere. Coffee bars, equipped with the new Espresso machines imported from Italy, could have been invented as teenage meeting places, being fashionable, non-alcoholic and often run by young proprietors of saintly tolerance. Social historians generally cite London, Soho in particular, when dealing with this phase of teenage culture, but the coffee bar, like skiffle itself, was a nationwide phenomenon. They were cheerful and, on the whole, orderly places, where young would-be musicians could play and sing among their peers. Indeed, parents, teachers and clergymen tended to approve of them, and to approve of skiffle as a harmless and creative activity for Youth. The Salvation Army started its own evangelizing skiffle group, called the Joy Strings. An Anglican priest, Father Geoffrey Beaumont, composed a "Folk Mass", incorporating a skiffle group. The newspapers the *Daily Herald* and *The People* sponsored a skiffle competition throughout Butlin's holiday camps. Magazines for housewives carried articles on catering for skiffle parties. All of which should have proved the kiss of death, but it didn't. On 16 February 1957, the BBC launched *6.5 Special*, its first regular television show determinedly aimed at teenagers, the signature tune being sung and played by the Bob Cort Skiffle group. The title referred to the transmission time, five minutes past six, which was itself quite a bold stroke, since the hour between six and seven in the evening had previously been left blank to allow parents to put small children to bed – the so-called "Toddlers' Truce". Quaint and patronising though it now seems, *6.5 Special* was instrumental in lifting skiffle away from its beginnings in jazz, blues and folk music and absorbing it into the popular music industry.

Skiffle groups appearing on television and with records to their name, even if they weren't hits, turned professional, and professional entertainers can't trade forever on rough-and-ready charm. Lonnie Donegan led the way and the rest followed him. Electric guitars began to replace acoustic guitars, real double basses ousted the broomstick and tea-chest, and grown-up drum kits saw off the washboard. It is interesting, in this context, to listen to Elvis Presley's first commercially released record, 'That's All Right Mama / Blue Moon of Kentucky', recorded on 7 July 1954 – eight days before Donegan's 'Rock Island Line' (15 July). Although Presley has drums, not washboard, the overall sound of his accompaniment could easily be mistaken for a skiffle group. Two years later, the sound has undergone the same changes as British skiffle groups were about to adopt as they turned themselves into proto-rock bands, with electric guitars, echo effects, and so on. Similarly, the two pieces on Presley's first record were, respectively, a blues by the African-American singer Arthur "Big Boy" Crudup and a song by an authentic bluegrass performer, Bill Monroe. Presley's later recordings, such as 'Hound Dog', were increasingly composed by professional songwriters. As long as it remained a largely amateur youth movement, skiffle was pretty well impervious to criticism or ridicule, but as soon as professionalism entered the picture it was a sitting duck. There is something inherently comic in the idea of Cockneys and Glaswegians and Liverpudlians earnestly singing songs about the rigours of the chain-gang in any case. But when they are doing it for good money, dressed in smart suits, they're really asking for it. The *coup de grâce* arrived a little late – in 1958 to be exact – but when it came it was neat, accurate and merciless. Peter Sellers was the executioner and the piece, a parody of Lonnie Donegan entitled 'Putting On The Smile', appeared on his album *Songs for Swingin' Sellers* – produced, incidentally, by George Martin. Donegan's later career was increasingly a matter of light-entertainment show-business. As the memory of skiffle faded, he turned to comic songs such as 'My Old Man's A Dustman' and 'Does Your Chewing-Gum Lose Its Flavour On The Bedpost Overnight?', prompting George Melly to remark, acutely if unkindly, that he ended up having more in common with George Formby than with Huddie Ledbetter. Donegan continued working in cabaret and in "pop nostalgia" touring shows almost until his death at the age of seventy-one. For old times' sake, he took part in the fortieth anniversary tour of the Chris Barber band in 1994.

By 1959 the skiffle craze had run its course. The washboard market never recovered, since this was the high summer of the affluent society and everyone was busy buying washing machines on hire-purchase. But what happened to all those amateur skifflers in all those coffee bars and youth clubs up and down the land? Most of them just gave up, the way young people have always given up last year's craze. The rest branched out in many directions, the majority into rock 'n' roll. It has been estimated that, by 1960, in the Liverpool area alone, there were 350 regular amateur or semi-professional rock groups. Assuming that they were all in their late teens and early twenties, which they were, there is only one route by which they could have arrived, and that's via skiffle. In effect, "Merseybeat" was electrified skiffle – typically two guitars, bass guitar (a 1950s invention) and drums. The subject has been exhaustively researched and recounted because one of these groups, a typical grammar-school outfit called the Quarrymen, eventually became the Beatles. One of the places where they gained their early experience was the Cavern, in Mathew Street, Liverpool. They started out there, in time-honoured skiffle style, by playing the interval for the top local traditional Mersysippi Jazz Band, whose members habitually fled to the pub as soon as the interval was announced. "One turn of the knob," remarked banjoist/guitarist Ken Baldwin, "and plaster came off the ceiling. Once this started happening, acoustic sound was lost and electronic sound took over. We got out before the end. Left them to get on with it."[3]

That is how skiffle is commonly represented, as an opening skirmish in the rise of British pop music. But there were other, less spectacular offshoots of the relationship between jazz and folk music. Take, for example, the Radio Ballad. This ambitious use of the radio medium, involving location recording, sound effects, song and instrumental music, was devised by the folk singer and theatre director Ewan McColl, the American folk singer and instrumentalist Peggy Seeger (sister of Pete Seeger) and Charles Parker, then Senior Radio Features Producer at BBC Midlands Region. Their aim was to tell epic stories about working people doing their everyday jobs. Their method was to record the voices of those actually involved in the story and weave them into an atmospheric musical narrative. The first, and in some ways the best, Radio Ballad was transmitted on the BBC Home Service on 2 July 1958. Entitled *The Ballad of John Axon*, it recounted the heroism of an engine driver who, earlier that year, had died fighting to control a runaway train when its steam-brakes had failed. Along with McColl, Seeger and other folk artists, the musical cast included the jazz musicians Bruce Turner and Bobby Mickleburgh, bassist Jim Bray, trumpeter Terry Brown and guitarist Fitzroy Coleman. Altogether, there were eight Radio Ballads between 1958 and 1964. Using what was then new technology, such as miniature tape recorders, and hugely complex and laborious editing procedures, they demonstrated what radio was capable of, given vision, dedication and resources. Most subsequent radio documentary features have owed something to the Radio Ballads.

Alexis Korner (1928–1984) claimed to have heard a record by the blues pianist Jimmy Yancey on the radio at the age of twelve and thenceforth dedicated himself to the blues. Born in Paris, of complicated Austrian-Jewish-Turkish-Greek parentage, and brought to London at the outbreak of World War II, he took up the guitar and played in various early revivalist bands. He played mandolin on Ken Colyer's first skiffle records and, in the mid-fifties, joined with the harmonica player Cyril Davies in starting a Thursday-night club called "Blues and Barrelhouse" at the Roundhouse pub in Soho. Such places regularly attracted young people who had started out with skiffle, become bored with its limitations and were ready for something to which they could give serious attention. The City Ramblers and, later, Ewan McColl, ran a similar club, devoted to English and other folk music, on Sunday nights at the Princess Louise in High Holborn. There were more scattered around London and other major cities. Although not an outstanding performer himself, Korner had great personal magnetism and the gift of leadership. He and Davies became underground heroes among the crowd of young blues followers which grew up around Blues and Barrelhouse towards the end of the decade. Korner himself took the unexpected line of reintegrating blues and jazz, but this time most of the players came from the fringes of the London modern jazz scene, figures such as saxophonist Dick Heckstall-Smith, bassist Jack Bruce and saxophonist and organist Graham Bond. Heckstall-Smith, an early protégé of Sandy Brown, was the first to take part, a rare modernist with a knowledge of the blues: "Though I was a bopper with a long way to go musically . . . ever since my Devon childhood I'd had a penchant for the blues. I'd heard Sonny Terry and Brownie McGhee, Muddy Waters, Lonnie Johnson, Josh White, Leadbelly – I loved them early and dearly."[4] The band which Korner eventually formed, towards the end of 1961, was Blues Incorporated, into whose orbit were drawn young singers and players of the generation which went on to launch the blues boom of the early sixties, among them Mick Jagger, Brian Jones, Keith Richards, John Mayall and Jimmy Page.

The interest created by skiffle in folk music generally, plus the sheer abundance of guitars among the youthful population, led to a great outburst of singing and playing of every imaginable kind. It is no accident that, quite apart from rock and pop, leading figures of the English folk revival, folk-rock, rhythm-and-blues, country-and-western, innumerable singer-songwriters, several jazz guitarists and bass players, occasional classical guitarists and the odd virtuoso, such as Davey Graham, who fits into no particular category, were all born around the year 1940, and were thus products of the skiffle years.

9 Six Months in a Palais . . .

Although it made remarkable advances over the course of the 1950s, modern jazz in Britain remained closely bound to the American original. Nevertheless, with growing mastery came growing confidence and by the middle of the decade the best British players were shadowing the stylistic developments in American jazz ever more intimately. With a plentiful supply of new recordings now available, the audience was up to date, too. The days when London fans could be "baffled and confounded" by John Dankworth's use of musical devices borrowed from Miles Davis were safely in the past. Indeed, the Miles Davis Quintet of 1956, with John Coltrane on tenor saxophone, soon became, along with the Modern Jazz Quartet, high fashion among those who prided themselves on being up with the latest trend – or "hip", as the rather slippery new jargon had it. The more frigid forms of cool jazz melted into restrained lyricism or playful good humour and, following the death of Charlie Parker in 1955, the neurotic fury of bebop was replaced by a new, forceful self-confidence under the name of "hard bop". All this found a faithful echo in Britain.

At the same time, the world of popular music, within which modern jazz had been living a fairly comfortable, semi-parasitic existence, was undergoing an uncomfortable change, as the advent of rock 'n' roll began to erode the edifice of dance-band culture. It was not the sudden cataclysm it is commonly made out to be, and most everyday music was unaffected. Ballroom dancing remained popular with many people. The annual Dinner and Dance continued to maintain its place in the calendars of social clubs, societies and commercial organizations. Hunt balls still took place, and whole families continued to flock to be entertained at seaside holiday camps. Of more immediate relevance, traditional jazz continued its upward trajectory. Yet there was a sense of foreboding in the air. An early scene in the film *Rock Around the Clock* (1956) depicts a conventional dance, with conventionally dressed couples moving decorously around the floor. The camera shows the bass player in the band glancing at his watch and yawning. This is followed by the scene of a floor crowded with happy, lively, casually dressed young people jiving to the rock 'n' roll of Bill Haley and his Comets. The juxtaposition was crude but effective – so effective, in fact, that teenagers in British cinemas reacted to it by jiving in the aisles, followed by jumping on the seats, smashing the fixtures and fittings and finally causing riots in the streets. The upshot was a classic example of moral panic, with teachers, judges, politicians and vicars holding forth on the Evil in Our Midst, and the rioters basking in the resultant attention. This being Britain, it was instantly noticed (but rarely mentioned) that these events involved exclusively working-class youth, and the "rougher" elements at that. The rest looked on fascinated, appalled but perhaps secretly a little excited. For a while there was a general feeling that rock meant riots. Buying rock records, or playing them on the juke box, was one way of partaking in the excitement at a safe distance. Once everything calmed down, it soon became obvious that the young crowds which had previously flocked to dance halls, weekend town-hall dances and the like, were melting away. Over the next few years, dance halls put on "rock nights", or hired second bands, playing rock, to alternate with the regular dance band. Large suburban pubs, working men's clubs and other social venues were soon doing well from putting on regular rock 'n' roll nights. These vied with traditional jazz, on something like equal terms, for the support of teens and twenties. It was dance bands, in particular touring "name" bands, who were really feeling the pinch. Jack Parnell, for example, folded his touring orchestra – the one featuring spectacular drum duets – in 1956 and took the post of musical director with Associated Television. The glamour which had surrounded the top big bands evaporated, and with the Premier League in disarray the whole elaborate structure began slowly to crumble. For jazz, the result was twofold.

The first effect was obvious. Big bands and popular dance orchestras had hitherto sustained Britain's modern jazz musicians, including some of the most prestigious, by providing them with well-paid jobs when finances were tight. This form of outdoor relief was dwindling daily and the only solution seemed to lie in the old adage, "If you can't beat 'em, join 'em". One of the first to act on this was Tony Crombie, whose plan to launch "Britain's first full-time Rock-And-Roll group" was front-page news in *Melody Maker* on 4 August 1956. The date is interesting, because towards the end of that same month Crombie was the moving spirit behind one of the most exquisite jazz vocal records ever made outside the US. *Annie By Candlelight*, featuring Annie Ross, with Crombie (playing piano), Bob Burns (clarinet), Roy Plummer (guitar) and Lennie Bush (bass), is a work of great delicacy, and Crombie's accompaniment unerringly subtle and appropriate. But a living had to be earned, and Tony Crombie's Rockets took to the road. They would, Crombie announced, limit themselves to two forty-five minute sets per night, in order to maximize the band's impact. More likely, said some, it was because that was as much as the musicians could take. Boredom and self-disgust in their ranks led to so much misbehaviour that their management was eventually reduced to checking them into hotels under a variety of pseudonyms, "Professor Cromberg and a party of students" being the favourite.

Unlike their traditionalist counterparts, the majority of modern jazz musicians possessed transferable skills. They could read music, play in any key, fill in a harmony and adjust their playing to fit a variety of contexts. When the first British rock singers came to make their first records, it was to these musicians that producers turned. Tommy Steele's first hit, 'Rock With The Caveman', for instance, contains a brief tenor saxophone solo by Ronnie Scott, who also makes a fleeting appearance in the film *The Tommy Steele Story* (1957). For Benny Green (late of the Ronnie Scott Orchestra), a chronic shortage of ready cash led him to become part of *Oh Boy!*, British television's first all-rock 'n' roll show. His account of the experience is a classic of its kind:

> No fiasco I ever lived through came within a million miles of the calamities of 1958, when, against my better judgement, I joined an orchestra called Lord Rockingham's Eleven, scheduled to appear on prime-time television each Saturday evening playing a sort of blend of primitive rock 'n' roll and sheer chaos. The reason I allowed myself to become involved was to do with money. I didn't have any, and they were offering £30 for each Saturday's show. At our first rehearsal, the show's producer, a Mr Good, listened to a few bars and stopped us, saying, "It doesn't sound fascist enough." We had no idea what he meant, and neither did he. Eventually he worked it out. He said we were playing in tune. And he wanted us to play out of tune. So we began to play hideously out of tune and an angelic smile lit Mr Good's face. We were now ready to be presented to the public . . . Within three weeks we were the new sensation.[1]

Concerned that his involvement in "this appalling travesty" might be recognized, Green donned a pair of sunglasses as a disguise, only for Jack Good to say approvingly, "Terrific! You look like a dope fiend. Keep them on for transmission!" Eventually, Green realized that "the times were leaving me behind, and that I ought to start thinking about making way for a younger man, say, somebody aged six."[2]

The second effect of the demise of dance-band culture involved the rising generation. Without the ramshackle apprenticeship provided by dance bands, and the value system inculcated along with the camaraderie, there was no obvious way for would-be modern jazzmen (it was still almost exclusively men) to get started. They might begin in the same way as would-be traditional jazz players, getting together with like-minded school friends, workmates or acquaintances, but there was a lot to learn and only people with exceptional talent could hope simply to pick it all up as they went along. However haphazard the old set-up may have been, it was better than nothing, and offered the chance of climbing the rickety ladder to ultimate professional status. Since the only way of attaining the requisite firmness and fluency of technique on any instrument is to play it a great deal, especially in the early stages, musicians who grew up in the later fifties tended to have an obsessive streak, grasping every possible opportunity to play in a band – any band, no matter how sad or unsuitable – and hanging around the stand at local jazz venues on the off-chance of sitting in. Thus, everyone's experience was more or less the same in general but unique in particular. This may explain the fact that jazz musicians of this generation display such a wealth of difference in their styles and attitudes. They were certainly a more diverse crowd of characters than those who had peopled Archer Street in the late forties, and they often lacked the full kit of craft competences possessed by those illustrious predecessors. One of the latter gave voice to the grumpy comment, later seized on as a catchphrase by Ronnie Scott: "Six months in a palais would do them the world of good!"

Examples abound, among that late-fifties generation, of players who came to prominence without having served a dance-band apprenticeship. To take just three of the best-known: Gordon Beck, pianist (1935–2011), trained as a draughtsman-designer in the aerospace industry. He was in his early twenties, working in Canada, and had gained his pilot's licence, when he became interested in jazz and began seriously practising the piano. Returning to Britain in 1958, he began sitting in at London clubs and was instantly absorbed into the jazz scene. Dick Morrissey, tenor saxophonist (1940–2000), while still a schoolboy, played traditional jazz clarinet with the Original Climax Jazz Band. Introduced to modern jazz, he switched to the saxophone and, although completely self-taught, was soon able to abandon his apprenticeship in the jewellery trade in order to play full-time. He was leading his own quartet by the age of twenty. Peter King, alto saxophonist (born 1940) suffered from nervous complaints which hampered his education. He attempted to design and build his own clarinet before acquiring a saxophone. By the age of 18 he was being talked about as a young jazz prodigy. His autobiography[3] reveals a complicated man with a quite extraordinary breadth of talents. These are three outstanding individuals, but in their diversity of background and early experience they are typical of the British jazz scene as it developed through the 1960s and '70s.

It was through dance bands that modern jazz had remained attached to the main body of popular music. Their whole style of presentation, including the type of vocalists they featured, chimed with most people's notion of popular entertainment. When that notion changed, as represented in *Rock Around The Clock*, the link was broken. A touching and astonishingly accurate depiction of the dilemma faced by young would-be jazz musicians at this exact moment is presented in the Swedish film *Sven Klangs Kvintett*.[4] A barely semi-pro teenage quintet plays for weddings and weekend dances in a small provincial town, most of its members nursing their devotion to jazz through nights filled with pedestrian dance tunes and novelty numbers. Their hopes of moving on to better things receive a boost when a very good bebop saxophonist joins them from the local army barracks, where he is doing his national service. At that precise moment, the bandleader (an older, more cynical man) discovers rock 'n' roll after seeing *Jailhouse Rock* at the cinema. A confrontation ensues, the band falls apart, its young members lose heart and abandon their dreams of a life in jazz.

But it was only the outermost fringe of the jazz audience that fell away. The committed audience for modern jazz was now fairly substantial, and its interest in even the biggest of name bands had been diminishing in any case. It had remained loyal to Jack Parnell and Ronnie Scott's nine-piece, but when Scott's subsequent big band proved a complete flop, despite being packed with jazz stars, the only big band to survive and retain a solid jazz following was Dankworth's. The recent developments suited him very well. They meant that he could pursue his ambition of leading a purely jazz orchestra without the distraction of catering to ballroom requirements. Dankworth's aims were higher and his vision far broader than most observers at the time realized and, despite his mild, dreamy manner, he possessed a flinty determination in pursuing them. He was particularly anxious about the public image of the band, as can be deduced from the billings of its broadcasts in *Radio Times*. In 1954, when the band was fairly new, we find it taking its turn in the weekly Thursday-night Light Programme show *The White Cockatoo* ("A nightclub at your fireside: Dancing to Johnny Dankworth and his Orchestra, with Theo Christididi and his Serenaders, plus cabaret by the Sapphires"). Dankworth's control over matters such as billings was then still quite weak. Two years later things were different. In 1956 came the series *Johnny Dankworth Plays*. The programmes were transmitted in two parts, with a fifteen-minute break for the sacrosanct *Book at Bedtime*. Part one was subtitled "Themes: a survey of popular music", with vocals by Cleo Laine, and part two subtitled "Variations: music of our time for the modern enthusiast". One can imagine Geraldo's name, or even Ted Heath's, in place of Dankworth's in the billing of *The White Cockatoo*, but only Dankworth could have devised the earnest, slightly schoolmasterly subtitles attached to his own show. He had effectively distanced himself from the expiring world of popular dance music. As part of the same policy, he also established a monthly newsletter, or "house magazine", *Off-Stand News*, mailed to subscribers from the band's West End office, price 2/6 (12.5p) a year, via a cut-out coupon in *Melody Maker*. (Interestingly, the only other well-known band to issue a house magazine to subscribers from its own West End office was Humphrey Lyttelton's.) Dankworth's later radio series, *Johnny Come Lately* (1957–58), was the most ambitious of all. Each programme was an hour and a quarter in length. At first it was subtitled "Dance music for late listening", a billing hastily revised, no doubt at Dankworth's insistence, to "Modern music for late listening". There was always a feature for Cleo Laine ("the vocal touch"), spots for bands-within-the-band (Dave

Lee Trio, Lawrie Monk Quartet, Dickie Hawdon Quintet and so on), a "jazz talking point" with a visiting pundit, and some often surprising instrumental guests. Veteran fans still recall the specially written tuba feature performed by the musical humorist Gerard Hoffnung. Dankworth had, in fact, invented his own very effective radio-magazine format, and been able to command the sizeable budget which it must have entailed.

The audience for modern jazz in Britain not only grew substantially but matured throughout the second half of the decade. The process was aided by the emergence of a number of knowledgeable and literate critics, notably Charles Fox and Alun Morgan, who contributed articles and reviews to *Melody Maker* and various specialist magazines. In 1956, together with Raymond Horricks, Morgan published the first balanced and succinct guide to the whole topic in a book with the straightforward title *Modern Jazz*, subtitled "A survey of developments since 1939".[5] As the factional heat cooled down and more sensible attitudes prevailed, jazz criticism in general took on a more adult tone. It marked a change in the public status of modern jazz, a change which seems to have been prompted partly by its acceptance in avant garde intellectual circles in the USA. For a large segment of young people in Britain – sixth formers, undergraduates and the like – traditional jazz was becoming too widely popular to have much appeal. These were the ones who now picked up the copious references to modern jazz in the work of Beat Generation writers such as Jack Kerouac, Gregory Corso, Allen Ginsberg and John Clellon Holmes. Their rejection of the materialism of fifties America, expressed in a mixture of defiance and romantic nihilism, had a powerful attraction. The music, as music often does, swept up the vague ideas, attitudes and scattered emotions surrounding this movement and handed them back in a form potent beyond words. One Beat Generation writer, Seymour Krim, even described his work as "typewriter-jazz".[6] The phenomenon was coldly received in more established literary circles. For instance, reviewing *Strike the Father Dead*, a novel by the British critic and novelist John Wain, Francis Wyndham wrote: "All the facile romanticism lavished on such figures as the Bohemian, the Gipsy, the Painter and the Poet in popular fiction of the past can now be concentrated in the Jazz Musician".[7] The Beats regarded jazz more as a useful emblem of their alienation than as an art in its own right. More generally, criticism and discussion about jazz was ceasing to be a purely parochial matter, confined to the trade press and publications for enthusiasts. As early as 1954, Dave Brubeck's picture appeared on the cover of *Time* magazine, accompanying a lengthy and admiring "profile" inside. Magazines such as *Esquire* and forward-looking periodicals like the *Evergreen Review* were regularly publishing articles on contemporary jazz during the second half of the decade. One of the first serious discussions of Thelonious Monk, for example, appeared in *Evergreen Review 7* (1959), written by Martin Williams.

In Britain, the seedy, *demi-monde* reputation which had hung around bebop in the days of Club Eleven gradually dispersed once it had become "modern jazz". A noteworthy stage in the process was the arrival of Benny Green as jazz critic at *The Observer*. (This was in 1958, the year of Lord Rockingham, making it simultaneously his *annus horribilis* and *mirabilis*.) His predecessor in the post was Kingsley Amis, whose appointment had clearly been a stratagem for bagging a celebrity author as a regular contributor. Amis's pieces were sharp and amusing, but proceeded from tastes acquired as an undergraduate at Oxford almost twenty years before and rarely visited since. This bore out one half of Green's contention that British jazz criticism was the work, on the one hand, of people who could write but knew nothing about the subject and, on the other, those who knew everything about the subject but were incapable of producing a literate sentence. With a few honourable exceptions, such as those mentioned above, he was right, and his presence on the pages of a prestigious national newspaper helped to change things for the better.

The increasing confidence and authority of British modern jazz over the course of the 1950s was boosted by the rise of a number of exceptional musicians. Although still closely attached to current American styles, they all possessed a spark of individuality which was to flourish in the following decade. Prominent among them was Tubby Hayes (1935–1973), whose instrument was the tenor saxophone, but who took up the vibraphone, apparently in a fit of absent-mindedness, and played it beautifully. He also became an excellent flautist in a similar fashion. He was born Edward Brian Hayes, in Raynes Park, south-west London, the only child of Teddy Hayes, a violinist in various popular light-music ensembles, including the BBC Revue Orchestra. Tubby had violin lessons from his father, and also learned the piano for a while, but became fixated on the tenor saxophone after seeing one in a shop window. At the age of twelve he was given one, and was able to play simple tunes on it by the end of the first day. He claimed only ever to have had one saxophone lesson – on how to take the instrument out of its case and assemble it. He began playing semi-professionally very soon afterwards, with the result that he was constantly missing school. He left as soon as he could and launched himself on a musical career. Since most of the available employment was on licensed premises, and he was only fifteen years old, life was not without its difficulties at first. He also indulged in the regular practice of hanging around and sitting-in, during which he played for the first time with Ronnie Scott, who was both startled and impressed. His professional career began close to the top, shortly after his sixteenth birthday, in a new band formed by Kenny Baker. There were two tenor saxophonists, the other being the veteran Jimmy Skidmore, who became his informal teacher and generally showed him the ropes. Hayes always spoke fondly of his six months' apprenticeship with "Skid" and the lasting benefit he had gained from their time together.

Despite copious mentions as a "boy wonder" in the music press, the remainder of Hayes's teenage years were mainly passed either in dance bands, including those of Ambrose and Roy Fox, or jazz-inclined bands such as the Tito Burns Sextet and the Vic Lewis and Jack Parnell orchestras. This, together with occasional solo appearances at modern jazz clubs, was the best that was available in the first half of the fifties. He did not record under his own name until March 1955. He can be heard soloing, however, on records by both the Lewis and Parnell bands. He sounds astonishingly mature, with none of the gaucherie displayed by his predecessors in their early days. He stood out, too, on account of his obvious youth and high spirits. He never even tried to conform to the deadpan, "cool" attitude fashionable among modern jazz musicians at the time. A chubby, cheerful lad with a huge, mischievous grin, he was a London "type" – larky, fizzing with energy, a bit bumptious and pleased with himself, but loveable with it. And he was obviously having the time of his life. But even this measure of self-assurance got him nowhere in seeking a pay-rise from Jack Parnell, who informed him that an extra pound a week was out of the question. He left the band in late 1954.

Musicians who found themselves suddenly unemployed usually resorted to picking up casual gigs, an activity known in *Melody Maker* parlance as "freelancing around Town". This did not prove difficult for the nineteen-year-old Hayes, with his growing reputation. His name was soon a fixture in the club columns of the paper, mostly in the West End and especially at the Flamingo. Booking arrangements in these London clubs, a question of matching musicians' availabilities to slots in the weekly programme, were necessarily quite fluid, but often settled into a mutually convenient pattern. One such pattern resulted in Tubby Hayes and Jimmy Deuchar forming a semi-permanent partnership. It was a happy accident which, as Hayes later admitted, forced him to reflect that getting by on youth, enthusiasm and natural ability was not enough.

> Jimmy was the one who made me start taking music seriously. I'd been on the road with big bands from 1952 to '54 and didn't worry much about anything, except having a ball. Then, that Christmas, came the group at the old Flamingo, with Jimmy and Terry Shannon, Pete Blannin and Bill Eyden. Jimmy was so good that I just had to try.[8]

Born in Dundee, Jimmy Deuchar (1930–1993), whose name has come up several times already, was indeed an outstanding jazz musician. A trumpet player of virtuoso technique and crackling tone, he also possessed great powers of musical invention. His improvised lines were not only fluent but beautifully constructed, the phrases coherent and subtly balanced. In addition, he was an arranger of legendary skill. Ronnie Scott, who readily confessed that, for his own part, he "couldn't arrange a vase of flowers", held Deuchar in awe:

> He was a brilliant natural musician. He could write an arrangement – and did – riding on the bus from, say, London to Manchester. He'd not only write the score, but all the parts in the score would be transposed to each instrument's key as he wrote it, so when you got to the gig you just put up the parts and played it. Everything fell under the fingers. Fantastic![9]

This combination of talents meant that Deuchar was in great demand by bandleaders, and later spent long periods away from the British jazz scene, particularly in Germany. Just as he had shown Dickie Hawdon the way into bebop, he now revealed to Tubby Hayes that he had only just begun to scratch the surface of his talent.

By early 1955, Tito Burns had given up band-leading and was setting himself up as an agent. He had seen how, even in Jack Parnell's high-voltage band, Tubby regularly stole the audience's attention. He predicted a bright future for him and proposed that he should form a band of his own, with the backing of the new Tito Burns agency. For various reasons, financial and logistical as well as musical, they planned a medium-sized band, small enough for lightness and mobility but big enough to have some of the impact of a full orchestra. After some trial and error, the Tubby Hayes Orchestra finally emerged, in March 1955, as an eight-piece line-up: Dave Usden and Dickie Hawdon (trumpets), Mike Senn (alto and baritone saxophones), Jack Sharpe (tenor and baritone saxophones), Harry South (piano), Pete Blannin (bass) and Lennie Breslaw (drums), with Tubby Hayes leading on tenor saxophone. The plan included a recording contract with Tempo, previously a small independent label but now relaunched as part of the Decca empire, and the band's public debut was preceded by the release of a 78 rpm single, 'May Ray / Orient Line'. This was later expanded to a four-track EP with two additional tracks, 'Jor-Du' and 'Monsoon'. Much was made of the similarity in line-up and presentation between the Hayes band and Scott's nine-piece. This did neither of them any harm, although actually there were considerable musical differences. The Scott band, a co-operative venture from the start, was an ensemble production, with every member featured equally. Tubby's band, on the other hand, was very much Tubby's band. The first thing one notices while playing through its records is the way the arrangements build up to his solo entry, almost always on a dramatic two-bar break. Neither band was particularly well served by its early recordings, Hayes in particular suffering from a "boxy" quality that radically suppresses the sparkle of live performance. Intonation tends to wander somewhat, too, and the rhythm section on these early records lacks lift. This was corrected later, when Lennie Breslaw left (reportedly following a spectacular "shout-up") and was replaced by Bill Eyden. The Hayes band drew particularly on the emergent New York hard-bop school for its repertoire. 'May Ray', by Horace Silver, recorded with Art Blakey's Jazz Messengers, and Duke Jordan's 'Jor-Du', recorded by Clifford Brown and Max Roach, were typical. Critics usually described Hayes's own style by referring to Sonny Rollins, Sonny Stitt or even Hank Mobley, to all of whose playing it bore only a passing resemblance at best. What it did share, though, was a stance, an approach, a mode of address which distinguished them all from the post-Lester Young line of tenor players. Vigorous, forthright, unambivalent, this was the tone of voice of the new jazz generation.

The Tubby Hayes Quartet at the Flamingo Club, c.1960–61. Left to right: Phil Seamen (playing Tommy Jones's drum kit), Jeff Clyne (bass), Terry Shannon (piano – obscured) and Tubby Hayes (tenor) (Photo: © Val Wilmer)

Over the next couple of years a kind of modern jazz élite formed around Tempo and its producer, Tony Hall. Thus, we find Hayes, Deuchar, Scott, the trumpeters Dizzy Reece and Dickie Hawdon, drummers Phil Seamen and Bill Eyden, pianists Harry South and Terry Shannon, bassists Jeff Clyne and Kenny Knapper, along with several others, recording in various combinations and under alternating leadership. The group was joined for a while in late 1956 by Victor Feldman, on a return visit from the US, where he had now settled. Taken together, the resulting records (now predominantly twelve-inch LP albums, although still including some singles and EPs) bear witness to the stature and self-confidence achieved by Britain's leading modern jazz musicians in that brief period. To pick out particular examples is probably unfair, but outstanding among them are: *Jimmy Deuchar Ensemble* (April 1956); *Victor Feldman in London* (December 1956 and January 1957), especially Vol. 2, containing pieces, predominantly Feldman compositions, for big band, quintet, and "nine-tet"; *After Lights Out* by the Tubby Hayes Quintet (July 1956); and *Progress Report* by Dizzy Reece, recorded at various dates throughout 1956. Almost the entire cast of Tempo's informal repertory company is to be heard somewhere on these four albums. This was a period in which stylistic development was proceeding in a fairly coherent direction. Despite a certain amount of journalistic falsetto in the music press about challenging convention, breaking down barriers, striking out in new directions, and so forth, the musicians knew what they were doing and their audiences were able to follow them. What we hear on these albums are players who have mastered the contemporary idiom. They are at ease within it, expressing themselves fluently and with a wealth of personal nuance. One piece on the Hayes album demonstrates this particularly well. It is called 'Message to the Messengers', composed by Harry South as a tribute to the American band, the Jazz Messengers, led by Art Blakey, when Horace Silver was its pianist and principal composer-arranger. The performance succeeds in recreating the distinctive atmosphere, subdued but intense, of those Messengers recordings with startling accuracy. The crucial point, however, is that this is not an *homage* to admired masters of the past. The Silver-Blakey Messengers were exact contemporaries of this Tubby Hayes quintet.

It is noticeable that the hit-or-miss approach to recording quality vanishes once a knowledgeable producer, such as Tony Hall, takes charge, with decent facilities at his disposal – in this case Decca's vast and venerable studios at West Hampstead. The Feldman album, with groups of up to fourteen players (including French horn and tuba) is especially good in this regard, with an aural perspective just about as good as mono recording was able to achieve. In particular, the full timbre of the vibraphone, notoriously difficult to capture, is immaculate. Despite having appeared with Glenn Miller at the age of ten and being dubbed "Kid Krupa" for his precocious drumming skills, Victor Feldman (1934–1987), whom we first met in Chapter 2, had survived the perils of being an infant prodigy unscathed. He rarely played the drums in adult life, becoming instead a virtuoso first of the vibraphone and then the piano, and a masterly composer-arranger. He emigrated to the US in 1955, to join Woody Herman's band, and returned home for quite long periods during the next few years. Benny Green recalled his eight-week visit in 1956–57, supposedly for a break and family reunion, as "a constant chase from recording studio to recording studio, a never-ending pursuit of sets of vibraphones from one jazz club to another, and desperate eleventh-hour attempts to find people to copy his scores in time for the next rehearsal."[10] Feldman later played with Cannonball Adderley, Shelly Manne and Wes Montgomery, among others. Miles Davis recorded his composition 'Seven Steps to Heaven', and he became the most sought-after exponent of tuned percussion in the Hollywood studios. A life-long asthma sufferer, he died at his Los Angeles home following an attack, aged fifty-three.

Alphonso "Dizzy" Reece (born 1931) came to Britain from Jamaica aboard the *SS Windrush* in 1948, settling for more than a decade in London but making lengthy working visits to continental Europe. An excellent trumpeter with a highly individual style, he was at the heart of the mid-fifties London jazz scene. He was a member of several bands, including one of Tony Crombie's (not the Rockets) and Kenny Graham's Afro-Cubists. He led several of his own quintets, in one of which Benny Green played tenor saxophone and declared it to have been among the most rewarding experiences of his musical career. Reece moved to New York in 1959, where he later recorded for the Blue Note label and toured with Dizzy Gillespie's big band. He was one of many jazz musicians to come to Britain from the Caribbean in the late forties and early fifties. Most of them, no matter how young, were technically polished performers when they arrived, impressive advertisements for the instrumental training of young people in the West Indies, which, judging by its results, was far superior to that available in Britain at the time. Prominent among the newcomers were the saxophonists Wilton "Bogey" Gaynair (1927–1995), George Tyndale (1913–1991), Harold McNair (1931–1971) and Andy Hamilton (1918–2012), trumpeters Pete Pitterson (1921–1994), Harry Beckett (1935–2010) and Ellsworth "Shake" Keane (1927–1997), bassist Coleridge Goode (born 1914) and vocalist-percussionist Frank Holder (born 1925). Most remarkable of all, however, was the intense and charismatic alto saxophonist Joe Harriott.

Joseph Arthurlin Harriott was born in Kingston, Jamaica, in 1928. His mother died when he was six years old and he was brought up in an orphanage run by the Sisters of Mercy. Attached to this was the Alpha School, famous for its Boys' Band, where Harriott studied the clarinet, and later saxophone. He came to Britain in 1951 and attracted much favourable attention when sitting in at the Feldman Club. He joined a new sextet being put together by the bassist Joe Muddell and was soon a familiar figure around the London jazz scene. By May 1952 he was appearing in a modern jazz concert at the Royal Festival Hall. Harriott's first recording, made in February 1954, reveals an accomplished player who had not yet fully digested his influences. Elements of the smooth, precisely articulated approach associated with Benny Carter and the high swing era alternate uncomfortably with an obvious attraction to Charlie Parker and bebop in general. A few months later he joined the Tony Kinsey Trio, replacing Tommy Whittle. (Kinsey's customary billing was "The Tony Kinsey Trio with . . .", thus ensuring name recognition for himself as leader and for the fourth member, or permanent guest.) From his very first recording with Kinsey it is clear that Harriott's style has settled firmly into bebop. His improvisation on 'How Deep Is The Ocean?' in particular, is superbly poised and confident. To say that it betrays a strong element of Parker is hardly necessary, since Parker's phraseology was now deeply embedded in the playing of every alto saxophonist who followed the bebop path. The impressive thing about Harriott at this stage is how at home he sounds, how natural and unforced his use of the idiom is. It is impossible, too, to miss the polished and spirited performance of the Kinsey trio, with Sammy Stokes on bass and Bill Le Sage alternating between piano and vibraphone. Harriott remained with the trio for a year and all their work together is still well worth listening to. Modern listeners should not be put off by the technical quality of these Esquire recordings, which is, admittedly, not brilliant. Recording technology was slowly but steadily improving and as it progressed it gradually outstripped Carlo Krahmer's capacity, as a one-man operator, to keep up with it.

Harriott was voted second in the alto saxophone section of the 1955 *Melody Maker* readers' poll, and appeared alongside Dankworth (the winner) in the personnel of that year's winners' EP, entitled *Waxing the Winners*. In the same year he recorded with the Jazz Today Unit, and Ronnie Scott recruited him into the new big band which he launched with high hopes, but at exactly the wrong moment. It lasted only a few months. Denis Preston, now well into his role as Britain's Norman Granz, recorded a "Joe Harriott with Strings" session, in emulation of Granz's successful "Parker with Strings". Harriott carried it off with great aplomb. He even recorded an album with Lita Rosa, the top female vocalist of the day. All told, by the end of 1955, Joe Harriott was established among the élite ranks of British modern jazz. It was at this moment that he went down with the first of several serious bouts of illness, a lung infection grave enough to put him into Pinewood sanatorium for a couple of months. He returned to work with Tony Kinsey and also with a quartet led by the drummer Allan Ganley. One of his recordings with the latter, a tricky version of 'I Feel A Song Coming On', taken at breakneck tempo, is a *tour de force* by any standard. In 1957 he formed his own quartet, expanded the following year to a quintet by the addition of Hank Shaw on trumpet. With a few changes, it was to form the basis for his most ambitious later work. Interestingly, in the midst of all this, and no doubt as a result of his connection with Denis Preston, he recorded an album, entitled *Al's Pals*, with what was essentially the Sandy Brown band, plus a few others, under the leadership of Al Fairweather. It is a good example of the openness to disparate styles and idioms which he maintained throughout his career. In 1961 he appeared as guest soloist with Chris Barber's band at the London Palladium, playing his own composition, 'Revival'. Barber went on to score a minor hit with a studio recording of this number, but Harriott was away on tour and unable to take part.

Despite further bouts of illness, Harriott led a successful quintet throughout the latter 1950s. British bands were now able to travel back and forth to continental Europe much more freely, and take advantage of its embryonic jazz-festival circuit. As a result of appearances at festivals in Frankfurt, San Remo and elsewhere, the Joe Harriott Quintet had achieved the beginnings of an international reputation by the end of the decade. The personnel of the band changed radically in 1960, with only Harriott and bassist Coleridge

Joe Harriott, with Booby Orr on drums, at the National Jazz Festival, Richmond, 1963 (Photo: © Val Wilmer)

Goode remaining. The new members were Shake Keene (trumpet), Pat Smythe (piano) and Phil Seamen (drums). This was the quintet which was to launch Harriott's revolutionary new "abstract" music, conceived during one of his periods in hospital. Often described at the time as "free-form jazz", it was by no means a free-for-all. Meticulously prepared, incorporating both written and improvised passages, each piece was planned as a single, coherent musical statement. Because it contained neither regular beat nor set harmonic sequence, the initial effect of Harriott's music was disconcerting for an audience which had always considered these two elements to be essential to jazz. So ingrained was the habit of spotting the American influence behind anything British, it was assumed Harriott must have been inspired by the US free-form pioneer, Ornette Coleman. Harriott vehemently denied this, saying he had never even heard of Ornette Coleman when he launched his new music. Comparing contemporary recordings by the two, now that the dust has long settled, it is hard to believe anyone could have found more than the occasional passing similarity between them. Joe Harriott died in 1973. His career had been much hampered by illness and, although he was widely admired during his life, some who had applauded him through the fifties could never accept his later innovations. His later audience was enthusiastic but not big enough to sustain the quintet beyond the first few years. His death came before his true importance could be widely recognized.

If one band could be said to epitomise British modern jazz in the late fifties, it would be the Jazz Couriers. A quintet under the joint leadership of Tubby Hayes and Ronnie Scott, the Couriers (named in reflection of the Jazz Messengers) took the popular form of a tenor saxophone duet, backed by a rhythm section – Terry Shannon, Malcolm Cecil (soon replaced by Phil Bates) and Bill Eyden, on piano, bass and drums respectively. In most cases, such as the celebrated pairings of Dexter Gordon and Wardell Gray, or Gene Ammons and Sonny Stitt, the two-tenor format constituted a staged confrontation, or "battle", although there were more friendly, conversational examples, notably the long-standing partnership between Zoot Sims and Al Cohn. In the case of Hayes and Scott the effect was more like a pair of acrobats, who leave the audience gasping at their dexterity, co-ordination and sheer pace. An alliance between the two best-known tenor players on the British scene looked like a promising idea, especially since both Scott and Hayes were keen to get involved in something more substantial than casual solo gigs in front of various rhythm sections. There was the added advantage of Tubby's growing powers as a composer and arranger, which promised to make this more than just a "string-of-solos" band.

The Couriers made their debut on 7 April 1957, on the first night of Jeff Kruger's Flamingo Club at its new premises in Wardour Street, sharing the bill with Joe Harriott and the Tony Kinsey Trio. The first record, entitled simply *The Jazz Couriers* came out on the Tempo label in August. Tubby's arrangements are cannily designed to maximize the excitement and drama inherent in two tenors flying in formation, taking off into solos and chasing one another from pillar to post. With the addition of Tubby's vibraphone at various points and a guest appearance on two tracks by Jimmy Deuchar, the whole album is very impressive. Interestingly, despite Tubby's penchant for bravura display, perhaps the finest of the eight pieces is his calm, mellow arrangement of Gershwin's *A Foggy Day*, in which Ronnie is particularly eloquent. It may have been accidental, the chance combination of two very different characters, but the Couriers possessed a kind of built-in drama. Ebullient and pugnacious, Tubby would astound everyone with his garrulous flow and impossible facility, while Ronnie, watchful and ironic, could catch the ear with a single thoughtful phrase. The contrast made a perfect partnership, and like many such partnerships, it had its uneasy side. Ever since encountering the fifteen-year-old Tubby, Ronnie had been awestruck not only by his precocious talent but by the thoughtless ease with which it was exercised. As they came to know one another better he began to wonder whether this was the unmixed blessing which it had first seemed:

I don't know what you'd call it. It was like you turned a switch and bang! It was always there, a bit – mechanical . . . I'm the complete opposite, go to pieces – psychological – nothing I can do about it. I can go for weeks feeling that the last thing in the world I should be is a saxophone player. Then there will come a time, maybe just one night or a run of nights, when I'm in my element.[11]

The contrast between the two even carried over into their appearance, as Scott's biographer, John Fordham, noted:

Though both were immaculately attired in suits – something that the sartorially-preoccupied [Scott] had always insisted on for bands he was in – clothes always looked as if they fitted him to the last fraction of an inch, while Hayes couldn't help resembling a schoolboy who had borrowed his father's Sunday-best.[12]

In their career of just under two and a half years, the Jazz Couriers gained as much of a public profile as a British modern jazz combo had so far managed. They even made a few appearances on *Six-Five Special*. There were three further albums, occasional radio broadcasts, brief trips to the continent, some one-nighters around Britain and tours in support of Sarah Vaughan and the Dave Brubeck Quartet. The vast majority of the band's appearances, however, took place in three West End clubs – the Flamingo, the Florida and the Downbeat – all within a few hundred yards of each other. The old problem of the modern jazz action being concentrated in central London persisted, and it was this as much as anything which caused the band to call it a day in August 1959. Decades later, when Dick Morrissey was complaining to Ronnie Scott about the tedium of tramping regularly around the same few dozen venues, Ronnie sympathized. "I know what you mean," he said. "That's what finished off the Couriers."[13] Probably, their finest hour took place on the Brubeck tour, at London's Dominion theatre (just a short walk from the above-mentioned West End clubs, as it happens). Officially, the Couriers were the "support act" opening the show, but Brubeck, then at the height of his popularity, confessed that they were a hard act to follow that night. Their set was recorded by EMI, and the subsequent album, *The Jazz Couriers in Concert*, turned out, despite a pronounced concert-hall echo, to be a British jazz classic, particularly the virtuoso performances of 'Guys and Dolls' and 'Cheek to Cheek' – both Hayes's arrangements.

When Ronnie Scott's nine-piece band broke up in August 1955, Pete King, drawing on his experience as its player-manager, retired from performing and went into full-time management and promotion, with the Jazz Couriers as his first clients. When, in turn, that band broke up, he and Scott fell to talking about a dream they had long cherished, of opening their own jazz club. It would not be the back room of a pub, or some Spartan rehearsal space rented by the hour, but something along the lines of a small New York club, such as the Half Note in Greenwich Village – friendly and comfortable, with food and drink available at sensible prices, where jazz lovers of all ages could feel at home. With Ronnie finding himself at a loose end, this could be the moment. They had the offer of a lease on premises in Soho, and took it. The basement of 39 Gerrard Street had housed many enterprises in its time – wartime bottle-parties, cab drivers' retreat, Chinese gaming parlour, various kinds of clip-joint and even, in the early fifties, a traditional jazz venue, the Delta Jazz Club. It was a smallish, oblong space, partly tucked in beneath the street and approached by a narrow, vertiginous staircase. Anything less promising as a cool, Manhattan-style jazz room it would be difficult to imagine. With the aid of a thousand-pound loan from Ronnie's stepfather, they made a down-payment, acquired a job lot of tables and chairs, had the place cleaned up and painted, hired a piano and opened for business on 31 October 1959. The opening was announced with what Ronnie later described as a "fusillade of publicity" – a small box in the classified section of *Melody Maker*, which was all they could afford. It offered, among other delights, "a young alto saxophonist, Peter King, and an old tenor saxophonist, Ronnie Scott", plus "the first appearance in a jazz club since the relief of Mafeking by Jack Parnell." A year's membership cost ten shillings (50p) and admission was set at 1/6 (7.5p) for members and 2/6 (12.5p) for non-members. Public confusion between the young (nineteen-year-old) Peter King and Ronnie's co-proprietor of the same name began at this moment and continued for many years.

Soho was a rough place in those days and any new establishment could expect a visit from "the boys", offering "protection". Ronnie and Pete, however, had been around long enough to be on friendly terms with most of the likely characters. Indeed, Ronnie claimed to have been at school with some of them. One of their first visitors was a much-feared underworld figure, Albert Dimes, an old friend of Ronnie's father, who arrived bearing a bottle of champagne to wish them luck. "If anyone comes around making trouble," he advised, "just ask them to come back tomorrow and discuss it with your associate, Mr Albert Dimes. I don't think they will." And they never did. The bottle of champagne was tucked away, to be opened in celebration when their debts had all been cleared. Thirty years later, long after the club had moved to larger premises in Frith Street, the "Albert Dimes memorial bottle" still reposed in the office fridge, awaiting that elusive moment. But the very fact that Ronnie Scott's club was still in being when its competitors were all long gone means that it must somehow have managed to overcome the problems that had dogged the presentation of modern jazz throughout the fifties. Principal among these was the claustrophobic smallness of the "scene" – the same few top players and bands following one another in and out of the same few clubs in London and the provinces. Most of these clubs were lodgers in premises devoted to other purposes during the day, which gave them an air of impermanence. Some were quite pleasant places; others weren't. Some were licensed to serve alcohol; others weren't. Apart from the Flamingo and the Marquee, none of them had any kind of name recognition – what would nowadays be called "branding".

King and Scott identified these problems and tackled them one by one. First, they managed to get a drinks licence, which helped, but only ran until 11pm. After much negotiation over matters of fire exits and so on, this was converted into a "supper" licence, requiring food to be served with drinks after 11pm. The pantomime with plates of ancient sandwiches which this involved was the origin of some of Ronnie's most venerable jokes ("Forty thousand flies can't be wrong" and so on). With Ronnie Scott's name attached, the branding took care of itself. But none of these measures addressed the main problem. The only way of dealing with that, they concluded, would be to bring in American artists that people were eager to hear. That, of course, raised the whole issue of work permits, the Musicians' Union (MU) and the American Federation of Musicians (AFM). American singers and solo pianists had been brought in, since they were regarded as variety or cabaret artists and were represented by different unions. It was also true that, by operating a strict one-for-one exchange policy, some American bands and package shows had been making brief concert tours in Britain over the previous few years. But these had been arranged through agencies with expert staff to deal with the labyrinthine detail involved. Nobody had even considered getting involved in all that international bureaucracy to bring single musicians to play in a basement in a Soho back street. Pete King decided on a direct approach. He flew to New York where, "in a room full of cigar smoke I met a lot of men with Italian names, all wearing trilby hats", and came away with an exchange deal. This was in November 1961, and the club's first American guest was the great tenor saxophonist Zoot Sims. He stayed for a month, playing to a packed club almost every night.

The appearance of the amiable Zoot Sims at Ronnie Scott's club marked a turning point in British jazz. He was followed by a parade of the finest living jazz soloists – the majority of them, oddly enough, tenor saxophonists (Dexter Gordon, Stan Getz, Ben Webster, Sonny Rollins, and so on), and later by whole bands. Contrary to the dire warnings which had formed the basis of the MU's argument, their appearance did not deprive British jazz musicians of employment. As for the contention that Britain would always be the loser in any large-scale exchange scheme, the rise of British pop music in the 1960s turned that on its head. As Pete King later observed, with justified satisfaction, "They got Freddie and the Dreamers; we got Sonny Rollins and Stan Getz. I'd call that a pretty good bargain."[14]

10 It's Trad, Dad!

Traditional jazz – or "trad" as it became universally known – grew in popularity towards the end of the 1950s. For young people of moderate habits, trad provided the perfect musical setting for socializing and fun. It was there to be taken casually – danced to, flirted to, talked above, listened to or simply accepted as part of the furniture – by clerks and schoolteachers, typists and students, shop assistants and apprentices. Even the Young Conservatives often had a trad band in attendance at their get-togethers. In short, trad was now fully accepted as social music. Virtually all social music at that time was played live, the idea of dancing to records being generally viewed with distain. This simple fact may well account for the extraordinary phenomenon known as the "trad boom", which marked the turn of the decade.

The first shock of rock 'n' roll soon passed, killed off, in George Melly's words, "by over-exposure in the press, by a mixture of bullying and flattering, by the crushing embrace of show biz".[1] Its British representatives, Tommy Steele and Cliff Richard, quickly turned soft and cuddly, and behind them came a string of identical youths calling themselves Shane or Ricky. Live rock 'n' roll was confined, for the time being, to bands of resentful older professionals, like Tony Crombie's Rockets, skiffle groups at various stages of electrification, and a kind of Falstaff's army of young semi-pros doing their best. Added to this was the fact that rock 'n' roll was firmly associated with "uncompromisingly proletarian and xenophobic" teddy boys.[2] As a result, by 1959 trad had very little competition when it came to live music for easy-going, informal socializing. It expanded to fill a vacuum, and as it did so it took on many of the features of a modern pop-music craze. Its followers developed characteristic attitudes, styles of dress and forms of dancing. Most importantly, they acquired a leader, a figurehead. This is where trad diverged markedly from the usual pattern and led baffled observers to ask the question – "Why Acker Bilk?" A more unlikely youth hero it would be difficult to imagine.

Aged thirty in 1957, Bernard Stanley Bilk came from the village of Pensford, Somerset, where his father was a cabinet maker and lay preacher. (The nickname "Acker", a local word meaning "pal" or "mate", was given him as a boy.) He had worked in a tobacco factory, as a builder's labourer and a blacksmith's apprentice. He took up the clarinet at age nineteen, while doing his National Service in Egypt, and later played semi-professionally around Bristol, where he formed his first band. In 1954, when Ken Colyer split from Chris Barber, Bilk was recruited into Colyer's new band, but hated life in London so much that he left after a few months and went home to Somerset. It was not until 1957 that he plucked up the courage to return, this time leading his Paramount Jazz Band. He was lucky in his timing. The demand for bands like his was growing and he was soon both busy and popular. His course from there to national celebrity was the result partly of good publicity and being in the right place at the right time, but just as much to do with his own personality and a talent greater than anyone would at first have guessed.

Acker Bilk was no teenager, but he never pretended to be. Instead, he was a kind of mischievous uncle, full of winks and droll remarks. Onto this was grafted a persona devised by his publicist, Peter Leslie. He had the notion of rigging the band out as Victorian, or possibly Edwardian, showmen, in shirtsleeves, striped waistcoats and bowler hats. Bilk was always billed as *Mr* Acker Bilk, and his publicity material, designed to look like a playbill of the 1880s, was couched in suitably orotund language. The band's music, for example, was described as being "in that Style much favoured in the American City of New Orleans: so Spirited in its Execution, so Subtle and Melodious in Conception . . ." and so on, for as long as space would allow. It was an affectionate send-up, but somehow it fitted with Acker's personal style. Peter Leslie also made sure that Acker's fans knew that his heart lay in Pensford, where boyhood adventures had cost him a couple of teeth and the top of one finger – neither of which seemed to affect his playing in the least – that he had done his share of poaching in his youth, was married to his childhood sweetheart, Jean, and was fond of cider. Meditating on all this, and what it might signify, George Melly came up with the following:

> My own feeling is that he may have represented some kind of chauvinistic revolt against American domination; that the mixture of Edwardian working-class dandy and rural bucolic came to stand for a pre-atomic innocence when we were on top . . . for the middle-aged he seemed a reassuring figure, and for the very young, a jolly uncle.[3]

It is certainly true that trad was never the kind of music which set out seriously to alienate parents or the older generation. They may have been a little mystified to find youngsters dancing to old music-hall tunes, like 'Yes, We Have No Bananas', and even jazzed-up military marches, such as 'Blaze Away', but there was certainly nothing threatening about it. Speaking for himself, Acker took a relaxed and realistic view of the whole business: "Don't matter what you wear. You could come on wearing a suit of armour, but if the music wasn't any good people wouldn't come back a second time."[4] And the music *was* good. Acker had what Humphrey Lyttelton (who admired him, and recorded duets with him in later years) called "that 'Here I Am!' quality". His warm, juicy, singing clarinet tone was instantly recognizable from the very first note, and, simple as it was, there was a robust lyricism in everything he played.

As 1959 turned into 1960, the sheer numbers of young people eager to join the ranks of trad fans brought about a whole new scale of presentation. While the usual venues up and down the country continued to do capacity business, advertisements for much bigger events, called "Jazz Jamboree", "Jazz Band Ball" and "All Nite Rave" or, if afloat, "Riverboat Shuffle", began to make their appearance in the music press. Indeed, the music papers, even the venerable *Melody Maker*, seemed to have turned into trad magazines more or less overnight. The notices promised "space for 400 jivers" or "eight hours continuous dancing" at events staged at such venues as the Royal Albert Hall, Alexandra Palace, Leicester's De Montfort Hall and Birmingham Town Hall. Unusual or bizarre surroundings were popular, too. In the Home Counties there was Eel Pie Island, in the Thames near Twickenham, and the labyrinthine Chislehurst Caves in Kent. In fact, underground hideaways were much prized, as witness Liverpool's Cavern Club, previously mentioned. In June 1960, a "Floating Festival of Jazz" promised a "jazz marathon" aboard the *S.S. Royal Daffodil* as it steamed down the Thames to Margate and back: "Tickets £2 – you can pay by instalments!" Such events brought out the exhibitionists in full trad regalia, a get-up that generally consisted of an ancient bowler hat (presumably in honour of Acker) and a strange ensemble, described thus by George Melly:

> The more extreme followers wore, not only a bowler, but army boots, potato sacks, old fur coats cut down to look like stone age waistcoats. This outfit became known as "Rave Gear", an expression first coined by an eccentric jazz promoter called "Uncle Bonny" who encouraged the wearing of it in his chain of southern clubs.[5]

Whimsical rather than threatening, rave gear bore a striking resemblance to the sketches that Spike Milligan doodled on his *Goon Show* scripts and which had been published from time to time. The total effect was of a bunch of mediaeval serfs, down on their luck. Often featured as part of rave gear was the Campaign for Nuclear Disarmament (CND) symbol, sometimes crudely painted on the garments and sometimes worn as some sort of badge. Traditional jazz had a long history of association with left-wing causes, and bands, notably Ken Colyer's, regularly took part in CND demonstrations and marches. Nevertheless, genuine CND supporters sometimes voiced disquiet at the use of their emblem in what seemed to them a frivolous context. A whole new and rather graceless dance style developed, too, which involved hopping from one foot to the other, and was called the "skip jive".

It was all remarkably well-behaved, on the whole, a fact which made trad's single outbreak of rock 'n' roll-style rioting all the more alarming. It took place in July 1960, during a jazz festival held at Beaulieu, Lord Montagu's seat in the New Forest. Acker's band were playing on a bandstand done up like a fairground roundabout, with an audience of a thousand seated on the lawn in front of Palace House, much to His Lordship's satisfaction. "He had not, at that point, looked at the queue outside," commented the *Observer*'s reporter. The queue was six hundred yards long and there were twice as many frustrated teenagers outside as happy ones inside. The riot, when it came, was caught on television, giving rise to predictable outrage. In fact, it was the scruffiness (and no doubt the rave gear) which caused the greatest scandal: "Some 3,000 of them have poured along the narrow lanes, and across the ferries, leaving a wake of startled citizenry in awed contemplation . . . 'I wouldn't mind so much,' confided one outraged hotel keeper, 'if they washed now and then'."[6]

By this stage there were an estimated forty professional trad bands grinding around the roads of a largely pre-motorway Britain. It is impossible to guess the number of semi-pro and amateur bands in cities, towns and villages. Everybody knew someone who played in a trad band, or wanted to. The uniformity which had taken hold in the wake of Chris Barber's sudden rise had become even more marked, with the pounding beat of the banjo even more prominent. "Show me a banjo and I'll show you a profit" was the promoter's watchword. To distinguish themselves from their virtually identical competitors, several professional bands tried to emulate Acker by adopting outlandish uniforms. Soon there were bands of Mississippi gamblers, Confederate soldiers, stockbrokers, and even old-time schoolmasters in mortar-board and gown. But it was just fancy dress, with none of the peculiar resonance of Acker's rig. Bands only wore it on big occasions, never at the ordinary jazz clubs which provided their regular bread and butter. And there was no escaping that round of village halls and corn exchanges, because the whole attraction of trad lay in its active, live, in-person nature. No doubt promoters would have been delighted if vans-full of live, argumentative and occasionally drunken musicians could have been replaced by one man playing records, but that was out of the question. The real fun of trad came, as it always had, from going out to where a band was playing and simply letting go. Unlike other popular crazes, trad was never heavily reliant on records. Total UK record sales actually went down slightly during the three or four years of the trad boom, and most of the hit records associated with it were not in any way typical. Chris Barber's one great chart success, 'Petite Fleur' (1959), did not contain a single note played by his trombone or trumpeter Pat Halcox's trumpet. It wasn't really trad at all, but a winsome little minor-key tune played as a clarinet solo by Monty Sunshine. Acker Bilk's 'Summer Set'

(1960) was similar, as was his huge success – with strings this time – 'Stranger On The Shore' (1961). Even as far back as 1956, Humphrey Lyttelton's 'Bad Penny Blues' was a trumpet-and-rhythm affair, and so thoroughly untypical of him that he later said he would probably have rejected it, on reflection, if he hadn't been in a hurry to get away on holiday. The band that did score a string of hit singles, earning itself the sobriquet "traddypop" as a result, was Kenny Ball and his Jazzmen.

Unusually for trad, Kenny Ball (1930–2013) had already been a professional musician for ten years, playing trumpet in a variety of contexts, including Eric Delaney's show-band and the Dixieland-styled "society" band of veteran clarinetist Sid Phillips. He formed his Jazzmen towards the end of 1958, joined the growing regiment of travelling bands and met with reasonable success. Early in 1961 the Jazzmen became the first trad band to oust rock-inflected pop music unequivocally from one of its strongholds – the BBC Light Programme's Sunday morning show, *Easy Beat*. According to producer-presenter Brian Matthew, when the band first appeared on the show it made a "colossal impact". In his book *Trad Mad*[7] he recalls that the show's listening figures "went up by leaps and bounds". Kenny Ball's original four-week contract was eventually extended to seven months, and 'Samantha', a single taken from the band's first album, went straight into the pop charts. Altogether, Ball was to have fourteen singles in the Top Fifty, stretching well beyond the few years of the trad boom, notably 'Midnight in Moscow', 'March of the Siamese Children', 'The Green Leaves of Summer', 'Sukiyaki', and even 'Teddy Bears' Picnic'. Listening to them now it is easy to hear what caught the popular ear. In the first place, they are all invincibly cheery, the tempos brisk but not breathless. Secondly, most of the tunes are already well-known, although in a different context, which lends a little spice to the treatment. Thirdly, the arrangements themselves, although always easy on the ear, are actually quite elaborate and tight, with textures changing from chorus to chorus. Solos, if any, are brief and the ensemble playing immaculate. Ball's early experience, especially with the meticulous Sid Phillips, probably had a lot to do with that. It all added up to what Philip Larkin neatly summarized as a "wrong-end-of-the-telescope version of New Orleans jazz".[8]

The triumvirate of the three "three Bs" – Barber, Bilk and Ball – was thus complete. Their images were quite distinct: Chris Barber, scholarly and slightly prim; Acker Bilk, avuncular and bucolic; Kenny Ball, the dedicated entertainer. These were the only bands to achieve wide name-recognition. The others: Terry Lightfoot, Bob Wallis, Mickey Ashman, Alan Elson, Dick Charlesworth, Mike Cotton, Mick Mulligan, Forrie Cairns, Jim McHarg – the list goes on – partook of the general popularity of trad without becoming anything like household names. *Boyfriend* magazine squealed: "It's Trad Tremendous . . . the music of the future . . . really zippy."[9] and *Marilyn* published a special pull-out supplement devoted to trad and its "earthy, beaty sound"[10] but, apart from noting Acker's "crazy striped waistcoats", the teenage media made no attempt to build star images around individual bands or their leaders. By 1962, not only was trad established as a major ingredient of all BBC radio's pop shows, it had even ousted all other forms of jazz from *Jazz Club* itself, a development which raised howls of anguish in the jazz press.

Riverboat Shuffle: Bob Wallis and his Band afloat, 1960 (Photo: © Val Wilmer)

All this was terribly confusing to an entertainment industry used to directing the traffic of popular taste and now reduced to dodging it. A particularly choice result of this confusion occurs in the film *Jazz Boat* (1960), which manages to muddle up big bands, rock 'n' roll and trad, to unintentionally hilarious effect. The film, starring Anthony Newley, along with British cinema stalwarts Lionel Jeffries and Bernie Winters, features a great deal of teenage jiving, in the style of current American rock 'n' roll movies, to the music of Ted Heath and his orchestra, playing first of all in what looks like a cave and then on a vessel which might be the *Royal Daffodil* – both venues strongly associated with trad. The smartly turned-out Heath, then aged sixty, looks thoroughly bewildered, as well he might. After this, all attempts to make sense of what was going on seem to have been abandoned. In March 1961 along came the Temperance Seven, not strictly trad, but somehow loosely attached to it. There were nine of them ("one over the eight", and therefore not actually "temperance" at all). Solemn-visaged relics of the Edwardian period, claiming to be habitués of the Pasadena Cocoa Rooms, Balls Pond Road, they appeared in smoking jackets, some with luxuriant facial hair and one wearing a fez, and performed songs of the 1920s in authentic style. Their vocalist was "Whispering" Paul McDowell, who sang in a light tenor voice, his face devoid of expression. The band had its origins in mid-fifties art schools, and a group of musical surrealists called The Alberts, allied to Spike Milligan and the *Goon Show*. One of their number was John R. T. Davies (1927–2004), a multi-instrumentalist who had played trombone with the Crane River Jazz Band in its early days. He was the one in the fez, and went under the stage name of "Shiek Haroun of Wadi el Yadounir". According to him, the band's first record, 'You're Driving Me Crazy', nearly didn't get released:

> I remember George Martin saying, "Well, there's no way we can put this out as a single, because the thing runs over four minutes", and at that time any single over two minutes fifteen seconds was immediately condemned to the trash can. But the people took it. They bought innumerable copies of that record. George was wrong, because he ignored the fact that we had something of a public image and maybe knew something that he didn't.[11]

The Temperance Seven were simply made for television, and 'You're Driving Me Crazy' actually reached number one in the pop charts in March 1961 on the strength of it – another atypical hit of the trad boom. John R. T. Davies went on to become probably the world's most revered restorer, and later digitizer, of the music on antique gramophone records.

Trad flourished in places where the revival-cum-traditional jazz movement had already taken root – the United Kingdom, West Germany, Scandinavia (Denmark especially), the Netherlands, Switzerland. One could speculate endlessly on why it should be these European countries and not others: northern, not southern; Protestant, not Roman Catholic; beer not wine; entertainment indoors more than outdoors; countries without a strong native popular music scene, unlike, say, France with its accordions and *chansons*, or Italy with its opera and Neapolitan songs. Whatever the reason, this was the case. It was often the practice for new British bands, before making their debut in Britain, to play themselves in by taking a residency at a jazz bar in Düsseldorf or Hamburg. The hours were more than excessive and the working conditions disgusting, but, within a few weeks, six individual players would have coalesced into a strong team, if they hadn't fallen apart under the strain. Colyer, Bilk, Ball and many others (although not Barber) went through this hardening process, as did their successors the "beat groups" of the sixties, including the Beatles. The world beyond this north-European terrain, having never "got" the revival, never really got trad either. Once the trad boom was under way it grew so rapidly that sheer momentum impelled it to keep growing. The logical move would be to expand into other territories, particularly the United States. But America had never heard of trad. There were some quite popular bands playing in that general style, such as the Dukes of Dixieland and Wilbur De Paris, and the Three Bs all had chart singles in the US – Barber with 'Petite Fleur', Bilk with 'Stranger On The Shore' and Ball with 'Midnight In Moscow', although the first two, as we have seen, were not really trad at all. Barber did tour successfully in the US on several occasions, but trad as a genre never attracted its own distinctive core following. The dilemma of how to sell trad to the Americans was never resolved, but attempts to tackle it were made, the most determined being a film entitled *It's Trad, Dad!*

COLUMBIA PICTURES presents **RING-A-DING RHYTHM** starring CHUBBY CHECKER with other international pop favorites, and introducing HELEN SHAPIRO.

Lobby-card for "It's Trad, Dad!" – retitled for US distribution – featuring Kenny Ball and his Jazzmen, 1962 (Photo: Courtesy Peter Vacher Collection)

From the point of view of plot, *It's Trad, Dad!* is pretty much identical to every teenage pop-music quickie of the period, viz: oldies try to stop teenagers having a good time dancing to their favourite music – trad, in this case. Teenagers enlist the help of some stars to put on their own show and change the oldies' minds. After a few predictable twists of plot, the oldies begin tapping their feet, signifying capitulation. The End. It was written by the producer, Milton Subotsky, a task which must have taken him all of half an hour, was filmed in black and white and runs for just over an hour and ten minutes. It cost a mere £50,000 to complete, which makes it not only a quickie but also a cheapie, even in 1962 terms. The teenage stars were Helen Shapiro (then aged fifteen) and Craig Douglas (twenty); the broadcasters David

Jacobs, Alan Freeman and Pete Murray played themselves, with the reliable Deryck Guyler playing the old misery in-chief. Trad was represented by the Three Bs, the Temperance Seven, Ottilie Patterson and the bands of Terry Lightfoot and Bob Wallis. None of the above meant a thing to American youth, and neither for that matter did the title. A few years later it might have been a different story but, in 1962, Britain had to give way to the dominant popular culture. To the list of musical attractions were added seven American acts, including Chubby Checker, Gene Vincent and Gary US Bonds, and the title was changed in the US to *Ring-a-Ding Rhythm*. And yet, that excellent critic, Philip French of *The Observer*, declared *It's Trad, Dad!* to be "one of the most imaginative British movies of the decade". The reason was the director, Richard Lester, whose only previous directorial effort had been *The Running, Jumping and Standing Still Film* (1959), an eleven-minute burst of Goon surrealism starring Spike Milligan and Peter Sellers. Lester turned what could have been a mere parade of bands and pop acts into a riot of cinematic tricks and jokes – speeded-up action, superimposed images, weird angles, faces emerging from the bells of trumpets. Two years later he did the same for the Beatles, with *A Hard Day's Night*.

And it was the Beatles who put an end to the trad boom. They were part of the army of electrified skiffle groups that had been growing all over Britain, but especially on Merseyside. They had been one of the groups whose amplification had brought flakes of paint off the ceiling of the Cavern Club, and caused members of the Merseysippi Jazz Band to flee to the pub. If one were to put a date to the end of the boom, it would be February 1963. In the first week of that month Kenny Ball's 'Sukiyaki' entered the charts at number 19. Just three places above them was 'Please Please Me', the Beatles' second release. By the end of the month 'Sukiyaki' had climbed to a respectable number ten, but the Beatles were at number two, and would soon be number one. The bubble didn't exactly burst; it deflated over the next few months. The BBC held a "Jazz 'n' Pop Festival" at the Royal Albert Hall in the spring, at which the Beatles appeared. According to George Melly, the screaming from the audience was so loud that no one could hear them. Bob Wallis and his Storyville Jazzmen were engaged to play a summer season in variety at the London Palladium. When the season finished, and they re-emerged into the real world, they found themselves without any work at all, and the band broke up.

Apart from unemployed musicians, the jazz world, by and large, was not sorry to see the back of the trad boom. You didn't have to be a killjoy or curmudgeon to find the endless corny old tunes and clanging banjos tiresome. Good bands that didn't toe the line, like Alex Welsh's and Bruce Turner's, had been crowded out of long-established venues by standardized trad, as promoters took advantage of the unexpected bonanza. Even jazz on the BBC had been wall-to-wall trad. Some musicians and commentators maintained that it had all been worth it; that this great wave of popularity would permanently raise the profile of jazz. Others, Humphrey Lyttelton for one, rejected this theory. He was convinced that the boom had done no long-term good at all:

> It was based on a fallacy, that it was jolly good if you wore funny clothes and played banjo-laden versions of old music hall songs because it brought a new audience in to listen to jazz. But I remember thinking at the time that it doesn't work like that. The audience you brought in was a sort of pop-oriented audience who are going to be the elder brothers and sisters of kids who are going to go on to something else, who are going to say, "We won't touch that music". So the next people who come in are going to follow the next pop phase. I never believed that that sort of popularisation was going to improve the general jazz club scene. I thought it was going to make it worse – and it certainly did.[12]

Indeed, it is doubtful whether more than a tiny minority of those who had become trad fans during the boom went on to take any further interest in jazz of any kind. More seriously, the *potential* audience for jazz, the kind of young people who had been its keenest supporters during the fifties, seemed to have deserted overnight. What happened? David Robson, a former editor of *Honey* magazine, summed up in simple terms what squads of sociologists have laboured over incomprehensibly for years:

> The Beatles had an effect everywhere, especially on the middle classes. Until the Beatles, rock 'n' roll was working-class territory. Until then middle-class students liked folk music or jazz . . . But the Beatles were clever, engaging and witty. A few years earlier Peter Sellers had lampooned rock 'n' rollers as thick – there was nothing thick about the Beatles.[13]

For jazz, perched in its anomalous position between popular entertainment and minority art, the fifties ended in 1963, with the end of the trad boom and the advent of the Beatles. But the popular entertainment side, bits of it at least, proved remarkably resilient. Take the case of Kenny Ball. His band returned to Britain, from a long tour of Australia, to find the boom over, but they had become so well recognized in the world of variety and light entertainment that they were scarcely affected. Beginning in 1968, they appeared in every episode of the first six series of the *Morecombe and Wise Show* on television, followed by eight years of *Saturday Night at the Mill*. Repeats of these, especially the former, continue to get regular airings, and probably will until the end of time. With these, plus international tours, to Australia, New Zealand, Canada, the US and even Russia, Kenny Ball and his Jazzmen simply kept going.

Acker Bilk pursued two virtually separate careers – three, if you count his status as a popular personality: a subject of *This Is Your Life*, panellist on *Juke Box Jury* and *Pub Entertainer of the Year*, and even participant in ITV's *Christmas Darts Spectacular*. He continued to lead his Paramount Jazz Band, while also purveying romantic clarinet solos with orchestral accompaniment. The latter grew out of his phenomenally successful recording of 'Stranger On The Shore'. This was his own composition, originally entitled 'Jenny', and named after his daughter. It acquired its new name when it was used as the theme tune of a serial on BBC children's television. The record was simultaneously top of the charts in Britain and the US, the first time this had ever happened. Two of his subsequent solo albums sold a million copies each and gained gold discs. With all this success, he didn't really need to keep touring with the band, but it was his life and he loved it. He gradually moved away from the trad formula to a loose, unfettered Dixie-mainstream style, but was careful always to close each show by donning the bowler hat to play 'Stranger On The Shore'.

Chris Barber, the man whose first album, *New Orleans Joys*, had set the trad bandwagon rolling in 1954, was by far the most adventurous of the Three Bs. He never became trapped in the formula which he had created, but constantly sought new ways of deploying those six instruments and fresh material for them to play. Early in the band's career he invited American blues artists Sonny Terry and Brownie McGhee, Big Bill Broonzy and Muddy Waters to join him on tour. The latter aroused great hostility among folk and blues purists with his use of the electric guitar and amplified harmonica. When, in 1960, the Barber band visited Chicago and experienced Muddy Waters's electric blues at first hand, in its native habitat, Barber was so captivated that he began to include an amplified blues set in the band's programme. This so outraged Monty Sunshine that he gave notice and left. Nothing daunted, Barber then took on the British blues pioneers Alexis Korner and Cyril Davies as supernumeraries, purely to play the blues set. When Chicago blues and R&B finally took off in the early sixties, it was partly thanks to a lot of initial boosting from Chris Barber. In 1964, with the permanent addition of the blues guitarist John Slaughter, he changed the band's name to "Chris Barber's Jazz and Blues Band".

Over the high jinks of the trad boom loomed, like Marley's Ghost, the stern figure of Ken Colyer, "The Guv'nor" to his followers. He did not conceal his scorn for the puerile side of trad, and thought most leading trad musicians were "capable of playing better stuff than they were playing", but never descended to personal denigration. At the same time, no one in the trad ranks, from the Three Bs to the obscurest band of semi-pro stompers, failed to acknowledge Colyer's seriousness and dedication. Most of them would have been secretly bound to admit that the difference between his methods and theirs was like that between "the handiwork of craftsmen and a branded product. The latter may be efficient but it lacks character."[14]

Colyer had always had a following. After the break with Barber, and as trad gathered strength through the fifties, that following acquired some of the characteristics of a dissenting sect. (Indeed, George Melly, in *Owning Up*, developed a mischievous and elaborate parallel, in which Colyer and the New Orleans purists were the dissenters, the original revivalists represented the Church of England, with Oliver and Armstrong as Bishops, and bebop played the part of Rome. Colyer, presumably, would be Luther.) In 1954, Studio 51, which had been one of the first *modern* jazz venues in the capital, became the Ken Colyer Club, in which his band and others of the same persuasion played on several nights of the week. In the mid-to-late 1950s, the atmosphere there on Colyer's nights, despite the space left for dancing at the back of the room, was intense and, indeed, reverential. These were the years not only of the "classic" Colyer band, but also of the skiffle group. For special occasions, Colyer would assemble his Omega Brass Band. Patterned after the parade bands then still to be seen and heard in the streets of New Orleans, this normally consisted of three trumpets, a couple of trombones, clarinet (sometimes also a high E-flat clarinet), a saxophone or two, sousaphone, snare and bass drums. Colyer's Omega Brass Band always turned out for special events such as the short-lived Soho Fair, CND marches and the Labour Party's Mayday celebrations. The brotherhood (and sisterhood) of the faithful was not confined to the London area, but spread across the nation. And they turned out in force for the Gov'nor wherever he appeared. It was well known among promoters that, no matter what the star trad competition, a Colyer gig was likely to prove a sell-out.

These and a few other survivors notwithstanding, trad was to all intents and purposes dead and buried by the end of 1963. But it shared one final attribute with pop music, which only revealed itself with the passage of time, namely its capacity as a source of "nostalgia". Most of us are subject to the potency of what Noël Coward called "cheap music", the popular music which surrounded us in our teens and early twenties, when, with any luck, we were enjoying life without too much in the way of responsibility. This potency normally comes to full strength about twenty-five years after the first exposure. It doesn't even matter if you weren't particularly fond of that music at the time; you will, however grudgingly, discover that you have a soft spot for it somewhere between the ages of forty and fifty. Those who were really keen are likely to become devotees all over again. That's how it was with music hall, big-band music, English light music, rock 'n' roll, folk music and all the myriad forms of pop music from the sixties onwards, even punk rock. And so it was with trad. Such devotion, once reignited, tends to be less ardent, less excitable, less fickle. It is steadier and more judicious. In other words, the enthusiasm is no longer juvenile but middle-aged, and middle-aged people, freed from the immediate cares of parenthood, often possess the time and the means to enjoy themselves.

The Second Coming of the trad boom, the boom-beyond-the-boom, which flourished in Britain throughout the 1980s and '90s and into the present century, was a remarkable social phenomenon. Unsurprisingly, since it involved middle-aged people of moderate habits, who behaved themselves, it attracted no attention whatsoever from the media, and thus remained invisible to everyone not directly involved. From early spring to late summer, in places as far apart as Bude in Cornwall, Keswick in the Lake District and Whitley Bay in Tyne and Wear, festivals of trad and allied styles attracted crowds of up to 5,000. Some went on for ten consecutive days. Never were patrons obliged to stumble around in muddy fields or stand in queues to use toilet facilities.[15] They stayed in hotels or bed-and-breakfast accommodation. Events were held in pubs, hotel ballrooms, village halls and the like, and festival-goers strolled from one venue to another. Rave gear, long abandoned, was replaced by the charming practice, derived from New Orleans parades, of decorating umbrellas. In true British holiday style, a prize was usually awarded for the best-decorated brolly. In winter the whole show decamped for "jazz weekends" at country or seaside hotels. Other popular styles had similar shadow lives, notably the big-band era (faithfully recreated by Syd Lawrence and others) and rock 'n' roll (the ageing Wee Willie Harris being much in demand), but these were either individual concerts or weekends in windy, out-of-season holiday camps. Nothing else matched the sheer size and enthusiasm of the second trad boom. It may have passed unnoticed by the rest of the world, but, in its modest, uncomplicated, innocent *joie de vivre*, it must surely stand as a perfect embodiment of the luckiest generation in British history – born during or just before the war, brought up amid rising expectations in living standards, education, work life and health care, and soon to embark upon a long and active retirement, funded by generous pension arrangements. Many a retirement party was enlivened by the playing of a trad band, most of its members well past retirement age themselves, and even New Orleans-style funeral parades were not unknown. The first trad boom, at its height, lasted a little over three years. The second lasted more than thirty.

11 Ominously into the Culture Belt

Humphrey Lyttelton died on 25 April 2008, aged eighty-six. At his funeral, eight days later, the multitude which came to see him off was greeted by a record he had made more than half a century before, in September 1957, when he was approaching his tenth anniversary as a bandleader. It was a version of 'Manhattan', by Rogers and Hart, a masterly performance which seems to sum up everything that his generation had learned from Armstrong. Along with its simplicity, clarity of line and easy grace it has the quality of directness, of reaching out and saying "listen to this!" And listening to it on such an occasion, one could not help reflecting on the distance that not only Lyttelton but the playing and general appreciation of jazz in Britain had covered in that first post-war decade. In 1947, Lyttelton had still been playing in George Webb's Dixielanders; John Dankworth and Ronnie Scott, following their adventures in Geraldo's Navy, were with Tito Burns; and the twelve-year-old Tubby Hayes was in the second form at Rutlish Grammar School, Merton. In the year 'Manhattan' was recorded, the innovative "MkII" Dankworth orchestra was on the road and broadcasting weekly. Dankworth's music was soon to become the distinctive sound of British cinema, not only feature films such as *Saturday Night and Sunday Morning* (Karel Reisz, 1960) and *The Criminal* (Joseph Losey, 1960), but commercials and documentaries – bright, upbeat and optimistic – for both cinema and television. Meanwhile, Scott and Hayes were co-leading the Jazz Couriers, and Lyttelton himself, keeping well away from trad, was presiding over one of the punchiest little swing bands in creation. And they all had an audience. It had grown and matured with them, content to enjoy what most of its members seemed to agree was an all-round good time for jazz. And, with musicians and bands such as the above, they certainly had no need to feel embarrassed or apologetic about the local product.

Indeed, Lyttelton's *Manhattan* could well have been a performance by an American soloist and band, recorded in the US – an observation which would have amounted to high praise in 1957. It is a curious fact that it was only when American musicians had, a few years later, come to be regular visitors to Britain that British jazz began to emerge from the shadow of American styles and assume its own identity. National characteristics in music are notoriously hard to define, and it did not happen all at once, but modern jazz in Britain took on a marked accent of its own over the next couple of decades. Interestingly, one of the leading figures in this was the man who was more directly involved than anyone else in playing day-to-day with American jazz musicians.

Once a regular flow of American soloists to Ronnie Scott's club seemed likely, the question of a resident pianist to lead the accompanying rhythm section became crucial, and the job went to Stan Tracey (born 1926). He was by no means an obvious choice. He had his own very characteristic style and stuck firmly to it, a practice which some of the guest soloists relished and others detested, but Scott always stood by him and Tracey kept at it for seven years, until sheer exhaustion caused him finally to step down. Tracey's early career had been typical of his generation: he was entirely self-taught, first on the accordion, then on piano while serving in the RAF. He had worked as accompanist to the comedian Bob Monkhouse, done a stint in Geraldo's Navy and been a member of Kenny Baker's band and the Ted Heath orchestra, in which he also played vibraphone. His musical development had been guided by the twin influences of Thelonious Monk and Duke Ellington, probably the two most distinctive and idiosyncratic pianists and composers in the whole of jazz. He had recorded prolifically throughout the fifties, on a few occasions leading his own trio, mostly playing standards. Then, in 1959, he came up with a trio album of eight pieces, quirkish and original, entitled *Little Klunk*, which announced his arrival as a composer and attracted much critical admiration. True jazz composers are rare. Most "compositions" are not really compositions at all, but themes for improvisation, often based on the harmonies of standards or the twelve-bar blues. By contrast, the work of composers such as Ellington, Monk or Jelly Roll Morton (Monk especially) is all of a piece – the theme and its treatment being inseparable. This was the case with *Little Klunk*.

It was while playing nightly at Ronnie Scott's, doing one of the most demanding jobs imaginable for a jazz pianist, that Tracey created that rare thing, a piece of music that is not only both startlingly new and instantly attractive, but which goes on to captivate succeeding generations of listeners. His *Jazz Suite: Under Milk Wood* arose from his having repeatedly both read and listened to Dylan Thomas's "play for voices", which spins a fantasy around a day in the life of a Welsh fishing-village. Characters and fragments of narrative caught his imagination and suggested ideas upon which the eight pieces are based. Recorded in 1965 by the indispensible Denis Preston, the suite is played by the quartet of Tracey, tenor saxophonist Bobby Wellins, bassist Jeff Clyne and drummer Jackie Dougan. Much of its charm comes from the combination of Tracey's mercurial piano and the extraordinary beauty of Bobby Wellins's tone, together with the delicacy of his phrasing. One piece in particular, 'Starless and Bible Black', has a brooding, melancholy quality that sets it apart from anything else in jazz. If there is a single moment when a distinctly British jazz voice can be detected, this is probably it.

One historically important point about *Under Milk Wood* is the fact that it owes its genesis to a work of literature. It was not quite Britain's first. John Dankworth recorded his suite *What the Dickens!* in 1963, and there may well have been a few others before that. But following *Under Milk Wood*, through the sixties and into the seventies, there came the most amazing and unexpected crop of new British jazz composers, and most of them had recourse at some time to literary and other artistic references. In *All What Jazz*, his collection of jazz criticism, Philip Larkin lamented the direction which jazz had taken in the 1960s: "full of compositional niceties and unexpected voicings, but I can't pretend that it is jazz as I understand the word". Jazz had, he concluded, "moved ominously into the culture belt". It is easy to sympathize with his unhappiness at the waning of the old ribald spirit, but, given the changes that had taken place, this was inevitable. If you turn loose in jazz a set of inquisitive, articulate, well-read and largely middle-class Englishmen, you are not likely to end up with a bunch of budding Fats Wallers or Dizzy Gillespies, or even Duke Ellingtons. You will have a quite different kind of artist, with an entirely different set of references and assumptions. You will have people like Mike Westbrook (born 1934), drawing on William Blake, D. H. Lawrence and Garcia Lorca, among others; Neil Ardley (1937–2004), with James Joyce, W. B. Yeats, Edward Lear and Lewis Carroll; or Michael Garrick (1933–2011), with J. R. R. Tolkien, Thomas Hardy, and even the Bible. It is also certainly true that, as the fifties ended and the sixties got going, the volume of solemn and pretentious nonsense being spouted about jazz sometimes reached distressing levels, but that too was inevitable, and a cure for it has yet to be found.

As to whether jazz was still an Unholy Row, that rather depends on the particular kind of jazz and the particular listener. Music becomes an Unholy Row when it violates the canons of acceptability – notions of melodiousness, harmonic consonance, tonal quality, volume, and so on. But these canons had been in a constant state of flux at least since World War I. For instance, the criterion of a "good singing voice" – a survival from pre-microphone days – was still often applied to popular vocalists in the fifties. One radio programme in particular offered a glimpse into people's differing notions of an acceptable voice. *Down Your Way* was broadcast in the Home Service (later BBC Radio Four) at teatime on Sundays for more than four decades, beginning in 1946. The format was simple: the presenter visited a different town or village each week, briefly interviewed a few inhabitants and invited each one to choose a favourite piece of music. The interviewees came from all generations and many walks of life, and their interest in music of any kind varied greatly. In the programme's early days, the oldest would have been born long before the advent of radio, or even effective recording. They often chose parlour songs of a comforting, religiose nature, such as 'Home Sweet Home', but rarely specified the singer. It was the next, middle-aged generation that went for the good voice, naming Richard Tauber singing 'You Are My Heart's Delight' or Peter Dawson's hearty 'Floral Dance'. These were the voices of ballad and operetta – full, theatrical voices. After this came interviewees who had been brought up with radio and the talkies, and there was no guessing what any of them might choose. The sheer variety unleashed by the advent of the broadcasting microphone must have been bewildering to older generations: Bing Crosby, Gracie Fields, Gene Autry, Carmen Miranda, George Formby – not one of them a conventionally good voice (except perhaps Gracie, when she was showing off). *Down Your Way* ended in 1987, by which time Frank Sinatra, the archetypal microphone singer, with a style rooted in swing, had long since taken the place of Richard Tauber as representative of the good singing voice among the middle-aged.

Similarly, the post-war years saw the Golden Age of English light music, the preserve of Vivian Ellis, Haydn Wood, Robert Farnon and late-period Eric Coates. This is now remembered, if at all, for providing the theme music to popular '50s and '60s radio and television programmes (*Hancock*, *Dr Findley's Casebook*, *Housewives' Choice* and so on), but at the time light music supplied a ubiquitous background to everyday life. The merest glance through *Radio Times* of the period will reveal this. The melodious, undemanding work of accomplished composers and orchestras, it was not the kind of thing to attract fanatical devotees, but its audience was enormous. Notable examples, such as Mantovani's recording of 'Charmaine' (featuring Ronald Binge's "cascading strings" effect) and Chaplin's theme from his film *Limelight*, played by Frank Chacksfield's orchestra, sold well over a million copies each in the early fifties. At the same time, the BBC retained five full-time regional light orchestras, each consisting of around forty players.[1] Yet the very term "light music" has fallen so far out of use that it is now barely understood. The distinguished light music composer Ernest Tomlinson, towards the end of his life, used to wonder why people no longer seemed able to tolerate music "without someone banging drums".

Such changes in taste creep in almost unnoticed, as one generation succeeds another, and they become clearly perceptible only in hindsight. The influence of Armstrong on jazz itself was direct and obvious from the start. Jazz music would not have existed in any of the forms we recognize today, were it not for him. But the indirect effect, although unrecognized at the time, was incalculable. He showed how a simple popular song could be made fluid, its melody bent into new shapes, set swinging above a springy beat, and sung in one's own, inimitable voice. Virtually every popular singer and dance-band player, from the late twenties onwards, had a bit of diluted Louis in them somewhere, even if they didn't know it. It was the discovery of the full-strength original which produced all those Armstrong moments that set off the revival of the 1940s. Bebop, by contrast, had a big impact on jazz, but nothing like the same transformative effect on popular music or culture generally. That had to wait until the end of the 1950s.

History rarely fits neatly into decades, but it is fair to claim that jazz began a whole new era in 1960. The immediate cause was *Kind of Blue*, an album recorded by Miles Davis in the spring of 1959 and released in August of that year. Young lovers of modern jazz, in particular, fell for it with the kind of mesmerised fascination that had overcome Lyttelton, Melly *et al.* on first encountering Armstrong. In 1960, just as in the 1930s, young heads crowded over the record player and, when the record had finished, played it again from the beginning. The machine was now powered by electricity, not clockwork, and *Kind of Blue* lasted a little over forty minutes, as opposed to the three minutes of Armstrong's 'Basin Street Blues', but its effect was the same. The typical reaction was something like, "I don't know what to make of it, but I love it." Musicians tended to add, "I must try to figure out how it works".

Instead of the mobile, chromatic harmonies of bebop ("changes"), which the denizens of Club Eleven had worked so hard to master, this new style was built on static chords which implied little or no forward momentum. Each chord contained within it its own distinctive scale. The musical term for such scales is "modes", and hence the type of jazz introduced by Miles Davis in *Kind of Blue* quickly became known as "modal jazz". Miles Davis was already a major figure, instantly recognizable by jazz listeners around the world, and no one could accuse *Kind of Blue* of "not being jazz". It was suffused with the accents of the blues, and the other players on the record[2] were all masters of the jazz art. In these respects it was as American as it could possibly be – and yet, along with all this, came strong hints of a European, particularly French, sensibility. Those cloudy harmonies, the restraint, the delicacy of touch, raised unmistakable echoes of Debussy, Erik Satie and "les Six". Miles Davis had, in fact, spent longish periods in Paris. He had met Jean-Paul Sartre, Boris Vian and even Picasso, created the music for Louis Malle's first film, *Ascenseur pour l'Échafaud*, and pursued an on-off love affair with Juliette Greco which lasted for more than ten years. Added to its other merits, it was this cosmopolitan flavour which made *Kind of Blue* attractive to the generation of educated youth who took to it so eagerly. In other words, it was something approaching a new, international jazz language, and its influence can be detected behind the work of the British jazz composers, bands and soloists of the following few decades. Furthermore, the ripples of its influence spread far beyond the jazz world. One of the reasons the popular music of the sixties and beyond sounds markedly different from that of the fifties and before lies in its harmonic practice. No longer did pop songs move smoothly through a series of largely predictable modulations, arranged in neat two-, four- or eight-bar periods. Commercial sheet music, which had for decades spelled out these patterns in commonly accepted chord symbols, now sprouted all kinds of variants and anomalous markings – evidence of the struggle which the publisher's arranger had experienced in an attempt to convey these new, "modal" harmonies in the old written language. By the end of the 1960s, clear traces of modalism could be found in the work of "minimalist" composers such as Philip Glass and Terry Riley, and from them it passed into the music of Brian Eno, David Bowie and the next generation of popular artists.[3] Bits of *Kind of Blue* are still regularly used as "mood music" on radio and television, well into the twenty-first century.

Just as with Armstrong in the thirties, much of this took place without any conscious reference to *Kind of Blue*, to Miles Davis, or even to jazz. It was as though people had been waiting for something that matched the mood of the times and felt that this was it. Miles Davis beat Louis Armstrong into second place in the trumpet section of the 1960 *Melody Maker* international poll – a result which caused a considerable stir. There would not have been time for *Kind of Blue* to make its full impact by March 1960, and Davis was already hugely popular, especially for his orchestral albums with Gil Evans.[4] A further stir was caused by Evans beating Duke Ellington to the top of the composer-arranger section. And that was another straw in the wind, because there was a distinctly European flavour to much of Evans's work.

Meanwhile, as if on another planet, the trad boom was taking off, and as it rose it seemed to pass through some invisible barrier, beyond the little world of jazz and into the enticing regions of pop. Another of the BBC's "Jazz and Rock Nights" took place at the Royal Albert Hall in January 1960, featuring Acker Bilk and several other trad names alongside Adam Faith, Craig Douglas and someone called Cuddly Dudley. (Lyttelton, when he discovered who else was on the bill, cancelled his appearance.) During the boom, trad would not really count as jazz at all in the estimation of many, and this was to have an unfortunate long-term effect. Later generations would come to regard all jazz before Charlie Parker, or even before Miles Davis, as old, tainted by association with trad, and therefore worthless. Specifically, any sort of loose-ensemble music, be it Armstrong's Hot Five, the Chicagoans, Fats Waller and his Rhythm, even the delectable Kansas City Six, would be dismissed as "trad". "How dreadful," wrote Philip Larkin in the introduction to *All What Jazz*, "to have lived in the twentieth century, but died before King Oliver led his men into the Gennett studios in Richmond, Indiana, or before Frank Walker auditioned Bessie Smith . . . or Bubber Miley joined Duke Ellington's Washingtonians." To which one might add: or before Lester Young met Billie Holiday, or Woody Herman assembled his Four Brothers band, or Gerry Mulligan, Gil Evans *et al.* hatched the *Birth of the Cool*. But none of this would mean a thing to someone whose idea of jazz begins in 1960. Modernists in the post-war years may have made fun of the revivalists and their lack of musical expertise, but would probably, if pressed, have grudgingly acknowledged that they were earnest in their endeavours. But once the revival gave birth to trad, and trad became pop, consorting with the likes of Cuddly Dudley, even that defence could be ruled out.

As the 1960s began, the jazz scene in Britain, as presented in the pages of *Melody Maker*, looked much the same as in previous years. Lyttelton and Dankworth remained the figureheads, their names widely familiar to the general public and their bands automatically top of the bill. Tubby Hayes and Ronnie Scott ruled the modern scene, while the Three Bs – Barber, Bilk and Ball – dominated trad. Jazz concerts on Sundays were still occasionally being banned by provincial magistrates. With National Service in the process of being abolished, army bands were desperately advertising for recruits, while bandleaders in holiday camps continued, as in days of yore, to seek "Lead alto, read/busk, no characters". When all else failed, a head of steam could always be raised by lobbing an indignant half-brick at the BBC. In the issue of 16 January 1960, reader John G. Taylor offered his contribution to the widespread conviction that the Corporation had it in for jazz. Having totted up every minute of radio music advertised in one week's *Radio Times* he came up with the following: classical music – 43h 20m; pop – 33h 40m; light music – 31h 25m; jazz – 2h 15m. Case proved. Except, of course, that it all depends on how you define jazz.

Which is more or less where we came in.

12 Envoi

In 1985 I had a brief correspondence with Philip Larkin, in the course of which he wrote: "Jazz does fascinate me as a kind of capsule history of art, rather like one of those snowstorms in a glass ball." This is a point often made or implied in his writing on jazz, particularly in the celebrated introduction to *All What Jazz*. As a metaphor it holds good throughout the period covered by this book. The saloon-bar pundits may have enjoyed debating what was or was not jazz, but there was really very little doubt about the contents of the glass ball. And the little storms inside it did enact, in brief and rudimentary fashion, the shifts and upheavals in Western art over the previous couple of centuries or so.

It seems to me, though, that developments from 1960 onwards force us to change the metaphor. When jazz ceased to be a purely American music it was no longer confined in its bottle and became increasingly difficult to define. It was now more like a river, which begins with a number of springs flowing together to make a brook. The obscure brook is joined by other, smaller brooks and springs until it becomes a substantial stream. Eventually, through many meanderings, rapids, deep pools and backwaters, the stream grows into a great river. Throughout its progress so far, there is no doubt that it is the same river, flowing between clearly defined banks. But as it nears the sea it opens out into a tidal estuary. Here it is often impossible to tell what is river and what is sea, especially when the tide is in, or what is firm land and what is impermanent sandbank. Eventually the river becomes engulfed by the sea. Of course, the river itself, in all its phases, is still there to be appreciated and enjoyed. Some welcome the bracing air and ever-changing aspect of the estuary; others prefer the green shades of the riverbank, or the springs and rivulets in the hills where it all began. I have never understood why people felt the need to quarrel over this.

During our exchange of letters I preferred not to tell Philip Larkin I was sorry to learn that he had found one particular record "not to be jazz as he understood the word", since I was one of the players on the record in question.

I was not particularly upset, partly because he praised the musicianship and originality, but mainly because from my position, a little further downstream, it *was* jazz as *I* understood the word.

I look back on life inside the fifties bubble with great affection. It would be sad if I didn't, seeing that it accounts for my teenage years. Mere existence is so exciting at that time of life, and it leaves impressions so vivid that it seems impossible that anyone else, at any other time, could have had such momentous experiences. Every generation goes through it, and it can lead to an anecdotage of Ancient Mariner proportions. One should try to avoid this, but, for me, there are some memories that simply refuse to lie down and be quiet: being exposed to the full force of Big Bill Broonzy's personality at the age of fourteen, for instance, or being part of the crowd, some openly weeping, which rose to greet Louis Armstrong's appearance in 1956 (and noticing how small and dapper this superman actually was). And there was that night in (I think) 1957 at 100 Oxford Street, the crowd so densely packed that condensation was running down the walls, the best Lyttelton band ever in full cry – and Jimmy Rushing out-front at the microphone, singing his heart out and looking as though, like me, he imagined he'd died and found himself in heaven.

Notes

References

OHJB refers to interviews in the *Oral History of Jazz in Britain*, compiled by the National Sound Archive and held at the British Library.

Jazz Prof. refers to www.jazzprofessional.com, a website launched by the late Ron Simmonds and now maintained by the National Jazz Archive.

Taylor site refers to http://vzone.virgin.net/davidh.taylor/bebop.htm (accessed June 2013), a large and well-organized website dealing with early British modern jazz, which unaccountably vanished from the web in late 2013 and, at the time of writing, has failed to reappear.

Chapter 2: Trumpet in a Handcart

1. Humphrey Lyttelton, *I Play as I Please* (London: McGibbon & Kee, 1954) .
2. Ibid.
3. George Melly, *Owning Up* (London: Weidenfeld & Nicolson, 1965).
4. Charles Delaunay, *Django Reinhardt* (London: Cassell, 1961).
5. Geoffrey Smith, *Stéphane Grappelli* (London: Pavilion, 1987).
6. *Philip Larkin Reads and Comments on "The Whitsun Weddings"*. Listen Records LPV6.
7. *Letter from America*. BBC Radio 4, 10 July 1971.
8. Lyttelton, *I Play as I Please*.
9. Don Rendell, *A Recap of 20 Years of British Jazz* (1967): text in *Jazz Prof.*
10. "Almost wherever you look across the spectrum of social attitudes and the cultural patterns which reflected them [in the immediate post-war years], you will find as much, if not more, in common with Thirties Britain than Fifties Britain." Peter Hennessy, *Never Again: Britain 1945–1951* (London: Jonathan Cape, 1992).
11. Lyttelton, *I Play as I Please*.
12. Ibid.

Chapter 3: Austerity Stomp

1. Melly, *Owning Up*.
2. Legon, *OHJB*.
3. Melly, *Owning Up*.
4. Legon, *OHJB*.
5. Melly, *Owning Up*.
6. Notes to CD *George Webb's Dixielanders 1943–1947* (Lake LACD128), extracted from a series of articles in *Just Jazz* magazine.
7. Ibid.
8. Ibid.
9. Ibid.
10. Legon, *OHJB*.
11. Conversation with author c. 2010.
12. Jim Godbolt, *A History of Jazz in Britain 1950–70* (London: Quartet, 1989).
13. Conversation with author c. 1990.
14. Lyttelton, *I Play as I Please*.
15. Ibid.
16. See note 6 above.
17. Lyttelton, *I Play as I Please*.
18. Melly, *Owning Up*.
19. Hawdon, *OHJB*.
20. Legon, *OHJB*.
21. Val Wilmer, *Mama Said There'd be Days Like This* (London: Women's Press, 1991).
22. Philip Larkin, *All What Jazz* (London: Faber & Faber, 1985).

Chapter 4: Welcome to Club Eleven!

1. John Dankworth, *Jazz in Revolution* (London: Constable, 1998).
2. The fullest discussion of the interaction of bebop with US racial and socio-political issues of the 1940s is in Scott DeVeaux, *The Birth of Bebop: A Social and Musical History* (University of California Press, 1997).
3. Presumably the version recorded in New York for the Guild label in 1945.
4. Fullado; see "Clubs" section of *Taylor site*.
5. Bill Burch, *Keeper of the Flame: Modern Jazz in Manchester 1946–1977* (self-published, Manchester, 2012).
6. Ibid.
7. Ibid.
8. Don Rendell, *Jazz Prof*.
9. Decca F8256.
10. *Letter from America*, BBC Radio 4, 10 July 1971.
11. Tito Burns, *OHJB*.
12. Ibid.
13. *The Goon Show*; see Chapter 5.
14. Laurie Morgan, *OHJB*.
15. The original eleven members were: Ronnie Scott, Hank Shaw, Lennie Bush, Joe Muddell, Bernie Fenton, Tommy Pollard, Tony Crombie, Laurie Morgan, John Dankworth, Johnny Rogers and Harry Morris.
16. "Sharp Schmutter," in *The Twentieth Century*, August 1959. Reprinted in Colin MacInnes, *England, Half English* (London: Hogarth Press, 1986).
17. Don Rendell, *Jazz Prof*.
18. Dominic Green, *Benny Green: Words and Music* (London: London House, 2000).

19. Don Rendell, *Jazz Prof.*
20. Kitty Grime and Val Wilmer, *Jazz at Ronnie Scott's* (London: Robert Hale, 1979).
21. Jack Parnell & his Quartet, *Scrubber Time* & *On the Sunny Side of the Street*, Decca Records, 29/12/46.
22. Dexter Gordon, quoted in Ross Russell, "Bebop", in *The Art of Jazz*, ed. Martin Williams (New York: Oxford University Press, 1959).
23. Strictly, a tenor saxhorn. It looks like a small tuba.

Chapter 5: New Orleans to London

1. *Downbeat*, June 1939.
2. Mike Pointon and Ray Smith, *Goin' Home: The Uncompromising Life and Music of Ken Colyer* (London: Ken Colyer Trust, 2010).
3. Ibid.
4. Monty Sunshine, *OHJB*.
5. Ibid.
6. Ibid.
7. Pointon and Smith, *Goin' Home*.
8. Ibid.
9. Ibid.
10. Ibid.
11. Ibid.
12. *Melody Maker*, 16 February 1952.
13. In Michael Sissons and Philip French (eds), *Age of Austerity* (Oxford: Oxford University Press, 1963 and 1986).
14. Quoted in Tony Bacon, *London Live* (London: Balafon Books, 1999).
15. Monty Sunshine, *OHJB*.
16. Pointon and Smith, *Goin' Home*.
17. *The Goon Show*, series 7, episode 18.
18. Monty Sunshine, *OHJB*.
19. Dominic Sandbrook, *Daily Telegraph*, 24 April 2010.
20. *The Jazz Scene* (London: Penguin Books, 1959).
21. *Melody Maker* Club Calendar, 30 January 1954: "Suffering from trad starvation?" (advert for Bob Dawbarn's Barnstormers).
22. *Daily Telegraph*, 23 April 2002.

Chapter 6: Couth, Kempt and Shevelled

1. Quoted in Alun Morgan's notes to *Stan Getz: Roost Sessions*, Vogue VJD 573, 1981.
2. *Melody Maker*, 11 March 1950; emphasis in original.
3. Lightly Politely / Strike Up The Band / Marmaduke / Little Benny. Jazz Parade Records, 18 May 1950.
4. Dankworth, *Jazz in Revolution*.
5. Ibid.
6. Graham Collier, *Cleo and John: A Biography of the Dankworths* (London: Quartet Books, 1976).
7. Ibid.
8. Ibid.
9. Notes to *Bundle from Britain*, Top Rank 614, 1959.
10. Dickie Hawdon, *OHJB*.
11. Obituary: *Daily Telegraph*, 9 August 2010.

12. Ibid.
13. Godbolt, *A History of Jazz in Britain 1950–1970*.
14. See entry on Ronnie Scott Orchestra at *Taylor site*.
15. *Jazz Journal*, February 1953.

Chapter 7: Let's Settle for Music

1. Take A Note From The South / Open House / Apples Be Ripe / Midnight Creep / Small Hour Fantasy.
2. *Graeme Bell, Australian Jazzman, his Autobiography* (New South Wales: Child & Associates, 1988).
3. Humphrey Lyttelton, *Second Chorus* (London: McGibbon & Kee, 1958).
4. Ibid.
5. Introductory note to the four-volume CD set *The Parlophones 1949–1959*, Calligraph Records, 1998.
6. Ibid.
7. Notes to *Accent on Swing* (1959), Lake LACD 310.
8. Lyttelton, *Second Chorus*.
9. Collected and reissued in 2000 as *Flook Digs Jazz*, Lake LACD 143.
10. Reissued as *Juicy & Full-Toned*, Lake LACD 12.
11. Notes to *Accent on Swing*, Lake LACD 310.

Chapter 8: Skiffle

1. See Chapter 5.
2. Typical items in Colyer's repertoire included 'Midnight Special', 'Casey Jones', 'Streamline Train', 'Muleskinner' and 'Ella Speed'.
3. Interview, BBC Radio 2 series *Traditionally British*, October 1993.
4. Dick Heckstall-Smith and Pete Grant, *Blowing the Blues* (Bath: Clear Books, 2004).

Chapter 9: Six Months in a Palais . . .

1. Quoted in Green, *Benny Green: Words and Music*.
2. Ibid.
3. Peter King, *Flying High* (London: Northway, 2011).
4. Dir. Stellan Olsen, 1976.
5. Alun Morgan and Raymond Horricks, *Modern Jazz: A Survey of Developments since 1939* (London: Gollancz, 1956).
6. Introduction to *The Beats*, ed. Seymour Krim (New York: Fawcett World Library, 1960).
7. *The Observer*, 25 March 1962.
8. See entry for Tubby Hayes at *Taylor site*.
9. See entry for Ronnie Scott Orchestra at *Taylor site*.
10. Album note to LP *Victor Feldman in London*, Tempo TAP 12.
11. Grime and Wilmer, *Jazz at Ronnie Scott's*.
12. John Fordham, *Jazz Man: The Amazing Story of Ronnie Scott and his Club* (London: Kyle Cathie, 1995).
13. Dick Morrissey, conversation with author, c. 1980.
14. The narrative in the final paragraphs of this chapter is the result of various conversations over the years between the author and the late, and much lamented, Pete King.

Chapter 10: It's Trad, Dad!

1. George Melly, *Revolt into Style* (Harmondsworth: Penguin, 1972).
2. Dick Hebdige, *Subculture: The Meaning of Style* (London: Routledge, 1981).
3. Melly, *Revolt into Style*.
4. Interview, BBC Radio 2 series *Traditionally British*, October 1993.
5. Melly, *Revolt into Style*.
6. *The Observer*, 31 July 1960.
7. Brian Matthew, *Trad Mad* (London: Souvenir Press, 1962).
8. Philip Larkin, *All What Jazz* (London: Faber & Faber, 1985).
9. *Boyfriend*, 25 November 1961.
10. *Marilyn*, 14 November 1961 (extracts from *Boyfriend* and *Marilyn* are quoted in an unpublished paper on the trad boom by the late Bob Wallis, held at the National Jazz Archive).
11. Interview, BBC Radio 2 series *Traditionally British*, 1993.
12. Ibid.
13. *Daily Telegraph*, 11 May 2012.
14. *Scene* magazine, 29 November 1962.
15. Although the damp and low-lying Upon-upon-Severn festival did, from time to time, threaten to turn into Upton-*in*-Severn festival.

Chapter 11: Ominously into the Culture Belt

1. The Musicians' Union may have been a villain in the eyes of jazz lovers, but it was the guardian angel of English light music. By restricting the BBC's use of records, through the "needle-time agreement", it kept these and other staff orchestras in being.
2. John Coltrane, Cannonball Adderley, Bill Evans, Paul Chambers and Jimmy Cobb.
3. A wide-ranging account of the long-term influence of *Kind of Blue* can be found in Richard Williams, *The Blue Moment* (London: Faber & Faber, 2009).
4. *Miles Ahead*, 1955 and *Porgy & Bess*, 1958.

Bibliography

Historical, Critical and Cultural

Bacon, Tony, *London Live*. London: Balafon Books, 1999.

Birch, Bill, *Keeper of the Flame: Modern Jazz in Manchester 1946–1977*. Self-published, Manchester, 2012.

Chilton, John, *Who's Who of British Jazz*. London: Cassell, 1997.

DeVeaux, Scott, *The Birth of Bebop: A Social and Musical History*. Berkeley: University of California Press, 1997. London: Picador, 1999.

Godbolt, Jim, *A History of Jazz in Britain 1919–50*. London: Quartet, 1984.

—*A History of Jazz in Britain 1950–70*. London: Quartet, 1989.

Green, Benny. *Drums in My Ears*. London: Davis-Poynter, 1973.

Harris, Rex, *Jazz*. Harmondsworth: Penguin Books, 1952.

Hennessy, Peter, *Never Again: Britain 1945–1951*. London: Jonathan Cape, 1992.

Larkin, Philip, *All What Jazz*. London: Faber & Faber, 1985.

Lomax, Alan, *Mr Jelly Roll*. New York: Duell, 1950. London: Cassell, 1952.

MacInnes, Colin, *England, Half English*. London: Hogarth Press, 1986.

Melly, George, *Revolt into Style*. Harmondsworth: Penguin, 1972.

Morgan, Alun and Raymond Horricks, *Modern Jazz: A Survey of Developments since 1939*. London: Gollancz, 1956.

Newton, Francis (Eric Hobsbawm), *The Jazz Scene*. London: McGibbon & Kee, 1959.

Ramsey, Frederick and Charles E. Smith (eds), *Jazzmen*. New York: Harcourt Brace, 1939. London: Sidgwick & Jackson, 1952.

Sissons, Michael and Philip French (eds), *Age of Austerity*. Oxford: Oxford University Press, 1963 and 1986.

Williams, Martin (ed.), *The Art of Jazz*. New York: Oxford University Press, 1959.

Williams, Richard, *The Blue Moment*. London: Faber & Faber, 2009.

Memoir, Reminiscence and Biography

Brown, Sandy, *McJazz Manuscripts*. London: Faber & Faber, 1979.

Collier, Graham, *Cleo and John: A Biography of the Dankworths*. London: Quartet Books, 1976.

Dankworth, John, *Jazz in Revolution*. London: Constable, 1998.

Delaunay, Charles, *Django Reinhardt*. London: Cassell, 1961.

Fordham, John, *Jazz Man: The Amazing Story of Ronnie Scott and his Club*. London: Kyle Cathie, 1995.

Gold, Harry, *Gold, Doubloons and Pieces of Eight*. London: Northway, 2000.

Goode, Coleridge and Roger Cotterrell, *Bass Lines: A Life in Jazz*. London: Northway, 2002.

Green, Benny, *Swingtime in Tottenham*. London: Lemon Tree Press, 1976.

Green, Dominic, *Benny Green: Words and Music*. London: London House, 2000.

Grime, Kitty and Val Wilmer, *Jazz at Ronnie Scott's*. London: Robert Hale, 1979.

Harris, Kenny, *Geraldo's Navy*. Brandon, Suffolk: KH Publishing, 1998.

Heckstall-Smith, Dick and Pete Grant, *Blowing the Blues*. Bath: Clear Books, 2004.

King, Peter, *Flying High*. London: Northway, 2011.

Laine, Cleo, *Cleo*. London: Simon & Schuster, 1994.

Lewis, Vic, *Music and Maiden Overs*. London: Chatto & Windus, 1987.

Lyttelton, Humphrey, *I Play as I Please*. London: McGibbon & Kee, 1954.

—*Second Chorus*. London: McGibbon & Kee, 1958.

—*Take it from the Top*. London: Robson, 1975.

Matthew, Brian, *Trad Mad*. London: Souvenir Press, 1962.

Melly, George, *Owning Up*. London: Weidenfeld & Nicolson, 1965.

Pointon, Mike and Ray Smith, *Goin' Home: The Uncompromising Life and Music of Ken Colyer*. London: Ken Colyer Trust, 2010.

Robertson, Alan, *Joe Harriott: Fire in his Soul*. London: Northway, 2003.

Smith, Geoffrey, *Stéphane Grappelli*. London: Pavilion, 1987.

Turner, Bruce, *Hot Air, Cool Music*. London: Quartet, 1984.

Wilmer, Val, *Mama Said There'd be Days Like This*. London: Women's Press, 1991.

Guide to Recordings

It has been customary to include a list of recommended recordings at this point, complete with label details and catalogue numbers. This information was often out of date on publication but, even so, readers found it useful. Things have changed in recent times, affecting both the form in which recorded music is presented and the manner in which it is made available to the public. Using the internet, music can be picked up via sites such as YouTube and Spotify, bought on CD, both new and second-hand, through Amazon etc., and also downloaded. With this in mind, I have drawn up a list of available recordings in the traditional way, but must add the following supplementary advice:

1. Almost everything released on CD can be found on Spotify, and much of it on YouTube.
2. Deleted material (such as the Esquire "Bebop In Britain" box) can often be found for sale second-hand.
3. A trawl using Google will often yield useful results.
4. There is bound to be some overlapping of material, especially with compilations.

All catalogue numbers given are UK.

Chapter 2: Trumpet in a Handcart

Compilations (pre-war, wartime, post-war):

Jazz in Britain 1919–1950 (CDx4, Properbox 88, compiled Jim Godbolt). Discs 3 and 4 apply specifically to this period.
> Artists and bands represented include: Disc 3: Ken "Snakehips" Johnson, Harry Roy, Johnny Claes, Harry Parry, HMV Public Jam Session, Buddy Feathersonhaugh's RAF Bomber Command Sextet, Vic Lewis / Jack Parnell Jazzmen, George Shearing Quintet, Leslie "Jiver" Hutchinson, Ted Heath & his Music, The Squadronaires. Disc 4: Harry Hayes & his Band, Melody Maker Columbia Jazz Rally, Graeme Bell & his Australian Jazz Band, Freddy Randall, Yorkshire Jazz Band.

Larkin's Jazz (CDx4, Properbox 155, sponsored by the Philip Larkin Society). A fascinating selection of the American jazz records which typically influenced wartime and immediate post-war tastes.

King Louis (CDx4, inc. Properbox 93). 99 classic Armstrong performances, from 1923 to 1929, including 'Basin Street Blues' and 'Drop That Sack'.

Kenny Baker: Birth of a Legend '41–'46 (Hep CD 58)

Harry Parry Sextet: Parry Opus (Vocalion CDEA6101)

Ted Heath & his Music: Listen To My Music, Vol. 1 [inc. Opus One] (Hep CD52)

Jack Parnell: Two Classic Albums Plus (CDx2 Avid AMSC1016)

It Always Rains on Sunday: DVD included in various releases of Ealing Studios material.

Dance Hall is also rumoured to be due for release.

Chapter 3: Austerity Stomp

Compilations:

*British Traditional Jazz: A Potted History 1936–63 (CDx3, Lake LACD300). This box, compiled by Lake Records proprietor Paul Adams, delivers exactly what the title promises. There are 73 tracks, some previously unissued, by bands and artists both famous and obscure.

The Great Revival (Single CDx4, Lake LACD 134/5/6/7). A good selection, including some of the best provincial bands. (134) Bobby Mickleburgh's Bobcats, Tony Short Trio, Cy Laurie Four & Jazz Band, Christie Brothers Stompers. (135) Brian Wooley's Jazzmen (Leicester), Bobby Mickleburgh, Mick Gill's Jazz Band (Nottingham), Acker Bilk's Pramount Jazz Band (the original, Bristol-based), Crane River Jazz Band. (136) Sandy Brown, Bobby Mickleburgh, George Chisholm, Lyttelton, Mike Daniels' Delta Jazzmen. (137) Les Jowett's Jazzmen (Brighton), Second City Jazzmen (Birmingham), Merseysippi Jazz Band (Liverpool), Chris Barber (early bands).

British Traditional Jazz at a Tangent, Vol. 3 (Lake LACD318). A selection, mainly from the mid-50s, of tracks by less well-known bands, including the Famous Southern Stompers, Mike Peters Band, Eric Silk's Southern Jazz Band etc.

George Webb's Dixielanders 1943–47 (Lake LACD128)

Humphrey Lyttelton & his Band:

The Parlophones (single CDx4, Calligraph CLG CD 035 -1/2/3/4)

Vintage Humphrey Lyttelton 1948–51 (Lake LACD172) [1st band recording + 1951 Royal Festival Hall concert]
    [More material from the 1951 concert was issued on long-deleted Dormouse 12" LP. No trace of any CD.]

Delving Back with Humph (Lake LACD72). First Lyttelton band plus "Chicagoans" session with Carlo Krahmer

Big Walkabout in London – Graeme Bell's Australian Jazz Band 1948–51 (Lake LACD166)

Chapter 4: Welcome to Club Eleven!

Compilations:

Bebop in Britain (CDx4, Esquire CD ESQ 100-4). Excellent anthology of early British modern jazz, now deleted but often available online. Artists and bands include: Esquire Five, Victor Feldman, Jazz at the Town Hall, All-Star Sextet, Ronnie Scott Boptet (Club 11), Quartet and Orchestra ("Nine-Piece"), Alan Dean, Johnny Dankworth Quartet (Club 11) and Seven,

Kenny Graham's Afro-Cubists, Norman Burns Quintet, Tito Burns Sextet, Vic Lewis New Music.

Bop-In' Britain (single CDx2, Jasmine JASCD637/8). Similar to the above, but of more obscure provenance, featuring (637) Bosworth Modern Jazz Group, Steve Race Bop Group, Alan Dean's Beboppers, Johnny Dankworth Seven (first recording), Ralph Sharon Sextet, Tommy Whittle Quartet & Septet. (638) Victor Feldman, Arnold Ross Quintet & Trio, Vic Ash All-Stars, Joe Harriott Quartet, Tony Hall's Hall-Stars.

Basement Bop (CDx2, Hallmark 330412). More Esquire material, deleted, rare. A somewhat random job-lot, but contains items by Melody Maker New Stars etc.

Ray Ellington Quartet: The Three Bears (Avid AMSC697)

Cleo Laine & John Dankworth: I Hear Music – a celebration of their life and work
   (CDx4, Salvo SALVOBX 403). Selection starting with Dankworth's first recorded solo
   (with Freddy Mirfield's Garbage Men, 1944) and ending in 2005.

Chapter 5: New Orleans to London

Bunk Johnson and the New Orleans Revival (CDx2, Jasmine JASCD635). A good selection, including his Brass Band and some rags.

Compilations:

British Traditional Jazz: A Potted History and *The Great Revival* (see Chapter 3) remain relevant here.

Vintage Crane River Jazz Band 1950–52 (Lake LACD182)

Christie Brothers Stompers (Cadillac SGC/MEL CD 20/1)

Ken Colyer's Jazzmen: New Orleans to London & Back to the Delta (Lake LACD209)

Chris Barber's Jazz Band: Complete Decca Sessions (CDx2, Lake LACD 141/2) (including album *New Orleans Joys* & Ottilie Patterson's debut)

Chris Barber's Jazz Band: Elite Syncopations (Lake LACD 294)

Ken Colyer's Jazzmen & Omega Brass Band: Marching Back to New Orleans (Lake LACD 21)

Goon Show Compendium Vol. 6 (BBC Audio, various editions)

Chapter 6: Couth, Kempt and Shevelled

Compilations:

Bebop In Britain, Bop-In' Britain & *I Hear Music* (see Chapter 4), and *Jack Parnell: Two Classic Albums Plus* (see Chapter 2) all remain relevant here.

John Dankworth & Cleo Laine Spread a Little Happiness (CDx2, AvidAMSC854)
   (including album *Cleo Sings British* plus Dankworth Seven & Orchestra)

The Vintage Years 1953–59: The Dankworth Orchestra through its various stages (Sepia RSCD2014)

John Dankworth Orchestra: Britain's Ambassador of Jazz (Harkit HRKCD 8345). The Mk II band recorded live at the 1959 Newport Jazz Festival.

Seamen's Mission – Phil Seamen (CDx4, Properbox 159). Seamen was at the heart of British modern jazz throughout the 1950s, and this marvellous anthology takes in his work with bands led by Jack Parnell, Jimmy Deuchar, Joe Harriott, Victor Feldman, Dizzy Reece, Stan Tracey and Tubby Hayes, along with Kenny Graham's Afro-Cubists, the renowned Ronnie Scott nine-piece and the Jazz Couriers.

Modern Jazz at the Royal Festival Hall (1954). Live concert with Don Rendell Sextet, Ken Moule Seven, Tony Crombie Orchestra (Jasmine JASCD627).

Jazz at the Flamingo (Fantastic Voyage FVCD 125). Anthology of bands and musicians who appeared at the club between 1953 and 1961, including Tubby Hayes, Jimmy Deuchar, Don Rendell, Ronnie Ross, Eddie Thompson and Derek Smith.

Meet Don Rendell. Don Rendell Quartet, Quintet & Sextet (1954–55) (Jasmine JASCD 613)

Playtime. Don Rendell Jazz Six, Jazz at the Flamingo and the Jazz Committee (1958–59) (Vocalion CDLK4284)

Tony Kinsey Quartet: Fascinating Rhythm. (Harkit HRKCD 8212) The classic Kinsey Trio plus Joe Harriott (1955) and Ronnie Ross (1955–56)

The Tony Kinsey Collection (CDx6, Acrobat ACSCD6001) A weighty compendium of his work between 1953 and 1961, featuring Bill LeSage, Tommy Whittle, Don Rendell, Ronnie Ross, Joe Harriott et al.

Chapter 7: Let's Settle for Music

Too Hot – The Best of Mainstream British Jazz (CDx3, Castle Music CMETD 992). Now deleted, but worth seeking out, this is an anthology of 56 tracks recorded by Denis Preston for the Pye Nixa label. Includes the Jazz Today Unit, Melody Maker All-Stars, Kenny Baker, Joe Harriott, Bruce Turner, Kenny Graham's Afro-Cubists and many others.

British Traditional Jazz at a Tangent, Vol. 1 (Lake LACD 316) & *Vol. 2* (LACD317). Bearing the subtitle "Breaking the Mould", these two compilation CDs amount to a wonderful testimony to the non-conformity that boiled beneath the uniform surface of trad. Vol. 1 has the Christie Brothers, Pat Hawes Band and Bertie King, among others; Vol. 2 contains some unlikely meetings between jazz, skiffle and the blues.

Humphrey Lyttelton: Humph Experiments (Lake LACD266). Contains all the Bell-Lyttelton recordings, the Grant-Lyttelton Paseo Jazz Band and the Lyttelton band with Ade Monsburgh.

Humph, Bruce & Sandy Swing at the BBC (Upbeat Jazz URCD182). Late 1950s broadcasts that catch the Lyttelton, Bruce Turner and Fairweather-Brown bands at their best.

Bruce Turner: Accent on Swing (CDx2, Lake LACD310). Mainly featuring Turner's Jump Band.

Alex Welsh and his Band: Music of the Mauve Decade (Lake LACD62)

Alex Welsh and his Band: Dixieland to Duke and The Melrose Folio (Lake LACD92).
    Some of this band's best work.

Alex Welsh and his Band: It's Right Here For You and Echoes of Chicago (Vocalion CDNJT5321)

Wally Fawkes: Flook Digs Jazz (Lake LACD143). The complete recording of Fawkes and the Troglodytes.

Turner, Fawkes, Brown: Juicy and Full-Toned (Lake LACD12)

Fairweather-Brown All-Stars:

The Incredible McJazz (Lake LACD229), *Doctor McJazz* (LACD211), *Al & Sandy* (LACD193). Their indispensible best.

Chapter 8: Skiffle

Compilations:

Lonnie Donegan and Original Hits of the Skiffle Explosion (CDx3, Big 3 Records BT 3008). Two discs covering Donegan from 'Rock Island Line' to 'Putting On The Style' plus third disc with Ken Colyer Skiffle Group, Alexis Korner, Nancy Whiskey etc.

How Britain Got the Blues 1 (CDx2, History of R&B Records R005). A collection of 56 original tracks by American blues and folk artists who inspired British skiffle and the later "blues boom". Includes Bessie Smith, Leadbelly, Big Bill Broonzy, Woody Guthrie, Washboard Sam, Robert Johnson etc.

Josh White: New York to London (CDx2, Jasmine JASMCD 3004-5). Includes much of the repertoire he performed during his early British visits.

Big Bill Broonzy On Tour in Britain, 1952 (CDx2, Jasmine JASMCD 3011-2). Live recordings from concerts in England and Scotland, complete with announcements etc.

The Radio Ballads. Complete series of eight programmes issued on single CDs, beginning with *The Ballad of John Axon* (Topic TSCD801); *Song of a Road* (TSCD 802); *Singing the Fishing* (TSCD 803).

Chapter 9: Six Months in a Palais . . .

The Dankworth recordings listed for Chapter 6 remain relevant here.

Tubby Hayes: The Little Giant (CDx4, Properbox 117). Follows his career through the 1950s, from early recordings with Vic Lewis and Jack Parnell, with an exemplary selection from classic Tempo albums cited in the text – including the 1956 Jimmy Deuchar Ensemble.

Dizzy Reece: Progress Report (Jasmine JASCD620)

The Joe Harriott Story (CDx4, Properbox 160). From early 1954 to his "abstract" jazz of 1960, plus a session from 1967.

The Jazz Couriers: First and Last Words (Jasmine JASCD626)

Tubby Hayes: Three Classic Albums Plus (CDx2, Avid AMSC1014) contains the albums *The Couriers of Jazz* and the live *Jazz Couriers in Concert*

Chapter 10: It's Trad, Dad!

Traditional Jazz: A Potted History (see Chapter 3) remains relevant here.

The really big hit records of the trad boom, by Acker Bilk, Kenny Ball, Temperance Seven etc., are constantly being recycled. Nowadays they can also be heard free on YouTube and other internet sites.

Numerous compilations with "Trad" in the title, fairly random assortments in the main, come and go. They can be found on the internet at quite low prices. A typical sample available at the end of 2012 was:

Golden Age of Trad (CDx3, no catalogue number), totalling 67 tracks by Barber, Bilk, Ball, Ken Colyer, Bob Wallis, Terry Lightfoot, Clyde Valley Stompers, Mick Mulligan, George Melly, Mike Daniels etc.

Acker Bilk Esquire (CDx2, Universal Classics & Jazz 546 458-2). Original albums *Stranger on the Shore* (1961) and *A Taste of Honey* (1962)

Mr Acker Bilk and his Paramount Jazz Band (Lake LACD48)

Best of British Jazz from BBC Jazz Club, Vol. 3 (Upbeat Jazz URCD 120). Radio shows (1960–61) by Chris Barber, Terry Lightfoot and the Temperance Seven.

A soundtrack album of *It's Trad, Dad!* has proved elusive, but clips from the film can be found on YouTube.

Chapter 11: Ominously into the Culture Belt

Humphrey Lyttelton:

I Play as I Please (Lake LACD189). Contains the cited track, 'Manhattan'.

John Dankworth:

Five Steps to Dankworth & Journey into Jazz (Vocalion CDNJT5303). Two albums from 1956–57, featuring the Mk II orchestra and small groups from within it.

The Collector's John Dankworth (CDx4, Sepia RSCD 2017-9). Four complete albums, including *What the Dickens!*

Stan Tracey:

Little Klunk (Jasmine JASCD639). Also contains the earlier album, *Stan Tracey Showcase*.

Jazz Suite: Under Milk Wood (Jazzizit JITCD 98150)

Miles Davis:

Kind of Blue (Sony/Columbia Legacy CK 64935)

Index

Note: page numbers in *italics* refer to photographs.

Lightning Source UK Ltd.
Milton Keynes UK
UKOW07n2121081214

242831UK00001B/81/P